HUTCH

HUTCH
Hard Work and Belief

The
Tommy Hutchison
Story

with Kevin Shannon

First published by Pitch Publishing, 2022

Pitch Publishing
9 Donnington Park,
85 Birdham Road,
Chichester,
West Sussex,
PO20 7AJ
www.pitchpublishing.co.uk
info@pitchpublishing.co.uk

A CIP catalogue record is available for this book
from the British Library.

ISBN 978 1 80150 191 0

Typesetting and origination by Pitch Publishing
Printed and bound in Great Britain by TJ Books, Padstow

Contents

To Irene for all the love and
support you have given me for
over 50 years

Foreword by Gordon Taylor

DURING MY 20-year playing career and 40 years running the Players' Union – the PFA – I came across not only great players with top-class skills on the field of play but such players who, once their playing career was over, contributed even more to the reputation of the game with their ability to impact so well on the lives of so many people, particularly youngsters, in the community of clubs that employed them. Tommy Hutchison was a prime example of such persons.

A great playing career of longevity and quality throughout football's pyramid to the very highest level for club and country. Such dedication was very deserving of the description from fellow colleagues as 'one of the very best community managers' and 'one of the finest and most deserving winners of the PFA Merit Award' for his contribution and service to football, alongside other pantheons of the world's greatest game!

Gordon Taylor OBE

Foreword by Gordon Milne

MY FIRST introduction to Tommy was when he joined Blackpool FC in 1968. His youthful enthusiasm and willingness to work and learn immediately caught my eye, plus his amazing physical strength and stamina in such a slight frame at that time. When I was appointed team manager of Coventry City in 1972, one of my first priorities was to sign Tommy; I had that assurance from the chairman that this would happen as soon as I had put pen to paper. Thankfully he was true to his word; Coventry City football club never did a better day's business in its history. He had a perfect temperament, and could handle any situation, was always available for selection and prepared to put himself forward when not 100 per cent fit, which was not very often. He looked after himself, had a Rolls-Royce engine and the strength and knowledge on how to handle it. Ron Wylie, our talented coach at the time, used to say that in bad days Tommy always gave the fans hope; how right he was. To be respected by supporters wherever he played, to be respected by his team-mates wherever he played, to be respected by his managers and coaches wherever he played, and to be respected by chairmen and fellow directors wherever he played takes some doing in a long football career. Very few players have ticked all those boxes; Tommy did that with dignity and style.

Gordon Milne

Prelude

I WAS taking a group of ten-year-olds for football at St Pius Primary school in Withywood, Bristol, one of the city's most deprived areas. They didn't know me; this was my first session with this group. Even if their teacher had said to them, 'Hey, this guy is Tommy Hutchison,' it would have meant nothing to them. I had been a football development officer for a number of years since finishing as a professional. I loved my job, in fact I loved it almost as much as I had loved being a player.

Almost!

I certainly loved working with kids like these, kids who came from a similar background to myself.

I had the drill off pat now; I wanted the children to develop independence, to work outside of their comfort zone.

'Okay, find a partner.' They all went with a friend, as expected.

'Right. One of you is number one, one of you is number two.' They identified their number. Now here was the cruel bit.

'Number ones over here, number twos over there. Ones: if you are a boy, find a new partner who is a girl; girls, a partner who is a boy. Twos, you do the same.' We would now generally have mixed-ability pairs who would not be used to working together.

The warm-up drill was a simple passing exercise. Stand four metres apart and side-foot a pass to your partner. As expected, within seconds chaos reigned, balls flying off everywhere. Those who could play the ball were frustrated that, quite often, their partner couldn't.

'Sir, she's useless, she can't even kick it straight.' The whinging and complaints came in from all quarters.

Now, football was my vehicle for teaching life skills to the children I worked with; skills they would need growing up in the areas of deprivation they called home. I'd had my fill of elite players during my time in the professional game. I wanted to work with children who were never going to make it to the academies of league clubs, but for whom football could still be a force for good if they gave it a chance. I was always on the lookout for those who were lacking in confidence, had low self-esteem and were often got at by other children. I wanted them to know that I understood how it felt to be undervalued. I wanted them to see that there is always a way to improve.

So, as usual, I sat them down.

'First of all,' I said, 'I'm not "Sir", the only "Sir" that I know is Sir Alex Ferguson.' Well, that made them sit up. They all knew of Sir Alex.

'You know Alex Ferguson?' a little lad asked.

'Aye, I know him well.' That impressed them. 'But even though I know Sir Alex, I still want you to call me by my first name, so you all call me Tommy, alright?' They all nodded.

'Now then, I want you to think about the passing session we just did. I want no names called out; I want no finger-pointing. However, if you can think of someone in that session that you thought was useless at football, I want you to put your hands up. You may even think that you yourself are useless at football. If that's you, you can put your hand up too. Hands up now!'

Every hand was up.

'Right then, hands down. You didn't know this, but I played over 400 games in the First Division for Blackpool and for Coventry.' I'd got their attention now.

'I played and I scored in an FA Cup Final at Wembley for Manchester City.' Well, Blackpool and Coventry may not have impressed them too much but the words 'Wembley' and 'Manchester City' had certainly hit the mark.

'I also played 17 times for my country, Scotland, and played in a World Cup finals.' I could tell that even those kids who knew nothing about football could see that this was something special.

'But do you know something?' They were all watching and listening. 'I never played football for my school team. Can anyone guess why?'

The hands shot up again. I pointed at a little girl. 'Tommy, were you ill?' she asked.

'No, never ill in my life.' I pointed to someone else.

'You were injured?'

'No, never injured. Okay, last guess.' I pointed at a little lad with wonky glasses.

'I bet the teacher didn't like you, Tommy.' We all laughed.

'Well, that may be true,' I said, 'and it's probably another story, but that's not the reason why I didn't play for the school team.'

'Well, why didn't you play then?' asked my friend with the glasses.

'The answer is simple,' I told them. 'I was useless at football.'

There was a second's silence as they took in what I had just said. Then they all fell about laughing. The idea that one of their teachers could be useless was a really funny idea. Some of them might not have believed me.

The fact is that I never did play for my school team. The genuine reason was that I was a useless footballer.

Chapter 1

God's Own Village

IF YOU are telling your life story, it's probably best to clear up any half-truths or misconceptions that may have been written about you. So here is one that I can sort out straight away. If you look me up on the internet or find my name in club histories it will always say: Tommy Hutchison, born Cardenden. This is both a half-truth and a misconception. I was actually born and raised in Dundonald, one of a number of villages that make up the small town of Cardenden. Now, you might think that such a small inaccuracy is hardly worth mentioning. Well, that would be a misjudgement of the pride each person has in their own small part of Cardenden. Indeed, there would be people living in Dundonald, even today, who would only be half joking when they say that anyone passing from Cardenden, under the railway bridge and up the hill into Dundonald should have to show a permit before they are allowed to enter 'God's own village'! To them and to most of its residents, at least when I lived there, Dundonald was a special place.

A stranger coming into the village in the 50s, when I was growing up, would perhaps not have been immediately struck by the thought that this was a village of God's own making. Dundonald, unlike the countryside that surrounded it, wasn't pretty. Looming over the village was a small mountain of black coal spoil that constantly gave off wisps of sulphurous smoke. The headstock, winding gear and railway sidings of the pit yard and the miner's raws (rows of terraced miners' cottages) would confirm the visitor's suspicions that they were in a mining village. Like many mining towns, the beauty of Dundonald was not to be found in its buildings, but in the hearts of the community that lived there.

I had a very happy childhood, largely due to my family; my dad Jock, my mum Liz and my elder sister, also Elizabeth (Lizabeth). My younger sister Ann, 13 years my junior, completed our immediate line-up. I say immediate as my mum, a Robertson before marriage, was from a long line of Dundonald folk, so the village was full of uncles, cousins, second cousins and the like. Perhaps it was a peculiarity of mining villages in Fife, but my mum, like other married women, was known by her maiden name even after her marriage to my dad, so Liz Robertson she was and Liz Robertson she remained to all who knew her.

Mum and Dad started married life in my Grandma Lieb's house on Main Road, Dundonald, and that's where both me, in 1947, and my sister Lizabeth, three years earlier, were born. (It was a good birthplace for a future Manchester City player, although the spelling of the street name could do with a tweak.) Undoubtedly it must have been a squash in a fairly small three-bedroomed house as, along with the four of us, there were my grandma and grandpa Robertson (who died before I got to know him) and several of my mum's brothers. It was probably a relief to everyone when the Hutchisons moved out and into a house of their own, a mid-terraced cottage in one of the miner's raws, less than a hundred yards from my birthplace. This is the first house I can remember.

The way of life we had back then is hugely different to that of today. I think that this is true for many aspects of my childhood. If I had to choose a word that best describes my early and even teenage years, I would choose William Wallace's catchphrase, 'freedom'. Mine, like every other child in Dundonald, was an outdoor childhood. The streets and the greens and the woods and the fields surrounding our village were our playground. The only spoken rule I was given by Mum or Dad was 'Dinnae be setting any fires noo.'

An unspoken rule was to always respect our neighbours and their property. Within these bounds we could do and go more or less where we liked. We would dam up the local burn (stream) called Den Burn and use the resulting pool for swimming, we would climb trees, sometimes for the fun of it, sometimes looking for birds' nests and for the eggs they would contain, we would play all manner of games in the streets, staying out until it was getting dark or our stomachs or our parents told us it was time to go home. It was a glorious time! When I finished playing football for a living, I worked with children in schools for over 20 years. The contrast between their young lives and mine could not have been starker in the things that I could do and the limitations on them. I wouldn't swap my upbringing for a more modern one. I think we definitely had the best of things.

Despite my happy life, I would have been aware that we were poor from quite an early age. However, it was never something that bothered me; why should it? Everyone else I knew was in the same hand-to-mouth boat as us. It's only in later years after leaving Dundonald that I realised how truly impoverished we were. There was a ten-bob note that floated around our family. On occasions it would be with one or other of my uncles if they were short, quite often it would be back with us, particularly if my dad was off work with one of his frequent bouts of illness. The main thing I suppose is that we never went hungry – there was always something on the table – or without clothes, however well worn or threadbare they might be. Mum, Dad and our wider family made sure we never went without the essentials.

Talking of wider family, it was the Robertsons of Dundonald that we saw the most of, usually on a daily basis. My mother had one sister, Nell, who had married a baker and for a while lived in Cupar, north Fife. She was always a welcome visitor coming back to Dundonald and not only for all the bread and cakes she would bring with her! Much more local were my mum's brothers. I never got to know Dave as he had died before I was born, having been kicked in the testicles in a local football match and developing complications which proved to be fatal. Her brother Richard also had an unfortunate story. Having been crushed by a roof fall in the local pit, he ended up with a broken back, was permanently disabled and unable to work again. Two of my uncles, John and Will, never married and eventually moved in with us after Grandma Lieb died.

My Uncle Flam (his real name was James) had an unusual skill which earned him his nickname. There would be occasional betting schools, groups of youths and men who would gather on the street to gamble around the village, and Flam would hold court in one of these. Two pennies would be tossed, or 'flammed', into the air by flicking them upwards with the thumb, Flam tossing one, his opponent the other. If the coins came down, say two heads, then Flam won both pennies. If it was two tails, his opponent took the cash. One of each side meant that they were flammed again. Now, Flam had got this down to a fine art, getting the penny to land almost every time on the side that he wanted. So good was he at flamming the penny that he very rarely lost, often making a tidy profit from the school. Such was his reputation that he was never short of opponents who were willing to risk losing money, if only to have a shot at beating a famous (of sorts) local champion!

My dad was a 'blow-in', a non-native of Dundonald who had come from Lochgelly, a village about three miles away. We visited Grandad and Grandma Hutchison on a regular basis but didn't see them every day as we did with the Robertsons. A highlight of a visit to Lochgelly was the chance to enhance my 'look' when playing cowboys and Indians with my friends. Grandad kept chickens down the back of his garden. Every time I went, me and him would collect some of the discarded feathers which I'd bring home, have inserted into a headband by my mum, and worn by me next time I wanted to be Geronimo! I doubt that the leader of the Apache nation ever wore feathers that came from the Scots Dumpy hen, but no one in my gang ever questioned the accuracy of my headband. My grandparents loved going to the pictures and would go almost every night to see a new film in the various local cinemas. This is an indication of how cheap it was to go to watch a film in those days, rather than of the wealth of the Hutchisons!

Birthdays were never really celebrated in our family. No fuss was made. Christmas, however, was an exciting time. I remember when I was younger getting a fort which came with little men dressed in the blue of the US army. They would defend the fort from other little men dressed as Red Indians, some on foot, some on horseback. It was magical! Lizabeth and I would also hang up our socks on Christmas Eve night and in the morning would find them filled with an apple, an orange and a chocolate Santa. The house would be filled all day with family and friends dropping in to say hello and to have a drink.

I remember one year when I was quite little, my Uncle Brickie telling me that if I wasn't good, Santa would fill my sock with hot cinders which would make the chocolate melt. This started me crying, which then meant that my mum gave Brickie a right tongue-lashing.

When I was older my present would inevitably be football related. I would either get a new pair of boots, which would require my dad to hammer home the leather studs using his cobblers last, or a new leather football. These balls, as heavy as a sack of concrete when wet, also came with a detachable bladder whose long nozzle had to be carefully squeezed into the leather casing with the handle of a spoon and then laced up when the ball was inflated. No matter how carefully this was done, the ball always ended up with a little lump around the laces caused by the nozzle.

Growing up with so much family around me meant that there was never a time when I felt unsafe being out and about. Even if my family hadn't been so extensive, then I don't think it would have made any difference really. Maybe it is just looking back through rose-tinted glasses, but I don't really remember any crime, or anti-social behaviour as we would now call it, in our village. It's a cliché I know, but people in Dundonald never locked their doors. True, this was partly to do with the fact that none of us who lived there had anything worth stealing, but it's also because you would have been taking from one of your own; it just wouldn't happen. If anyone did step out of line at all, matters were usually sorted by the people of the village themselves. There would be very few instances where the police would need to be involved in things.

Many of the sights and smells of 1950s Dundonald are very much in the past and unlikely to be seen again. A familiar scene in those days would be the women of the raws (men and women had much more defined roles in those days), my mum included, taking out the mats that would be spread over the floor of the cottage, hanging them over the washing line, and then giving them their weekly sound beating with a hefty stick or the coal shovel. The shower of dust this caused was evidence that we didn't possess a vacuum cleaner. Once clean, the mats would be returned to the floors of the cottage.

As a toddler I can remember sitting and playing on these mats, much more comfortable than the cold lino floor. My dad was very handy around the house, good at fixing and making things. He obviously saw great potential for the same in me, his only son. We had little money for any of life's luxuries, and there weren't many toys around in our house. My dad improvised and he would give me one of the clugs (pieces of scrap wood he would bring home from work for kindling) and a small hammer and I would happily while away my time bashing the clug with the hammer.

I must have impressed him with my dexterity as he next introduced me to some nails. Now there was a purpose to my hammering as I could turn the clug into some form of woody, naily hedgehog. Can you imagine the outcry today if I had hurt myself, hammered a nail into my finger instead of the clug for example? Back then such activities never caused an eyebrow to be raised. As it happens my early explorations into carpentry were ended by my mum the day that she came to take out one of the mats for a beating and found that someone had nailed it to the floor!

The miner's raws themselves are long gone, demolished and consigned to history, replaced with houses that are bigger and more comfortable. As you won't be able to visit the house of my childhood, let me take you back to the 50s to take you on a tour of our cottage in the miners raw. It won't take us long.

Chapter 2

The Miner's Raw

WE'LL CROSS over Main Road, walk around the side of the miners' institute building and into the raw. The first thing to notice is that the rows of terraced cottages are right beside the road. There is no footpath. Don't worry though, as in Dundonald in the 1950s there were very few motorised vehicles. Hardly anyone had a car, milk was delivered from a very slow battery-powered van, the baker delivered bread from a horse-drawn cart and although coal was delivered by lorry, it would only trundle along the village roads. The streets were very safe and popular playgrounds for us kids.

If we walk halfway up the terrace, we will come to our old house. Here it is. The terrace had 16 houses in it and, as you can see, they were single-storey buildings. Living mid-terrace probably wasn't the ideal position in the raw, as you will find out later. To enter our house, you need to step off the tarmac road onto the small, cobbled courtyard in front of us. You see those two doors leading into the cottages? Well, the one on the left will take you to Mary Davidson's house, so we will take the one on the right into the Hutchison household.

Before we go in, however, you might be wondering why every cottage in the raw has a half-sized beer barrel standing on a plinth beside the door. Well, the barrels had two purposes in our lives, one of which I will talk about later. Once a week the barrel would be filled with hot water from several kettle trips and my mother would scrub our clothes clean in it using a washboard. All the women of the raw would do the same on their wash days.

If we go in through the door, we are straight into the scullery. You can see we have a sink by the window, that metal tub over there is a gas boiler where my mum could boil the washing before finishing them off in the barrel outside. We also have a gas cooker. There are two doors on your right; one that leads into our small pantry, the place we store our food, and the other is to our toilet.

If we take the door on the other side of the scullery, we go into the living room, which could be described as cosy! It's a bit dark in here you say? Well, don't be looking for the electric light switch, as there isn't one! We won't get electricity in our cottage for a few years yet. We light each room from a gas mantle in the ceiling. We have to be careful to make sure the meter is topped up now and then with another shilling as we will be rummaging round in the dark for a coin if we are not sharp enough and the gas runs out.

Behind the table at the back of the room is a curtain running wall to wall. If we pull back the curtain, you can see the two beds separated by a partition; that's where Lizabeth and I go to sleep. We keep our clothes (we don't need many) in our mum and dad's bedroom. There is only one bedroom in each cottage in the raw. Ah! You've noticed we only have the one door, the one we came through off the street; that's right. And that's why it's a bit of an inconvenience to live mid-terrace like we do. Glance through my mum and dad's bedroom window now. You see that grassy area out there with the upright poles? Well, that's the drying area.

If you live at the end of the terrace, you can just nip around the back of the raw to hang out the washing. Live mid-terrace and it's quite a trek, particularly with a heavy basket. So what my mum does is carry the washing through the house to the bedroom window. She then climbs through the window to the drying area and my dad then passes the basket out to her. When she collects the dry washing, it's back out and then in through the window, remembering to untie and bring our washing line in with her. It's not that anyone would pinch it, it's just that us kids from the raw often play out there and if we were running around there after dark, she wouldn't want any of us to be decapitated!

Well, that's the end of the tour. That's our little home! A compact place to live I think you will agree!

You can see from the description of our cottage that we didn't have a lot of money or material possessions. What we did have was our family and our community. I knew everyone in our raw and most of the people in the other raws too. They all knew us. Word would spread and we would know when someone was in need. My mother in particular would always help out our neighbours in any way that she could. Likewise, if we were struggling at any time, family and neighbours in the raws or the other areas of Dundonald would make sure that we never went under. We, as a community, had our own unofficial social services.

If a neighbour was sick and bed-bound, my mum would often go round to their house and help out with cooking, cleaning, or even sit with them through the night if they needed around-the-clock care. Her services would also be called upon if there was a death in Dundonald. She would help with the laying out of the person who had died, washing the body, combing their hair and dressing them in their best clothes. She did this to help the family save some of the costs of the undertaker but, also, she believed that people like us deserved to have their dignity preserved, even in death.

Her generosity really did know no bounds. She would literally give away anything we had if someone's need, she thought, was greater than ours. This extended to money too, not that we ever had any to spare. If someone asked her, 'You coudnae lend us ten bob coud ye Liz?', she would say, 'Oh aye. Nae bother, here's a pound hen,' and away they would go.

Now the custom in our village was that when the man of the house was paid on a Friday, the pay packet was handed over to his wife. She would then give him a few bob back for the week ahead while using the rest of the wage to take care of the family finances. My dad, knowing of my mum's overgenerous nature, had learned to 'skim' his pay packet; to open the envelope without tearing it, take out a few bob and then reseal the envelope so no tampering could be detected. My mum suspected and would accuse him of skimming, but he would always deny any such underhand dealing, knowing we had a small emergency fund if Mum's generosity got the better of her.

We stayed in the raws until I was about ten and we were allocated a bigger house in Dundonald Park, a house literally around the corner from my Grandma Lieb's house where I had been born. For all its deprivations, I wouldn't change my time living in the raws. This time, as with almost all of my childhood, I was happy and content, despite us being poor. Living as part of that community has left me with many happy memories of events and the characters we lived with. Before we leave the raws, I have to tell you of one such event and of one such character.

The source of heat in our cottage, not surprisingly being a mining village, was coal. We had a coal fire in our living room that was surrounded by a range which had a hob and a small oven either side of the fire. This was our only heated room, although you could heat up the kitchen a little when using the gas cooker. My mum would often use the hobs or the oven for cooking, thus saving a few shillings from the gas meter. The kettle would always be steaming away on the hob ready for the next pot of tea. Now, the problem with using the fire so much was that the chimney often needed sweeping. Don't sweep your chimney and you run the risk of the gathering soot catching alight, causing a chimney fire.

We only had one sweep in Dundonald, a chap called Jock Mason. Jock was a nice, simple sort of a chap but as a sweep he was no great shakes. You would think that sweeping a chimney successfully couldn't be too hard a task. Well, oft times it was for Jock. His appearance didn't help. By the nature of his job, the fact he went round the village with a face totally blackened with soot wasn't too surprising. It was his bright red hair, a total contrast to his dirtied expression, that would startle folk. His appearance didn't inspire confidence, and this lack of faith in him by his customers was often justified.

Anyway, one day, my mum decided to bite the bullet and rather than risk a chimney fire, she called Jock in to sweep our chimney. In preparation for his visit, and knowing his ability to conjure up sooty disasters, we had covered the furniture with old sheets. Jock arrived with his set of ladders, and propping them against the wall, he gave my mum and me an old coal sack and instructed us to use this to cover the fireplace and catch the soot when he shoved his brush down our chimney. Those coal sacks were porous old things at the best of times, so my mum and I knew that we and our living room were going to be plastered in soot whatever happened. As Jock made his way up onto the roof ready to insert his brush into one of the two pots on our chimney (the other belonging to Mary Davidson in the adjoining cottage), my mum and I, following his instructions, made our way to the fireplace with the sack.

From the roof, Jock called down, 'Are yous ready doon thare?' 'Aye,' Mum shouted back and we both braced ourselves against the range, sealing as much of the fireplace as we could with the coal sack. For an instant nothing happened, no soot hit the bag, and my mum and I looked at each other. It was then we heard shouts and curses from Mary's house next door. Rushing outside, we were just in time to see Mary and her husband Ralph emerging from their very dusty cottage, coughing,

24

spluttering and blackened with soot. As Mary told us later, 'We were sat by th' fire when all o' a sudden we were hoaching with soot.'

Jock did eventually find our chimney pot and swept our chimney. The best of it all was when he said to Mary, 'Ah'll nae be charging ye fur the' sweepin' th'day. We'll say tha' this one's on th' hoose, Mary.' Jock Mason, a legend in many a Dundonald living room!

I've told this story many times to lots of people over the years and a common reaction is that it reminds them of the chandelier scene in *Only Fools and Horses*. It is my hope that somehow writer John Sullivan got to hear it second-hand and that Jock Mason is responsible for one of the great TV comedy moments of all time!

Coal was an ever-present feature of life in Dundonald. It was used for cooking and heating in our homes, it was the source of employment for 90 per cent of the residents and the architecture of the mine dominated the landscape of the village. It was also central to us as a family.

Chapter 3

Son of a Miner

MY DAD, Jock, was a miner. This is a statement that even 40-plus years after his death fills me with pride. He worked in the pits for the whole of his working life knowing that his job was slowly killing him. As a chronic lifelong asthmatic, my dad should never have worked as a collier. Most miners, able-bodied at the start of their working life, would have some form of breathing condition by the time, at 65 years of age, they had completed their final shift. My dad had breathing difficulties before he set foot underground, so the toll on his body of breathing in coal dust every working day became increasingly apparent the more years he worked.

The reason he did it, the reason he carried on when the state of his health was telling him to stop, was the same for him as for most men in our village. He had no choice. In Dundonald, if you needed to earn a wage, if you needed to feed, clothe and shelter your family, then the pit was the only place for most men. I can never remember a time when my dad was really well. February was a month that we came to dread in our house. It was just inevitable that my dad would take ill with a bout of pleurisy, an inflammation of the lungs, that would see him forced to his bed for several days.

My mum would put a kaolin poultice on his chest to ease the pain and his breathing. I can still smell those things, even today. After my dad had died, February was a month that would often see my mum feeling down and sad. Dad had many prolonged spells of poor health where he would drag himself from his bed and off to the pit. If he didn't work, he didn't get paid and we as a family were in danger of going without. It still makes me sad when I think of how he often sacrificed himself so that we didn't go short.

Every time my dad, or any other miner for that matter, went underground they knew that they were putting their lives at risk. The health and safety of miners in the 40s, 50s and 60s, despite the nationalisation of the mines in 1945, was still a poor second to profit. As a young man, my dad had suffered a broken leg from a roof fall. There were very few miners in Dundonald who had never suffered a work-related injury.

When the Dundonald mine closed in the 60s, my dad, with most of the other men, went to work at the nearby Bowhill pit. Where that mine once stood in the middle of the village of Bowhill, there is a memorial to those who worked and died in that pit. In the almost 70 years that the mine was in operation, over 300 miners lost their lives. More than four men a year, on average, died while at work.

In my mind's eye, I can still see my dad walking up the road when we lived in the raw. It was obvious from the way he moved how weary he was. Like all the men who worked underground, he was coated from head to toe in coal dust. His first task on arriving home would be to clean himself up. This is where the half beer barrel came into play again. My mum would have been back and forth filling it with hot water so he could have a wash when he got home from his shift. In those days I can never remember my dad ever looking properly clean. He also always had red-rimmed eyes, a legacy, I would imagine, of the irritating dust. All along the raws this washing ritual was repeated as the men returned from work.

I remember well, as a ten-year-old, the great day in 1957 that the newly built pit head baths were going to be officially opened at the Dundonald colliery. It was a summer day but the heavens opened and a storm of Biblical proportions descended on our village. Despite the weather, a huge crowd gathered to witness this historic event. We weren't there to listen to speeches by whoever the local bigwig was who was conducting the ceremony. We were there to see the opening of a facility that would transform the lives of every family who had someone working in the mine. The opportunity to change out of dirty clothes, to shower and be properly clean after a shift cannot be overstated. It took over 60 years from the opening of that mine, 12 years from the date of nationalisation, to install something as simple as a set of showers at Dundonald Colliery. At last the colliers would be able to leave their place of work with a bit of dignity, freshly washed and cleanly dressed. The barrels, at least for the miners if not for their wives, were finally redundant.

My mum, when she left school, worked at the pit too. She worked in one of the surface sheds beside a conveyor belt. Her job was to pick out the lumps of rock that had got mixed up with the coal. This was a hard old job and very poorly paid. She would be on her feet for hours, stood beside the belt with a group, mainly women, sorting through the coal.

By the time I came along, she was working on a local farm doing whatever the season dictated. For example, she would be part of a group of women who would harvest turnips when they were ready to be picked. We called this 'shawing neeps'. She would stand with feet astride the turnip drill. She would pull the plant from the soil, chop off the roots and the 'shaw' (the top of the turnip bulb and its shoots). The shaw and the roots would be chucked one way into a cart to be used for sheep food. The 'neeps', the turnip bulbs, were placed in another cart on the other side of the drill ready to be taken to market. It goes without saying that this was also a back-breaking job conducted outside in all weathers. My mum would often say, however, that she only ever had a cold when she had left the farm and stopped working outdoors.

Having low-paid jobs and my father's poor health often meant that we had to supplement our needs in inventive ways. A shortage of coal in the winter months would mean that I would be sent to the nearby railway sidings to fill a couple of buckets from the wagons full of coal waiting to leave the village. No vegetables? Well, a trip to the nearby fields could see Mum and Dad return with a bag of potatoes or a couple of turnips. After one such escapade, my mother realised that in pulling up the turnip, she had somehow lost her engagement ring. An extensive search failed to find the missing piece of jewellery. If anyone is treasure hunting on Harley's Farm in Dundonald and comes across an old engagement ring, one with very few diamonds, you will know who to return it to! At Christmas we would have a walk to the local Den Wood, choose a small tree and take it back home to decorate. We would never have felt that we were pinching stuff. We were using the resources of our area in order to keep our head above water as many others around us did too.

The move from the raws to the house in Dundonald Park saw an upturn in our fortunes. Firstly, we now had a house with both hot and cold running water and three bedrooms, so for a while Lizabeth and I had our own rooms. The big boost to our table was that we now had a garden front and back and my dad soon set about planting both gardens with a variety of vegetables. My mum had suggested to my dad that the front garden could perhaps be planted with flowers. My dad wasn't going to waste any room where food could be grown. 'The ainlie fleurs in that garden will be cauliflowers,' was his reply.

My mum, as soft-hearted as ever, took a shine to the cows who grazed in the field at the back of our garden. If she had any bread that had gone stale, she would break it up and feed it to the cows. The cows now knew that our garden was an alternative food source to grass. They discovered that if they came looking for my mum and that her and her bread weren't available, they could crane their necks over our fence and help themselves to a few tasty cabbages instead. My dad wasn't best pleased that, due to his wife's kindness to local farm animals, he now had to extend the height of our back fence by a couple of feet in order to protect our precious veg!

There were occasions when my dad wasn't able for the garden. He would say, 'Tam, could ye dig over the wee bit o' garden for me, son?'

I would gladly have done anything to help my dad and so would often be out there digging over a patch ready for some vegetables. However, as a young lad growing into my teenage years, I never found any kind of manual work easy. I was a tall but spindly boy who lacked any sort of muscle definition. My mum was concerned enough about my skinny frame to arrange an appointment with a paediatrician in Edinburgh. He couldn't find anything wrong with me and he remarked to my mum that she wasn't very big. He then asked how big my dad was. Now, both Mum and Dad were on the small side, and when the doctor heard this he said to my mum, 'Mrs Hutchison, two sparrows won't make an eagle.' That was the end of the consultation!

My mum was the kindest of people, she had a heart of gold. However, she was quite a volatile character, quick to lose her temper. This was the opposite of my dad, who was calm and even-tempered but who still had a steely nature when it came to discipline. As a miner's family we were entitled to a delivery of coal. This was supplied by lorry and loosely dumped on the road outside the Dundonald Park house. If my dad was ill then I would have to barrow the coal to the bunker we had behind the house.

I remember one occasion when I started down the garden path and the barrow overbalanced slightly. I hadn't the strength to correct it and the coal spilled onto the garden. This caused my mum to fly into a rage and she tried to skelp me with the flat of her hand. On that occasion, as with most of these incidents, I was quick enough to dodge. If I had upset her and I wasn't in range of her hand, then I knew that a slipper, or a baffie as we would call it, would be winging its way towards me. I was pretty nifty on my feet and rarely got caught. My mum would tell me to return the baffie to her. I knew better than that, as from past experience I knew that, once returned, it would be heading back in my direction and at speed!

I would leave her alone and her anger would subside as quickly as it had risen. Her volcano of a temper and her use of physical force as a means of discipline didn't bother me particularly. It was just the way she was and I learned quickly when it was a good time to leave her alone. My dad, in contrast, never laid a hand on me ever, but he had a tongue like a razor when he chose to use it. He had a much more effective method of discipline as far as I was concerned.

I remember once, when I was 16 or 17, I had been in Bowhill with a few mates and they decided they would go into Pyatts, one of the pubs in the village. Some of them ordered beer but I had a pineapple juice; I'd never had a drink and was very conscious of the need to stay fit for football. When I got home, a neighbour, Tam Hughes, was in the house chatting with my mum and dad. He asked me what I'd been up to so I said, 'Oh, we just dropped intae Pyatts.' My dad gave me that steely look of his. 'Oh, so ye were in th' pub were ye? Ye think ye'r smart. Do you want tae play fitba or be a drunk like some aroond here.' I told my dad that I'd only had a soft drink, but he was on a roll and didn't want to know, 'Ye were in th' pub.' I was now in tears like I was most times that my dad was upset with me. My mum, however, was having a go back at him, 'He's tellt ye he wis na drinkin. He wid nae dae that.' That's all he needed to do, to let me know that something I had done or said had disappointed him and that would bring me to tears.

Soon after moving into our house in Dundonald Park, my grandma, Lieb Robertson, died. The days following her death were sad ones. I attended her funeral and even though I was only ten, I remember one of my uncles passing me one of the straps that supported her coffin and with which we lowered her slowly into the ground. She had been the central figure in the family, her house the hub of family gatherings.

With her passing, that mantle now passed to my mum and to our house. Just as my grandma had been worshipped by her sons, my mum was worshipped by her brothers. At first, my mum looked after her brothers, John and Will, still living in my grandma's house, cooking, cleaning and washing for them. It became clear she was running herself into the ground and eventually it was agreed that the two brothers, both miners, would move in with us. Although this meant an overcrowded house, particularly when my second sister came along, it also meant two extra wages in the house and our financial situation improved considerably.

I got on well with my uncles. They shared my passion for cowboy films and cowboy books. One of my jobs was to recycle these books, taking them from one uncle to another until they had all had the chance to read them. This shows the innocent nature of the times; these were men in their 30s who were entertained by reading stories of the Wild West, with its train robberies, range wars and cavalry battles against the Red Indians. Partly as a result of my dad's skimming of his wage packet and partly because we had my uncles' two wages coming into the house, we were able to afford a Philips TV set. This meant that my uncles and me had the added bonus of being able to watch the adventures of the Lone Ranger and his mate Tonto once a week.

Making sure that we saw the latest film by Gary Cooper or James Stewart was important to all the males on the Robertson side of the family, as was picking up the latest novel by Zane Grey. However, the most important thing in all our lives, with the exception of family, was football.

Chapter 4

Eating, Sleeping, Football

I CAN'T remember a time when I didn't play football. My earliest memories would be of kicking a ball around on the streets, or the grassy areas of the village. Playing football was as much a part of my life as going to bed or sitting down to eat. I played every day. I would only need to step out of the house to find a game going on and I would often play all day. Playing on the green, outside of our house in Dundonald Park, or in The Square, my lack of physical strength wasn't a problem. I was skilful enough to hold my own in the endless games we played. In fact, on the crowded pitch we played on, close control was needed as space was in short supply. Taking part in these games, I am sure, helped me to develop both my touch and dribbling skills.

If we fancied playing with proper goals, we could nip into the Moorside, the ground at the top of our road where Dundonald Bluebell played. On the very odd occasion that none of my friends were around, I could use the corrugated fence that surrounded Moorside to kick the ball against and have it come back to me, practising passing, shooting and trapping the ball.

Even running messages for my mum gave me a chance to practise. I'd go the long way to the store, the local Co-op, along Main Road. On the way down I would play the ball against the wall that ran the length of the road, with my left foot. I'd pop into the store to pick up my mum's message, and if I had a few pennies, I'd get myself either a Penny Dainty, a small chocolate bar, or if I was particularly flush, a bar of McGowan's 'big coo' toffee. On the way back, I would pass with my right foot, collect the rebound and pass again. I just loved having a ball at my feet (and a mouthful of toffee!).

At school, I never excelled. I behaved myself and got by, but for me the real purpose of school were the games of football that we would have in the yard at breaktime and dinnertime. I went to Denend Primary School, a few minutes' walk from home. The highlight of my time there was in a class taught by Mrs Cuthbert. One day she brought in a heavy yellow goalkeeper's jersey. Mrs Cuthbert called me and another lad out to hold up the shirt. I couldn't believe the weight of it. She told us that it belonged to her uncle, John Thomson, a goalkeeper for Celtic and Scotland who had died after an accident on the pitch.

I later found out more about John. He was born in Kirkcaldy but grew up in Cardenden. At 14 he was working at Bowhill Colliery where his job of coupling and uncoupling coal wagons helped him to develop strong hands and wrists. He was spotted by Celtic playing in junior football. Unusually for a goalkeeper, he was small in stature and had small hands but was agile, athletic and had a huge leap. The accident Mrs Cuthbert referred to was a collision on the Ibrox Park pitch. Thomson was a brave player and he had no hesitation in diving at the feet of onrushing Rangers forward, Sam English. Unfortunately, Thomson's head contacted the knee of English, bursting an artery in his head. John died in hospital that night at the age of 22. His grave and memorial stand in Bowhill Cemetery. Apparently, a crowd of 30,000 people lined the streets on the day of his funeral, some of them walking the 70 miles from Glasgow.

My primary school had no football team, but my secondary school Auchterderran High certainly did. However, I was never considered good enough to play in it. This wasn't a decision I necessarily disagreed with as I never really believed I was good enough to be picked. We never had trials for the team, teachers chose players based on performances in games sessions. As I couldn't kick the ball hard enough to make it travel from the touchline to the goal – I just didn't have the strength – it wasn't surprising that they never considered me. In the year above me there was a real star player. Willie Johnston, future Rangers and Scotland winger, known to us as Billy or Bud, was certainly playing for the school team. I knew him well and there wasn't a doubt that he was going on to great things.

Had anyone suggested that Tam Hutchison would also one day play for Scotland, it would have raised a smile from teachers and classmates alike. Yet, here's the thing, I can't remember a time when I didn't know that I would play football for Scotland. It wasn't a vague notion that I had.

It was as certain to me, even when I couldn't make the Auchterderran side, that one day, just as sure as the sun would rise tomorrow, that I would become a Scottish international. I didn't share this with anyone, I wasn't that daft. I remember on one occasion being lined up for a games session and the teacher asking if any of us thought we would become professional footballers. A few lads put their hands up, but I certainly wasn't one of them.

As at primary school, I never pulled up any trees academically at the high school. I kept my nose clean, did what was asked of me, and waited for breaktimes when I could have a ball at my feet again. I do remember one teacher, a Mr Garland, who taught PE and English. He decided he would nip in the bud any future possible discipline problems with my class by showing us what would happen if we did misbehave.

He lined us up, boys and girls, and whacked us one at a time across the palm of the hand with a belt, the belt having two splits at the end which meant it wrapped around your hand giving an extra little sting of pain. Remember, we hadn't done anything wrong, hadn't broken any rules. He was just demonstrating what would happen if we did! Such was the joy of the Scottish education system in the 50s!

However, being at the high school had an unexpected bonus for me. The school did not provide school meals so for some of my time there I would go home for dinner. However, at one stage, the nearby Bowhill Colliery started to allow us to use their canteen to buy a meal. My dad was working at Bowhill as the Dundonald mine had closed. So, depending on his shift, I would sometimes eat with him at lunchtime.

My dad had got me a second-hand bike to get to the high school. On one occasion Billy Johnston asked me if he could borrow it to go down to the shops one lunchtime to buy some sweets. I had no problem with that so away went Billy and the bike. Unfortunately for me, for Billy and for my bike, he wasn't as nifty on two wheels as he was jinking up and down the wing. Turning back into school after getting his sweets, he failed to spot an approaching bus in the way he would an onrushing full-back and the bike became a mangled wreck. Luckily Billy was thrown clear and unhurt so that he didn't suffer the same fate! Unfortunately, it was me that had to carry what was left of the bike home all the way back to Dundonald.

I continued to play football all of the hours that God sent, determined to improve, determined to fulfil my dream. Billy Johnston had been taken on by Rangers and he told me how the players there improved the strength in their legs by running in heavy pit boots. I needed to improve the strength in my legs but my feet were already too big to fit into the boots my dad or uncles wore. I decided to improvise and so I would put on two pairs of heavy woollen football socks, soak my feet in a bucket of water to make the socks heavy, squeeze into my football boots and then run endless laps of the Bluebell pitch. I have to say I was dedicated and I did all I could to improve physically and to improve my ball skills. I still didn't play any properly organised football but my ambition never wavered.

As lads growing up in Dundonald, football was king. However, there were brief interludes when other activities would happen. If tennis was on the telly, we would tie a rope across the street between two lamp posts and, using homemade plywood bats, we would have our own Wimbledon competition. Drawing wickets on the corrugated fence around the Bluebell, a stick and a tennis ball would enable us to play cricket. A baked beans can, sunk into the grass outside our house, and a shared putter would give us our own putting green.

One of the other sports that I started to play had long-term benefits for my football career. My sister Liz and myself started to take part in badminton sessions at the nearby miners' institute. I became good enough to play at various tournaments around the district. I feel that all the stretching that I did in reaching for shots stood me in good stead in my career. I never suffered from pulled or strained muscles, never had to warm up before training or games. I remember teasing Tommy Caton, my team-mate at Manchester City. I went out to training one day and there is Tommy going through his stretching exercises. I said to him, 'It's strange Tommy that there's ye doin' all that stretching and you're forever pullin' muscles, an' here's me, never dae a stretch and ner' so much as a strain!' My Uncle George, who for some reason had the nickname Spank, helped with the running of the badminton sessions. He would encourage me not to keep stretching, but to move my feet in order to achieve more power and direction in my shots. This was a skill I was able to transfer to football.

When I was about 14, my mates and I hit upon a scheme to raise money so we could buy ourselves some kit. I got permission from my Auntie Beth, who looked after the hall, to start running a disco or, as we called it, a 'hop', in the institute. We borrowed some records and a record player and charged people a few pennies to come in. We would split our profits with some money going towards the kit and the rest being used to buy new records. I remember the first record we bought was 'Telstar' by the Tornados. We named our team, if you can call it that, Dundonald Athletic. We would play games against boys from other local villages, Cardenden or Jamphlars. It was all very informal. Whoever turned up played, whatever their age, with jerseys for goalposts and no referees.

The same miners' institute was the venue for one of the more organised types of football I was involved in. Each Friday there would be a five-a-side competition held there with up to ten teams of boys taking part. Ten boys playing on an area the size of a badminton court meant that close control and touch were important if you were going to play well and make an impression. The boys from the eight non-competing teams would sit on the stage. One set of goals would be drawn on the stage front, the other goals were the double doors at the other end of the hall. The prize of a box of Maltesers, to be shared between the five lads in the team, was a huge incentive to win.

Eventually, at the age of 15, my dad heard of a local team that was looking for players. This team, CISWO (Coal Industry Social Welfare Organisation), was run by a man called Brigham Young! In a community where most people had a nickname of some kind or another, it's perhaps surprising that Brigham's name was the one he was born with but as far as I know he was no relation to his famous namesake from Utah! For the first time, I was playing proper organised football and, over a season, I played several games for Brigham's team.

I must have been getting better as a player. However, luck would still play an important role in my becoming a Bluebell and taking what would be my first small steps towards a career in professional football.

Chapter 5

Bluebells

AFTER FOUR years at Auchterderran High, at the age of 15 I was able to leave school. I never took an exam and had no academic qualifications. In the early 60s that was no barrier to getting a job. Most kids were able to leave school and walk into a job of sorts. I had applied for a couple of things, didn't get them but wasn't particularly worried. I had a safety net, if you could call it that, because there was a job waiting for me and for any other Dundonald lad down the pit. The reality of life in our house was that if you were living there and eating there, then you had to earn your keep. If there was nothing else, then it would have to be the colliery for me. My dad had made it clear that he didn't want me to follow in his footsteps. I didn't really need much persuading to agree with his way of thinking.

When I was 11 or 12, my Uncle Spank took me underground at the Dundonald mine. I don't know if he got permission for me or if he just managed to sneak me in. It was a Sunday so the colliery wasn't operating. The speed of the cage and the duration of its descent terrified me. Emerging from the cage at the bottom of the shaft I was hit both by the overpowering smell of coal and the humid atmosphere. It was awful. I couldn't wait to get back to light and air. If I didn't know before how bad the working conditions of my dad and the other miners were, I certainly did after this little visit and, even then, I hadn't moved far from the cage and had been nowhere near the coalface. I knew without any doubt that I did not want to be a miner.

I bought myself a little time by enrolling at the Lauder College in Dunfermline. For three months I was able to have taster sessions in various trades such as bricklaying, carpentry, and painting and decorating, which did give me an idea of what I might like to do. However, at the end of the three months, I still had no job and I was given a start date for the colliery. Luckily for me, Spank heard that a local decorator was looking for an apprentice, so a week before I was due to start in the pit, I found myself in a pair of dungarees about to start a career where a paste or paintbrush would be the tools of my trade rather than a pick and a shovel. Both Dad and me couldn't have been happier.

Having a job made not an iota of difference to my ambition to one day be a professional footballer. The conviction that I would line up at Hampden Park in that dark-blue shirt still burned as brightly as it ever had. I may now have been a working man (or at least a working teenager) but I still played football every evening and every weekend. My passion for the game was undimmed and that passion was about to be rewarded.

One Saturday afternoon I was having a kick about with some pals on the green when I saw Jock Bradford marching towards us. Jock was a relative of my mum and we knew each other well. He was also a member of the committee at Dundonald Bluebell who picked the team to play each week.

'Tam, away n' get yer boots, we need ye tae play the' day son.'

It turned out that a car bringing some of the players from Methil, a shipyard town about 12 miles from Dundonald, had broken down and they weren't going to make kick-off. I played that afternoon and I must have done okay as I kept my place for the next few games. After that little run, I found myself in and out of the side for a spell before later in the season finally establishing myself as a regular. I felt that the hours of practise, the endless laps of the Bluebell pitch and the strength training had finally started to bear fruit. This bit of success only made me redouble my efforts.

Bluebell played in the Fife Junior League. The players I played with and against came from mining communities and shipyards; they were tough, tough characters who were hard and aggressive on the football field. For someone with a physique like mine, playing with characters like these was going to be a challenge. There were occasions when my team-mates would fire the ball out to me on the wing and I would almost be skittled over, both by the power of the pass and the weight of the old leather ball.

I still struggled to kick the ball any sort of distance and so crosses to the back post from my wing were a rarity. I had two qualities that both earned me my place in the side and the respect of my team-mates. Firstly, I could play. I was skilful, could beat an opponent, had a good touch and could pick a pass. Secondly, I wouldn't allow myself to be intimidated. It didn't matter how many times I was brought down or I was kicked. The next opportunity I had to run at the opponent who had fouled me, I would be taking him on again. I really enjoyed seeing their sense of frustration at the fact that, despite trying to kick me to kingdom come, here I was, on the ball and coming at them yet again. My legs were often black and blue but also extremely thin. My sister Lizabeth bought me a pair of shin pads but, because my legs were so spindly, they wouldn't bend enough to fit me. My mate in the team, Alex Carswell, laughed at me and told me to take them off as they made my legs look like Popeye's after he had had his spinach. I never wore them again.

Another of my uncles, Uncle Brickie, was a regular at these games. I couldn't have wished for a more vocal supporter both in the encouragement he gave to me and in the warnings of violence that he issued to the more physical full-backs that I faced (which in the Fife Junior League was all of them!). These threats I took to be welcome but empty bluster from my uncle. However, a few years after my time at the Bluebell, I was talking to Drew Davidson, a friend since boyhood, who knew everything there was to know about the Bluebell and the Fife Junior League. He told me he had come across some documents from years ago about an incident at a game at Valleyfield that resulted in a lifetime ban being issued by the league to a spectator who had run onto the field, incensed by the referee's decisions, and chased the poor man up and down the pitch. 'You know who that was?' Drew asked me. Not thinking of my time at Dundonald, I shook my head, I hadn't a clue. Of course, it was Brickie, who, when telling my opponents what he was going to do to them, should have been nowhere near the Moorside or any other stadium in the Fife League!

We were watched by crowds of upwards of 200 people. They were never slow to air their views on the players they watched. They also had some fun with members of the committee. Eighty per cent of the Bluebell pitch was a pristine, bowling-green surface. Unfortunately, the remaining 20 per cent, the strip that ran the length of the field from goal line to goal line in front of the clubhouse where most spectators stood, was like a bog. It was continually waterlogged.

To make the surface playable, bucketloads of cinders from the nearby railway sidings were liberally poured on to the mud until, at last, players could move over that part of the pitch without sinking up to their ankles. Now, playing on sharp gritty cinders not only tested a player's ball control, the ball bouncing and running differently to how it did on the grass, but it also tested a player's courage, to the limit. It took a special kind of player who was willing to try a slide tackle on that side of the pitch. Any full-back or centre-half daring or foolish enough to go to ground on the cinders certainly bore the marks of their actions through the scars on their tattered and bloodied arms and legs.

Having a cinder surface also caused problems for the officials. The grass part of the pitch could be marked out using the usual white paint. This didn't work on cinders. The solution that the committee came up with was less than satisfactory. It involved an unfortunate committee member, ten minutes before kick-off, emerging from the clubhouse. He would have a bucket of sawdust in one hand and a trowel in the other. He would then attempt to mark out a touchline with the sawdust. As he shuffled along the pitch doing his best against impossible odds to produce a thin, straight line, he would have to run a gauntlet of advice, jibes and insults from the spectators gathered in front of the clubhouse, their mood brightened from a couple of hours drinking.

I think for many there was more entertainment to be had in the pre-match marking-out ritual than there was in the game itself. You may wonder why the touchline wasn't marked out a lot earlier while spectators were safely inside having a drink, so saving the unfortunate committee man the trauma of facing the public. The answer is that the sawdust had a very limited lifespan. Any sudden gust of wind would scatter the most carefully drawn line. The referee and the linesman also had a near-impossible task of judging when a ball was in or out of play on that side of the pitch due to the rapidly disappearing sawdust. Not that the Dundonald public had any sympathy for them. They were fair game in the same way as the committee man was; their ineptness in judging the ball in or out of play only added to the afternoon's rich entertainment.

It could be said that I was now a semi-professional footballer as players at the Bluebell were paid five bob (25 pence) each time we played. However, a shilling (five pence) of our match fee had to be spent on the weekly club raffle. Just like my dad, I handed over my wages, both as an apprentice painter and as a semi-pro footballer, to my mum and got a few bob back for the week. This meant I had the means to enjoy the lively but innocent social life of our town.

I visited our two cinemas on a regular basis, sometimes going to the first house at the Goth and being out in time to go to the second house at the Rex on the same evening. In those days there was always two films on the bill: the B-movie, which after an interval to buy an ice cream or sweets, was followed by the A-movie, the main feature. An evening like this at the pictures would mean watching four films.

Cowboy films were still my movie of choice with anything by John Wayne being a favourite. In the next two years I would not only watch films at these two cinemas but I would also visit them in a professional capacity in order to paint and redecorate them. The fact that in those days people could smoke in these places meant that the services of someone like me was required every few years to brighten up walls and ceilings that had started to yellow.

At this stage, girls were starting to appear on my radar but, if I was at a dance, it would be with some pals and we would spend a lot of time trying to get a friend to talk on our behalf to a girl we might quite like, to see if she might be willing to chat or even to dance. I can't remember too many conversations with females and even less dances. As a way of finding a girl, our methods, at least as far as I was concerned, were pretty useless.

On the field (and on the cinders too) my footballing fortunes continued to improve. Some of the matches I played in were fierce affairs against teams from local villages. For Bluebell, this would be games against Bowhill or Lochgelly. Many senior Scottish clubs recognised the value of playing their young players in a league such as ours in order to toughen them up. I remember playing against Billy Johnston when we played Loch Ore, a club that Rangers had loaned him to.

Billy was a frequent visitor to the Bluebell and would often join in training sessions. On one occasion he had to borrow a pair of boots from one of the Dundonald lads as he had been asked to go for a trial at Manchester United (this must have been before his Rangers days). At that time Billy used to play games with a boot on his right foot but only a training shoe on his left; I don't know the reason for this, but he didn't want to turn up to United with only one boot, hence his need to borrow. The boots on this occasion didn't do the trick as his trial was unsuccessful.

Throughout his career, Billy would get into trouble due to having a short fuse and an explosive temper. He was sent off numerous times in his career, sometimes for violent conduct. As boys growing up, there were frequent fallings-out and the odd bit of fisticuffs, but I never saw any other lad react quite like Billy. On one occasion when we were gathered in the institute a boy named Bobby Torbot said something to Billy that he took exception to, and Billy laid him out with one punch straight in his face. I know Billy's dad was killed in a car crash travelling to watch him play in a game. Perhaps this tragedy added to his anger issues.

There were other young lads of a similar calibre to Billy playing in Fife. Inevitably, if the quality of the players in the league was good, then scouts from bigger clubs would be watching these games. The first approach I had was from someone after a game asking if I would be willing to go for a trial to Sheffield United. Nothing came of that but soon afterwards I travelled down to Blackburn, invited by them, again for a trial. I left dejected. It was like men against boys and I just couldn't cope with the physical nature of the game. I could beat a player with skill but I just didn't have the power or the pace to get away from them. Funny how things work out, but in just a few more years Blackburn would be a club that I loved playing against.

Another trial in Lancashire came along, this time at Oldham. This also ended in failure. They sent me a nice letter which I have still got to this day, saying that although they thought I was a good footballer, they also thought that I would never have the strength to stand up to the demands of league football. They wished me well in whatever future career I pursued. (They were obviously very confident that that career wouldn't be in football!) I used that letter many times with children on my football development courses. I told them that I had two choices. I could agree with the coaches at Oldham and give up. Or I could use it to fire myself up, to give myself the extra motivation of proving them wrong. Which is obviously what I did.

I was soon off on my travels again, this time on the train with my dad for a trial at Scottish First Division club Dundee United. This time I didn't need a letter to tell me that things hadn't gone well. As me and my dad queued to get a cup of tea in the little refreshments hut, I felt dejected. I just couldn't seem to perform when given a trial. When we got to the table, an elderly lady was pouring the tea from a huge brown teapot. Despite never lifting her head from her task, she managed to get as much tea in each saucer as there was in the cups. Still without lifting her head, she said to me, 'Well, how did ye play th'day, son?' Before I could answer, my dad replied, 'Na he ne'er played very well th'day hen.'

What she said next, I have never forgotten. 'Well, ye must hae something, son, or ye wouldnae be here.' I took her words of wisdom away with me, little knowing that in just a few weeks she was proved correct when a Scottish League club did indeed think that I had 'something'.

Chapter 6

Becoming a Wasp

I HEARD whispers that Rangers were taking a look at me. A similar rumour circulated that Tommy Docherty, the manager at Rotherham, was about to make a move. If either club were lining up to make an offer, then they were going to be too late. Another invitation to trial arrived, this time with Alloa Athletic, a team from Clackmannanshire who played in the Scottish Second Division. I had been to several trials, but this one was going to be different. At other clubs I had either played in their youth team or in a specially arranged trial game. Alloa had no youth or reserve team and I had expected to train with them as part of the trial. I was in for a shock as I was informed that the trial was to be a first-team game against Albion Rovers. When I arrived, I was listed on the team sheet as 'A. Trialist'.

A horrible incident happened in this game. One of our players, Bobby St John, went down after a tackle. As the trainer came on, Bobby said, 'Nai bother. It's just mah shin pad snapped.' The trainer was looking down at Bobby's leg and told him, 'Bobby, son, ye'r nae waring ony pads.' His leg was so badly broken that he was never to play again.

After something like this, the result scarcely mattered but we did run out 4-0 winners.

For me, the game proved to be a watershed moment. I knew that I had played well and that I had impressed, scoring one goal and setting up two others. So, on the Sunday following the game, I wasn't too surprised when the Alloa secretary turned up at our house with the forms needed to sign me on. I didn't hesitate to write my signature on the dotted line. As Alloa played in amber and black hoops, I was to become a Wasp!

Like many teams at this level, Alloa were part-time. I would still be working as a painter and decorator during the week. However, instead of training one evening a week as at the Bluebell, I would now be training twice a week at Recreation Park in Alloa. I remember, once, some of my Dundonald team-mates gathering round one of the committee men one evening after training to ask why a certain young lad kept being invited back to training despite being, in the words of these boys, 'absolutely boggin'.

The answer was straight to the point, 'Well, lads, dae ye want tae train in the mirk or in the light?' The boy in question worked at the shipyard and had access to five or six freestanding floodlights. His participation at Bluebell training was never in question again as the players realised that a player's worth to the team couldn't just be measured in terms of his footballing ability!

Moving to Alloa, I thought I would be leaving the freestanding lights behind and I wasn't to be disappointed. At our ground, we had no need of temporary lighting. Those of you thinking of Recreation Park in the 60s will probably imagine a floodlight pylon at each corner of the ground in traditional fashion. You'd be wrong. Just like the Bluebell, Alloa had no lights. We relied on the floodlights from the bus station behind one of the stands to illuminate the pitch. These were great when you faced away from the lights; you could see everything. Face the other way, however, and all you could see was silhouettes of players and ball. It was a case of having to make do.

Recreation Park also had a significant slope from one goal to the other. I really enjoyed playing on the main stand side of the ground as this meant I was playing downhill. One other feature of the ground was the brewery on the opposite side to the bus station. When beer was being brewed, there was an overpowering yeasty smell in the air, not the best atmosphere for playing football!

I didn't know whether I would be a regular in the first team straight away or not but the bad luck of other players meant that the manager, Archie MacPherson, had limited options in terms of team selection. In my second game, a 2-1 win against Queen of the South, a lad called John 'Bud' Flanagan also suffered a broken leg. This was a life-changing injury for John in more ways than one as he had just been told before the game that Rangers were going to bid for him and take him to Ibrox. His injury put an end to their interest.

In the third game, we played at home to Forfar Athletic, and the curse struck again when Jim Bailie, one of our best players, also went down with a serious injury, torn knee ligaments, that ended his season. With Flanagan, St John and Bailie all being out, my chances of staying in the team had increased due to their misfortune. In fact, due to the injury situation, there were games in my initial run in the team when the manager was forced to play five 18-year-olds in the forward positions. It did no harm, however, as we went on a fantastic run and won seven of my first nine games for the club.

MacPherson was a nice, soft, old lad. He had been Alloa's manager for a good few years and had played for a number of teams, including Rangers and Liverpool. He was quite a shy man and he didn't seem to relish talking to the players. He was almost embarrassed to take a team talk or even have a face-to-face conversation. If I had thought that now, playing for a Scottish League team, tactics would be part of training and team talks, then I was wrong.

Archie, who had retained the nickname Curly from his younger days despite no longer having a single curl on his head, picked the team but did very little else. He seldom made an appearance at a training session and his team talks rarely went beyond urging us to 'get stuck in'. The season was already ten games old when I joined but I have to say the players certainly did what the manager asked and gave their all in every game.

My financial situation had suddenly greatly improved. As an apprentice painter and decorator, I was earning £3 a week, not forgetting my four shillings from Bluebell! At Alloa I was on £6 if I played plus another £4 if we won. That first season at Alloa was a reasonable one with the team finishing eighth, which meant a fair number of win bonuses being paid. My dad, who was earning about £9 a week for his 40-plus hours in the pit, had a chat with me when I signed for the club.

I had intended giving my wage packet to my mum in the way that I had when I started as an apprentice. However, my dad advised that I open a bank account and give half of my football wages to my mum and keep the rest for myself, and this is what I did. He knew that my mum would still give away anything that was asked of her and he wanted to safeguard things for me. He was aware of the precarious earning power of a footballer and we both knew that this was possibly as good as it would get for me, particularly with the ever-present risk of injury being a real and continuing threat. However, my good fortune financially was reflected by that of my parents too. My dad was able to buy a second-hand Honda 50 motorbike. For the first time, he and my mum had a bit of freedom. They would go off on little trips on the bike, Dad driving and Mum riding pillion. They could go shopping at stores in Kirkcaldy rather than being limited to those in Cardenden. They would also both come to the occasional Alloa game to watch me play.

There was very little glamour in playing in the Scottish Second Division. However, if I had at all started to get a bit big for my boots, then living and working among the people in Fife would quickly have put me in my place. My mate Alex Carswell, who I had grown up with and who I had played with at the Bluebell, now worked in the Methil shipyards. When Alloa were due to play the local team, East Fife, Alex talked one of his friends from the yard to come along to the game.

I think he must also have talked me up a bit as, back in the pub after the game, he asked his friend for his verdict on Tam Hutchison. 'That was th' string bean laddie oot oan th' wing?' his mate asked. 'Aye, that was him,' confirmed Alex. 'An' he's a painter 'n decorator, is he?' 'Aye, that's his job,' said Alex. 'Well, tell him tae stick at it,' advised his mate! When Alex told me about his friend and his advice on not giving up the day job, I just put it down to Fifers being a hard people to impress!

The passion that I had for playing football certainly didn't come from my mum or dad. Their interest in the game really only extended as far as me, what I was doing on the pitch and who I was playing for. My uncles, my mum's brothers, were much more interested and knowledgeable about the sport. It was also true that there was an athletic gene running in our family as living across the road from us in The Square was John Ritchie, a cousin of mine who went on to have a long career in football, albeit sometimes in a part-time capacity. He mainly played as a goalkeeper, for several clubs including Dundee United and Bradford. I say mainly as a keeper as he also had a short stint as a centre-forward for Cowdenbeath and scored a few goals for them. He was also a coach and managed Brechin City for a spell too.

The nearest thing to a sporting activity that my mum and dad did was to go dancing. I can see them now, all dressed up on a Saturday night, off to a local hop. My mum would be wearing a pair of high heels but have a pair of sandals tucked under her arm. She could only bear the discomfort of the heels for so long, so sandals would come into play at some stage during the evening.

You would think that someone who needed to have quick feet on the football field would also be fairly adept at moving with grace and rhythm on the dance floor. Certainly, this wasn't true in my case. I hadn't inherited my mum or my dad's dancing genes and Fred Astaire had nothing to fear from me. However, it was at local dances that you were most likely to find a girl and so, despite my lack of ability on the dance floor, like my parents I would be at a local hop on a Saturday night, just not the same one as them.

I was at a dance at Bowhill miners' institute one Saturday night. They had a local band on, playing the popular songs of the day, doing their best to sound like The Beatles or Gerry and the Pacemakers, only with Fife accents. On this particular night, I saw two girls, obviously sisters, who I had not seen before. I asked one of them, Dot, to dance, and that went fairly well. Later in the evening I asked her sister, Irene, to dance with me and that went very well, so much so that I spent the rest of the evening chatting with her, and at the end of the night we had agreed to meet up again.

The girls were Irene and Dorothy Adair. They lived with their family at Ballingry, a village outside of Cardenden. I really liked Irene and, using a term that today is very old-fashioned, we started courting. We would go on dates to the local dances and to the pictures. Sometimes she would get the Kirkcaldy bus on a Saturday evening from Ballingry and as it passed through Bowhill I would get on and join her and we would go dancing in the town.

I took her to meet my family and I was introduced to hers. She had a sweet, kind and gentle nature that very much appealed to me and was quiet and easy-going in everything she said or did. I couldn't fail to notice that she was also a very good-looking girl who dressed in a really attractive way. I was smitten and I very soon realised that Irene was the one for me.

She worked in the offices of the Linoleum works in Kirkcaldy, a huge employer of local people at the time, which is now long gone. Every working day she would catch the bus from Ballingry, which just happened to pass through Cardenden. I would often be working at some of the properties on the High Street. I would make sure that, as her bus passed by, I was out on the street and we would give each other a wave!

Irene, unlike her brothers and her dad, wasn't interested in football. She would have been more impressed that she was now going steady (another outdated 1960s term) with a painter and decorator than with someone who kicked a ball about on a Saturday afternoon. Perhaps she could see a lifetime of perfectly painted and wallpapered living rooms and bedrooms stretching away into her future!

I was fortunate that a couple of the Alloa players, Alec Hodge and Jim Bailey, were local boys and so every Tuesday and Thursday, straight after work, I would hop into a car, get taken to training and be dropped back later in the evening. I would often catch the bus and go over to Irene's house in Ballingry. I was sometimes so knackered after my day at work, my two hours of training and all the travelling about that I would fall asleep on her mum's settee, only to be woken up so I could get the last bus back to Dundonald. She must have seen something in me because, despite my sleepy ways, we continued to go out together.

I have said that Irene was a very easy-going girl and the following story shows this perfectly. On spring and summer evenings after work, when I had no training and when the evenings were light until late, I would turn up to Irene's house to see her. Inevitably, one of her brothers would produce a ball and say, 'Come on, Tam, we'll have a wee kickaboot.' Opposite the house was a cemetery which stood next door to some football fields, and it was to these that we headed. (Irene's mum, Betty, would regularly have flowers on the table on a Monday. I used to joke that this was because they lived opposite the cemetery!)

The 'wee kickaboot' would last for a couple of hours and usually involve the rest of her brothers and sometimes her dad. At nine o'clock, we would troop back into the kitchen where Irene's mum, assisted by Irene herself, would have homemade tea and cakes ready for the household. A chat with everyone around the table would take us up to 9.55pm when I would take my leave to catch the ten o'clock bus back to Dundonald!

Irene never complained about me disappearing to play football with her brothers on the nights I had come over to see her. Perhaps she was just pleased that I got on well with her family and that they seemed to like me. If she had grumbled about the 'wee kickaboot' she would have been given short shrift from her dad Joe. He, like her brothers, was a big football fan, who loved Glasgow Rangers. Having a prospective son-in-law who played in the Scottish League was just about as good as it could get, and if Irene didn't appreciate the prospect of having a footballer in the family, Joe certainly did.

He hated losing at anything – cards, dominoes or football – so on our evening kickabouts I was always on Joe's team and he expected me to ensure he was always on the winning side. I often joked with Irene after we were married that ours was a shotgun wedding except, in this case, the imaginary gun held by her dad was pointing at her not at me! Under no circumstances would she be allowed to let a footballer escape, not that I would ever have wanted to be free from Irene.

Joe would sometimes come down to see me play when I was at Blackpool. A keen photographer, he would cart his heavy old camera, set it up in the stands and take pictures of me in action. When developed, the grainy old black-and-white prints would require some explanation. 'Tha's your fut there Tam,' as a leg was just visible sticking out from behind a full-back, or 'Ye see the ball flyin' ore the bar, well tha' was your shot Tam,' in a picture where perhaps only ball, crossbar and the crowd were to be seen. He was never going to win the sports photograph of the year.

He could, however, be quite a difficult man, who seemed to be shy and embarrassed in company. He would sometimes sit in his chair, bonnet on his head, morose and unwilling to talk. He also had a quick temper. All of this is not surprising when you find out that during the war he was captured by the Japanese and spent years in one of their prison camps. He never said what happened to him there but with the history of these places now well known, it's not hard to imagine.

After we were married and had our first baby, Lynn, Irene and I were wary of how her dad would react to Lynn's crying. As it happens, he was fine with her, a lot more patient than he would have been with an adult who was disturbing his peace. Animals too, particularly dogs, never felt the rough edge of his tongue. They loved him and would do anything for him.

My mum could also manage to bring him out of himself. We were all together at Irene's brother Josie's wedding. Irene's dad was sat in his chair not really joining in anything. My mum went over to him and took his hand, and said, 'C'maoan noo Joe oot o' yer chair, lets shaw thae young ones how tae dance.' He grumbled and moaned for a bit but he allowed her to lead him on to the floor. After a bit he was all smiles and laughter and never sat down!

In later years, during the close season, when Irene, the children and I came back to Fife, I would take him out down to the pub for a drink. I would slip him a tenner before we got inside so that he could always buy his round and not be embarrassed by lack of funds. He always appreciated that. I was never able to take my own dad out in the same way which is something I regret. He did take a drink, the occasional bottle of beer or a Drambuie at Christmas, but he was never one for going into pubs. I think that's a shame as I know he would have enjoyed meeting friends and acquaintances while having me in tow and being able to show off his son who played for Scotland.

In my second and third years at Alloa, the amount of win bonuses that I was taking home gradually decreased as the team were less successful. The eighth place we achieved in my first season there was followed by finishes of 13th and 17th in the next two seasons. The small crowds that Alloa could attract always meant that we would struggle to bring in or hold on to the players who could have seen us push for promotion. The gulf between ourselves and clubs who had full-time pro players was shown when we played a League Cup tie at Hibs the season I joined. Alloa lost the game at Easter Road 11-2. Fortunately, this game took place a few weeks before I signed on.

Being part of a league club meant I travelled to many parts of Scotland that I had not seen before. It also meant that I was given the chance to play at some historic venues. At Alloa, I fulfilled part of my Scottish dream by playing at Hampden Park for the first time, in a Scottish Second Division game against Queen's Park, who owned and played in the national team's stadium. On that occasion there was only a few hundred people there to watch us beat the home side 3-1. I was also one of the last visiting players to play at Cathkin Park, the home of Glasgow club Third Lanark who, soon after we played there in February 1967 and lost 3-0, went out of business.

Playing for Alloa gave me the chance to play with and against better players than those I had encountered in the Fife League. Peter Smith was a good centre-half who had played for Hearts. He was ultra-competitive and would kick his granny if it meant the team would win. Jim Bailey, who lived in Lochgelly and who I relied on sometimes for lifts to training, was an excellent left-half, a defensive midfielder in today's terms. We also had Harry Rutherford who earned himself a transfer to First Division Ayr United. I 'won' my first piece of silverware, at Alloa, although when you hear the bizarre circumstances of this win you will understand why we were not issued with medals.

Each season Alloa played in the Stirlingshire Cup, a competition for clubs who played under the jurisdiction of the Stirlingshire County FA. We are probably unique in football history as being the only club to have won a competition without scoring a goal. We received a bye in the first round which put us straight into the semi-final, a game we drew 0-0 with Dumbarton but won on the toss of a coin. The final should have been against Stirling Albion. For some reason, they pulled out of the game and we were awarded the cup!

Things with Irene were progressing nicely and I decided it was time to ask her to marry me. I was hopeful that she would say yes; after all, a qualified painter, decorator and part-time footballer would be an excellent catch! So, one evening when we had just come out of the pictures in Lochgelly, I popped the question and Irene said yes. The setting wasn't very scenic. Downtown Lochgelly on a wet Sunday wasn't really a rival for Paris or for Venice but it was good enough for us! I didn't go down on one knee as it was damp and I had a good pair of trousers on, but Irene didn't seem to mind. The bus stop and the wall which were the backdrop to my proposal are still there.

Whenever we pass the site these days, I will often remind Irene of how I saved her from a lifetime of carrying lino in the Kirkcaldy factory when she said yes to my question that far-off day in 1967. She will come back at me by stating the fact that she never had carried a roll of lino, as she was an office worker! We bought our engagement rings from a jeweller in Kirkcaldy but our official engagement took place in Edinburgh on 17 June 1967 under the Scott Monument. If you are impressed that I know the exact date, don't be. On the inside of our rings we have inscribed 'Irene and Tommy 17-6-67'. No date was set for our wedding as at that time there seemed no need for any urgency.

I had played more than 60 games for Alloa in the two and a half years that I had been at the club. I felt that I could certainly play at a higher level, something that would have to happen if I was to fulfil the ambition of wearing that dark-blue shirt, an ambition that still burned brightly. I knew that players in this league were being watched and were being moved on to higher things. Tony Green, who I had played against when he was at Albion Rovers, and Cowdenbeath's Henry Mowbray had both been picked up by English Second Division club Blackpool. I was hoping that something similar might happen to me. I wasn't to be left disappointed.

Chapter 7

I Do Like to Be Beside the Seaside

I HAVE often felt that not having gone through a club's youth system, the 1960s equivalent of today's academies, has given me more of an appreciation for what life is like outside professional football. At the age of 20, I was doing okay. I had been earning money as an apprentice painter and decorator for four years and I had been playing part-time football (and paid for the privilege) for Alloa for the past two and a half years. I also had a girl that I was mad about and eventually wanted to marry. My love of playing football had not diminished with adulthood. The passion I had for the game was as strong at 20 years of age as it had been when I was five. The only fly in the ointment was how my job would sometimes get in the way of me being able to produce my best. Take a certain Saturday in February 1968 for example. Alloa were due to play at Love Street against St Mirren.

At ten o'clock that morning I would be at the arranged meeting point to get on the team bus that would take us to Paisley. None of that seems to be problematic until you find out that I am painting the post office in Cowdenbeath. Now, the post office has to be open during the day and so it could only be decorated at night. The night before the St Mirren game I am up a ladder, paintbrush in hand until six in the morning. By the time I get home, I can just manage an hour in bed before I am up again and off for the bus. Not the best preparation for 90 minutes of athletic endeavour!

It's a good job that on that day I did not know that someone had travelled to Love Street with the express purpose of watching me play. I say this, but if someone had said to me, 'Tam, Stan Mortensen is watching ye th' day son,' my response would have been, 'Who is he?' That wouldn't have been me being disrespectful, it would have been me showing my lack of knowledge of the wider game of football. I didn't know that Stan was the manager of Blackpool or that he had been one of the most famous players of his era.

My love of football has always been for playing the game. When I finished playing, my motivation was in trying to get young children to fall in love with the game in the way I did, or at least to feel better about themselves through what they achieved on our school courses playing football. I have never been, even to this day, a great lover of watching football. I had only ever been to two or three live matches and the only live game on the TV in those days was the Scotland v England game. For me, nothing could ever replace the thrill of playing. On the day that Stan came to watch me at St Mirren, I wouldn't have known him from Adam.

As a team, we had been on a poor run, winning only one of our last eight games. Our prospects of a good result that day were made even more unlikely by the form of our opponents. They had already beaten us at home earlier in the season and by this stage were really flying, well on the way to the league title that they would clinch in May. I didn't realise as we kicked off that in three months, when the St Mirren players were celebrating their title, I would be living nearly 250 miles south of Dundonald and a full-time professional footballer.

At full time, as we trooped off the Love Street pitch having been trounced 6-1, the prospect of a move anywhere seemed remote. The following week we were at home to Montrose and we redeemed ourselves a little as we won the game 2-1. I didn't know at the time that this would be my last game for Alloa. I also didn't know that scouts from Blackpool had watched me again.

You can imagine my surprise when, on the Monday following the game, a telegram arrived at our house. It was exciting enough that we had a telegram. I'm not sure anyone in our family had ever had one before. But it was the contents of the note that raised our excitement levels to fever pitch. It was from Alloa telling me to call the secretary urgently. We all thought that the need to ring could only be for one reason. We were right! When I got through to him from a phone box at the bottom of the road, trouser pockets filled with coins so that we didn't get cut off, I was told that an offer from Blackpool of £6,000 had been accepted by the club and that Blackpool would be in touch.

This represented good business for Alloa. They had signed me for nothing, had two and a half years of committed service and were selling me for a nice profit. (If I played 15 first-team games for Blackpool, the fee would rise to £10,000. I had completed the 15 games within a few months of joining.) It goes without saying that this was also good business for me. My family, Irene and I could scarcely take it all in. If things weren't already exciting enough, then sure enough, the next day another telegram arrived. Two telegrams in two days! It read: 'Phone me Blackpool 31107 7pm this evening. Mortensen.'

I still have both telegrams. By this stage, I was fully aware who 'Mortensen' was. In actual fact I never made that phone call. It was arranged through the club that I would meet Stan Mortensen at a hotel in Alloa the following night, a training night. Me and my dad, who was coming with me for moral support, could get a lift with Alec Hodge. While the boys from Alloa were training, we would be at the hotel meeting the man who would hopefully be my next manager. Stan certainly made a good impression on Dad and me. He was really good company, put us at our ease and made us smile at his stories. He was also the best-dressed man I had ever seen with his well-cut suit, expensive tie and highly polished shoes.

There was no negotiation in terms of wages, or anything else for that matter. Stan told us how everything was going to be. My basic wage would be £25 a week. If I played in the first team, I would earn another £15. I would also receive £300 as part of the fee paid to Alloa, with another £300 when completing 15 games. The money was great, but what really had me walking on air was that, as from the following Monday, I would effectively finish work. There was no way that I could ever think of playing football as work. I was going to be paid for something that to me was simply a joy. How good could life get!

Driving back through Dundonald, I asked Alec to pull over when I saw my long-time pal Drew Davidson on the street. I had good news and bad news for him. The bad news was that because of my impending move south I would not now be able to attend his upcoming wedding. The good news, as he pointed out to me, was that he now had somewhere to stay on holiday (once I got a house). Irene, my family and her family could not have been more delighted. The only downside was that for the first time since we started going out, and certainly since we became engaged, we were going to be apart. This was something that set us both thinking.

I had to tell my boss, Bandy Mathison, that Friday would be my last day. He was a football fan, an East Fife season-ticket holder, and he could not have been more supportive; he told me not to worry about working what should have been a month's notice. However, a local union official wasn't quite so easy-going. He insisted that if I was not at work on Monday and every working day until my notice was served, then, as he put it, 'Ye'll ne'er paint in Scotland agin.' There was no way that I wouldn't be in Blackpool on Monday so I asked him if I could have his threat in writing. I didn't want to have to paint for a living in Scotland or anywhere else for that matter, ever again!

On the Monday, Mum, Dad, Irene and me caught the train to Preston where we were picked up by Harry Johnston, who introduced himself as Stan Mortensen's assistant. We were taken to Blackpool's ground, Bloomfield Road, and given a tour. In the boardroom, I saw a photo of a young-looking Harry Johnston on his team-mate's shoulders holding the FA Cup. When I enquired with a staff member, he confirmed that Harry had captained the team to victory in the game labelled the Matthews Final. My football knowledge was improving all the time.

We were taken to what would be our digs for the next few days, an establishment right across the road from the stadium, run by Kitty and Horace, a train driver. It was a posh place, tablecloths on the tables, cutlery impeccably laid out for each meal. We were all impressed. For the couple of days that we were together in Blackpool, we had a great time. Once training finished at midday, I was free to explore my new home. My dad was a big fan of Tony Bennett and we got tickets to see him live in his show. My mum was also catered for as also appearing in Blackpool was the Musical Muscle Man, Tony Holland, who had won *Opportunity Knocks*. They loved it. For me, it was wonderful that through my football I was able to start paying them back a little bit for all they had done for me.

I was sad to see them go back to Fife, particularly Irene, who I was going to greatly miss, but I was also really excited about what lay ahead. The first thing I had to do was to pack up my few belongings and walk with them a few hundred yards up the road. I found out that Kitty and Horace's house was a bit of a show place for new and prospective signings and their families. It was meant to impress and show the club in a good light.

The place I was moving too was a bit more down to earth and not quite as posh. It had five other young Blackpool players living there, three of whom would be my room-mates. The digs were run by Mabel and her husband Frank, who was also a milkman. Mabel was wonderful. As well as looking after all of us, cooking for us, doing our washing and ironing, she also had her own young family to cater for. We paid £5 each per week to stay with Mabel and it was worth every penny; she was a typically kind and hospitable Lancashire lady.

My room-mates, all young lads, were Brian Dean, Tony Green and Henry Mowbray. The latter two were Scots and I soon settled in with them. Poor old Brian, a Manchester boy, didn't have a clue what we were talking about half of the time. There were the usual pranks and practical jokes that you would expect from young lads away from home for the first time. Looking back, it was all very innocent. None of us drank. After training we might head to the Tyldesley Conservative Club on Palmer Avenue, across the road from the digs, to play snooker. Next door to this was a Crown Green bowling club, so we also tried our hand at bowls. We would often take a football down onto the beach and simply practise passing and shooting.

It was great being at a big club with a historic stadium and proper floodlights. Each day we would turn up at Bloomfield Road, get changed and get into cars, those who didn't own one sharing with someone that did. We would drive to the training ground which was south of town near the Squires Gate airport. There were no changing facilities at the training ground and it wasn't ideal getting back into someone's car covered in mud to go back to Bloomfield Road to bathe and change.

The baths were huge old things with stone floors and no tiles. So, you'd climb in there and hunt for a piece of soap. Old Harry the groundsman would come in wearing his waistcoat and one of the boys would say, 'Harry, we're needing soap.' 'Are you's eatin' it?' was his usual response, and off he'd go grumbling. He'd come back in with a huge length of red carbolic, but pare off the smallest of slithers with his knife. 'Watch you don't cut it too thick there, Harry!' one of the boys would shout.

Those baths were so lovely to lie in after a hard day's running and you'd come in absolutely catholed. I was getting to know all the other players and just like those at the Bluebell and at Alloa, there was a lot of mickey-taking that went on. It was important as the new boy to show you could take it and that you could give it out. At training, both the home and away dressing rooms would be used; the first-team players would be in the plusher home dressing room, the reserves in the away dressing room. Tony Green had progressed from the reserves and earned his place in the first-team room. Henry Mowbray and I changed with the reserves.

One day soon after I arrived, we were having our weight checked; first-team players first, then us reserves. When I had been weighed, I was walking past the open door of the first-team room when Alan Skirton, a Cockney right-winger from Arsenal, shouted out, 'And what was your weight, today, Hutchie?' which started a barrage of jokes and comments from the other players at my expense. I was well aware of my less-than-impressive physique, which had already been the butt of the player's humour. However, I had to give as good as I got, so I poked my head in the door, looked at his rather chunky midriff and said, 'So, Skirty, and what weight should you be?' As I walked back to our dressing room I had to smile as I could hear the other players now ribbing Skirton.

I played my first game for Blackpool in the reserves against Newcastle reserves at Bloomfield Road. It may have been the reserves but the attendance was still the biggest that I had played in front of, with several thousand turning up to watch 'the stiffs'. I was in direct opposition with Newcastle right-back John Craggs, who went on to have a long career at Newcastle and Middlesbrough.

Craggs, like me, knew that his manager and his coaches would be carefully watching his performance. He didn't want someone like me making a mug of him and so he set out to kick lumps out of me. I played really well, however, and felt I had the beating of him whenever I had the chance to run at him. I loved it: the crowd, the noise, the stadium and the standard of players I was playing with and against. I wanted more. If it was this good playing for the reserves, just how good would playing for the first team be? It wouldn't be long until I found out.

Chapter 8

Tangerine Dream

I PLAYED a few more reserve games and felt that I was playing well. I certainly didn't feel in any way out of my depth. I think Morty must have thought the same. I had arranged with some of my reserve team-mates to go and watch a game at Blackburn during our free time. Morty got wind of this, had a quiet word with me, telling me not to go as he might need me for the first-team game at home to Plymouth.

A month after signing I made my full Blackpool debut and John Sillett, a former Chelsea and Coventry player, was the full-back I was facing. He had been a very good footballer but was coming to the end of his career and that night I gave him a real chasing, running him ragged for 90 minutes. I got to know John well in later years, frequently meeting up with him at Coventry legend days. He would often announce to anyone willing to listen, arm around my shoulder, that he was the person, due to his performance that night, who set me on the road to fame, fortune and international glory! He also told me that Plymouth tried to buy me from Blackpool based on that performance.

We beat Plymouth that night, but it would take an extraordinary run if we were to achieve the ambition of gaining promotion back to the First Division from which the club had been relegated the previous season. I stayed in the team for the rest of the season, displacing left-winger Graham Oates. This was a surprise to me, as when he signed me, Morty had told me that I would be taking Alan Skirton's place on the right wing. Over my first few months at the club, I saw what a good player Skirton was in training and in games. It dawned on me that this was Morty baiting a hook, telling me I was going to replace one of the club's best players, a subtle way of flattering me, telling me how highly

59

I was rated. The problem with that plan was that, with my football ignorance, I had no idea who Skirton was or how good a player he was until I saw him for myself.

The game that followed my debut was away at Blackburn and the defeat we suffered there seemed to have ended any realistic hope of promotion we may have had. However, we went on a tremendous run that mirrored the start I had at Alloa. We won the next six games on the trot and when we came to the last game of the season at Huddersfield, we knew that if we bettered the result of our rivals, Queens Park Rangers, we would be promoted to the First Division.

The pitch at Leeds Road was a quagmire that got worse the longer the game went on as the rain that had started the previous day continued to pour down. It was so bad that at one point the referee ordered Tony Green back to the changing room for a new strip as he couldn't tell whether Tony's shirt was Blackpool tangerine or Huddersfield blue and white. Huddersfield had the best of the first half and scored just before half-time. It looked like our promotion was slipping away until we learned at the break that Rangers were also losing at Aston Villa. A draw might be enough to take us up.

We had much the better of the second half and we dominated proceedings. We were well on top and scored three times without reply. As our match ended, we heard that Rangers had equalised at Villa Park. Their game was still being played but, as things stood, we were up. Some of the 4,000 travelling Blackpool fans invaded the pitch to celebrate. They were too quick off the mark, however. The dreadful news came through that Rangers, through an own goal in the last minute, had won and would be promoted in our place. It was a crushing blow for everyone. Morty looked stunned when he came into our morgue of a dressing room. He thanked us for our efforts and told us we should be proud of ourselves for coming so close and that next year would be our year.

I may have only been a part of the team for a couple of months but our failure hit me as hard as anyone else. I had allowed myself to daydream that I would be taking the field with players like George Best, pitting my wits against all the top full-backs and really putting myself in the shop window with regard to the Scotland selectors. My bubble had burst, my dream was gone, my mood not helped by the fact that our points total of 58 was the highest total by a team who failed to win promotion.

I didn't really have time to dwell too much on the season ending. Back in Fife, the biggest date in my life so far was fast approaching. When I would arrive back in Blackpool after the summer break, it would be as a married man and I would have my new wife with me.

When it came around, our wedding day was as simple as our engagement. We had booked the registry office in Kirkcaldy and only close family and friends attended. However, as we both had quite a lot of close family, the attendance wasn't bad! I had my best man there, my cousin and long-time friend George Campbell, and Irene had her bridesmaid, her best friend Ann Geddis. Irene looked lovely in her new white two-piece suit.

At Blackpool, we often had visits from lads who were selling lengths of material for the local Lancashire mills. I chose a length from a pattern I liked and the lad arranged for my wedding suit to be made. The actual wedding itself is a blur. I couldn't believe how quick the ceremony was and remarked on this to the registrar, who was a bit of a dour Scot, 'Aye,' he said, 'it will tek ye a lot longer to get oot of it than it did to get in.'

The reception was back at Irene's mum and dad's house in Ballingry. The food, sandwiches and cakes were ordered from the local Co-op and my Auntie Nell's husband, the baker from Cupar, had made us a fantastic three-tiered cake, covered in tangerine icing and tangerine ribbons, obviously because of our Blackpool connection. The day may appear to be low-key, but everything was simply done, without a fuss and turned out just the way that we wanted it. It was a lovely family occasion, and one that we both look back fondly on because of the happy memories that we have.

I was able to buy both my mum and my dad's wedding outfits for them. As we stood together having a cup of tea in the garden, my dad said something to me that I have never forgotten. He said, 'Ye ken Tam, th' day was th' first day tha' a've ever had a pair o' lither shoes oan mah feet.' While his wistful comment made me sad to think how hard a life he and my mum had had, I was so pleased that my new career meant that I could help make life a little bit easier for them. I knew that if things continued going well for me, that I would be able to slip a few quid my dad's way every time that I came home. He would then dripfeed my overgenerous Mum. We left our little reception to catch the 2pm train from Cowdenbeath – not to go off on honeymoon – we weren't having one – but to start our new life together in Blackpool.

Returning in that summer of 1968, this time with Irene by my side, the world was an unsettled place. In France there were huge student riots. In the US there were ongoing protests about the Vietnam war. For me, however, the world was a wonderful place. Could life get any better? The thought that I would soon be going back to work was enough to almost make me laugh out loud. For me, at least for the time being, the concept of work simply didn't exist. I loved training. I loved playing. I was being paid to do both! I knew that in many ways I was such a lucky boy. But I also remembered the hours of running, training and practise that had got me to this point. The saying 'the harder I worked, the luckier I got' was true for me.

We were also going to get our first house, a Blackpool club house, which was situated close to Stanley Park and which we were to live in rent-free. It was a big old airy place with huge bay windows. With the free time I had after training each day, it wouldn't take me long to have it painted and decorated in the way that Irene wanted. We furnished it initially with bits and pieces of furniture donated by family members. However, we did have a stroke of luck in the flooring department.

One of the Blackpool directors had a business dealing in antiques and second-hand items. When a show home was being sold, he would often have the chance to buy the carpet. He told me to let him know if we wanted any, which we did. It was great! It cost us £45 to have the whole house, upstairs and down, fitted with virtually new carpet. We had to take all the doors off as the carpet was so thick.

My dad came down from Fife to shave and refit these a few weeks later. When Irene and I next went back to Fife we were instructed by my mum to bring an offcut of carpet with us so she could see. This we did. If you have ever watched the musical *Fiddler on the Roof*, you will remember a scene where all the family and the neighbours visit the son-in-law and daughter of the main character, Tevye, to see their 'new arrival'. The couple do in fact have a new baby but the interest of family and friends is on the newly arrived sewing machine which will allow the son-in-law, a tailor, to better earn a living.

Well, it was a bit like that with Irene, me and the offcut of carpet. It was viewed, examined, stroked and admired by family and neighbours alike who had heard all about it from my mum, who marvelled at how thick it was. It says much for the Dundonald folks who came around as they seemed genuinely pleased for Irene and me, no hint of jealousy at our good fortune. The carpet was green and I did expect a bit of stick from Irene's dad, him being a Rangers boy, but even he never said a dicky bird against it.

On the football front, things seemed to be on the up as well. We had missed promotion by a whisker the previous season. I could see no reason why this couldn't be our year. We had a good squad of players who I genuinely felt would do more than just okay. Our captain was former England right-back and captain Jimmy Armfield, who was a good, experienced player. We also had former England international Gordon Milne, who had won trophies in one of Bill Shankly's great Liverpool teams.

These were the sort of players who would never be afraid to tell any one of us if we weren't doing things right or if we were letting the team down. Something that always stuck with me was a comment that Jimmy made about never coming off the field having let the fans down. He wanted us all to know who it was who paid our wages. We had solid players in every position but the best of our bunch by a mile was attacking midfielder Tony Green. My former room-mate was easily the best footballer that I had played with, perhaps second only to George Best in players that I had seen. With Tony in our team anything was possible. I could never understand why any of the really top teams never came in for him. Perhaps the only reason was that he didn't score enough goals.

I felt lucky too that I played for a manager like Morty. To the players, he was a father figure who cared about us as people as well as players. In my first few weeks at the club, he had on a couple of occasions given a tenner each to Tony, Henry Mowbray and me and told us to go home to Scotland when a weekend game was over, and not to come back until the following Wednesday.

He would notice when you were a little bit off in training or in a game. Having moved away from his family in South Shields to Blackpool as a young lad, he understood that we might suffer from a little bit of homesickness. Little acts of kindness like this made a huge difference to team spirit and loyalty to the manager. I think everyone in our squad would have given every last ounce of energy for the Blackpool cause because of him.

Stan had said when appointed to the job that he would be a tracksuit manager. However, I don't think that this was ever going to be his style. I never saw him in a tracksuit in the 18 months we worked together.

He was a dapper fellow who really liked to dress smartly in his suits. One Friday in that close season of 1968, Stan arrived, his usual elegant self, for training, after our session had started. Knowing Stan, he had probably just come from Sands Casino. Friday sessions, which were held at Bloomfield Road, were all about running, some endurance work and a lot of short, sharp sprints. Stan was watching the sprints and he said to Tom White and John McPhee, 'Boys, when I was playing, I was quicker than you two. In fact, I think I still am. Fancy a race?' Now neither of these two lads was a slouch when it came to sprinting, so Morty wasn't choosing an easy option by offering to take them on. All the lads were watching as Stan, dressed to the nines in suit and highly polished shoes and in his late 40s, lined up on the cinder track next to the pitch. The two boys, wearing boots, were on the grass beside him. Credit to Stan, it may have only been a 15-yard sprint and perhaps he did get a bit of a flyer, but he outpaced the two boys to the cheers of all watching.

This was typical Morty, a clever way to keep team spirit really high. As far as we were concerned, we had an excellent manager who was respected and admired by everyone in the club and who we fully expected to lead us to promotion. We would have been shocked and saddened had we known that, within the year, Stan would be sacked.

Chapter 9

Morty

STAN WASN'T cut out to be a disciplinarian. He was just too nice a chap. However, with the good bunch of players he had at Blackpool, particularly having senior pros like Armfield and Milne to help keep everyone in line, on most occasions only a light touch from him was necessary. When you have a squad of young men, many of them in their late teens or early 20s, there will be times when high jinks happen. Henry Mowbray was a practical joker who was always up to mischief. One night when we got back to our digs, during my early Blackpool days, Henry thought it would be a funny to hide the pram that our landlady Mabel had for her toddler. He lifted it over the fence into the entryway at the back of the house.

When we went down to breakfast next morning, Mabel was going potty, looking here, there and everywhere, wondering what could have happened to it. Henry went to collect the pram intending to shout 'surprise'. To his horror he found that the pram had gone. We later found out that the scrap man had been around the area that day. We scarpered into training only to be told by our trainer Les Graham that the boss wanted to see us. The other players had somehow found out what had happened and thought that our discomfort at having to go and see Morty was highly amusing.

As we trudged down the corridor to Stan's office, Tony and I were giving Mowbray pelters as we had done nothing wrong. Stan wasn't happy with us at all. Mabel had phoned and told him we had lost her pram. We were stood like naughty schoolboys while Stan sat and glared at us behind his desk. 'What do you mean, you were only joking? Why touch the pram in the first place? And who was the stupid sod who thought it would be a good idea to lift – ' In the middle of his tirade, he had noticed his desk drawer was open.

He reached in and pulled out some ties, obviously new and still in their wrappers. 'Oh, boys, what do you think of these? I was given them in the market this morning. Nice ties, aren't they?' 'They're smart, Boss,' said Henry, glad to be off the subject of the pram. 'Think you can make use of them lads? Yes? Here you are then,' said Stan, handing us the ties. 'Off you go and make sure your landlady gets a new pram. A good one, mind.' He just couldn't stay mad for long.

We strolled back to the dressing room, up the same corridor, feeling a lot lighter than when we had gone down it. A group of expectant, smirking faces greeted us as we entered, but we said nothing. 'So, what did the boss have to say then?' asked one of our team-mates, impatient to have details of our dressing-down. 'The boss?' queried Henry. 'Oh, he just wondered if we'd like a new tie,' he said, holding up his gift from Stan. The players just looked at each other and shook their heads. Henry was lucky that Tony and me were so easy-going and the three of us put together for a new pram. But at least we did have some nice new ties!

Some of the players knew how to knock Stan out of his stride if he was annoyed and having a go. I had been at team-mate John Ingram's 21st birthday party, held at his digs. Everything was going well until someone decided to use one of the small trifles on the buffet table like a custard pie and pushed it in somebody's face. Soon the remaining trifles and cakes were airborne, being thrown willy-nilly by the players at each other. Now that wasn't my sort of thing and as soon as the desserts started flying, I took my leave.

Our next game after the party was in London and we caught our train from Blackpool South. I usually sat with the younger players having a game of cards. Older players like Gordon and Jimmy would be in a different compartment. Stan came down the aisle, immaculately dressed as always, and slid open our door. 'You boys get me into some bother with these directors,' he grumbled, standing in the doorway. 'I honestly feel like I'm in charge of a bunch of naughty kids. It's cost us nearly £30 to redecorate the room and clean the carpet. So, who decided to throw – ' Alan Skirton, who knew what Morty was like, interrupted him mid-rant. 'Boss, excuse me butting in, but that suit. It's fantastic. I'd like one of those.' We all nodded our appreciation at Morty's sartorial elegance. Telling-off forgotten, Morty grasped the edges of his suit jacket and said,

'Oh, you like it, boys? Well, I wore it last night in the casino too. You wouldn't believe the amount of money floating about in there.' And off he would go, telling us of his gambling exploits.

Morty was a gambler. Before he had taken up the Blackpool job, he was a bookmaker, which he had to give up to be a manager. He loved spending his time and some of his money in Blackpool's casinos. He told us that one night he had been on a roll and had stayed out long past the time he had agreed with his wife to be home. In fact, he was so late that it was early morning before he got back to his house.

He crept in the front door of his bungalow, then along the corridor and into the bedroom. He was hoping to sneak into bed before his wife woke up and found out that he hadn't been home. His plan looked to have failed when his dog came to say hello and the fuss caused his wife Jean to stir. Thinking quickly, Stan reached into his wardrobe and pulled out his golf clubs, 'Just off for an early morning round, dear.' 'Have a lovely time,' was Jean's reply. His bacon had been saved!

Stan's willingness to gamble saved Blackpool some money when he signed Tony Green from Albion Rovers, the year before he signed me. Tony told me this story. Rovers at that time had an owner, Tam Fagan, who was also a car dealer and by all accounts, a bit of an Arthur Daley character. The club's pay structure meant that a player in the team earned £8, if the player was injured, £6, and if he was dropped and left out of the team, only £4. One of Rovers' best players, Kenny Jenkins, a first-team regular, was injured in a game against Stenhousemuir and was going to be missing from the team for a few weeks. When he checked his pay for the first week of his spell out injured, he found that he'd only been paid £4 instead of the £6 which as an injured player he was due. He goes to see our friend, Tam Fagan and says, 'Gaffer, you've made a mistake wi' mah pay. Ah'm injured so Ah shood be oon' six poond.' His boss was ready for him and says, 'Nae mistake, son. It's four poond as Ah was droppin' ye fur th' next game anyhow. On ye go, son.' And with a wave of his hand dismissed him.

This is the guy Morty negotiated with for Tony's transfer. They agreed a fee of £13,500 as the initial payment but they couldn't agree on the further payment Rovers would receive when Tony had played 20 first-team games. Stan was holding out for £2,000, the guy from Rovers wanted £4,000. In the end Stan suggested that they toss a coin for one fee or the other. Morty won and Blackpool saved a couple of thousand quid.

The season that promised so much for us started fairly well. With almost a quarter of the season gone we were unbeaten, although six of those ten games had been draws. We then lost three games on the trot. We never really recovered and never put together the sort of winning run needed to propel us into the top two. We did have a good run in the League Cup where we reached the quarter-final stage. In a second-round replay with Wrexham I scored my first Blackpool goal. We then went on to play the reigning First Division champions, Manchester City, in the next round. City had a fiery winger, Tony Coleman, who I clashed with a few times before he finally lost his rag completely, headbutted me and sent me sprawling to the floor.

Incredibly, neither the referee or linesman saw it and he escaped what should have been a certain sending off, even in those lenient days. I had the last laugh though as a Tom White goal gave us the win and our 20th game without defeat, then a club record. In the next round another First Division team, Wolves, came to Bloomfield Road. They went away beaten too. Results like these showed the quality we had in our team. Unfortunately, that quality wasn't so much on show in the next round as we went down 5-1 to Arsenal at Highbury.

Our goal that night was scored by Tony Green. It was bad luck for him and for us as a team that Tony often played in pain from his Achilles tendon. He had been to see a specialist, a Mr Barnes, who told Tony that there was nothing he could do until the tendon snapped. He was warned that the tendon would snap at some stage and that if he wanted to make this happen sooner rather than later, he should go running over a ploughed field. Tony ignored the advice and carried on playing.

It didn't help our cause that our best player wasn't fully fit, and the eighth-place finish we achieved that season was disappointing. We all felt that we would do better the following season. If nothing else, our cup matches against First Division teams showed that we could beat the best. Stan felt the same, that promotion was within our grasp and that we would achieve it next year. Unfortunately, he wasn't given the chance to see it through.

Citing dressing-room unrest, the board sacked Mortensen soon after the season finished. The reason they gave wasn't true. As far as the players were concerned, there was no need for Stan to go. None of the players had a bad word to say about him. My own point of view was that Stan was a lovely man and a good manager, even though he wasn't one for tactics or for studying the opposition. For him, a good team was made by having the best players that the club could afford playing in their correct positions. As long as you tried your best and did the job that your position dictated, then you were okay for him.

Stan was a legend in Blackpool, both at the club and in the town. He held no bitterness for what had happened to him. In retirement he lived in the area and was frequently seen at Bloomfield Road watching his beloved Tangerines. At one stage, when the club were in serious financial difficulties, Stan auctioned his medals and gave the proceeds to the club to fend off the prospect of liquidation. He is someone that myself and an awful lot of other people would look back on with gratitude and affection.

And so we would have a new manager. As Irene and I headed back to Fife that summer of 1969, my future seemed a little less certain. Who would the board choose and would he, in an era when some managers chose to play without wingers, see value in someone like me? If I had known what was to come the following year, my worries would have vanished.

Chapter 10

Promotion

A LIVERPUDLIAN, Les Shannon, was to be our new manager. He had just got Bury promoted from the Third Division. As a character, he was chalk and cheese when compared to Mortensen. He was quiet, reserved and distant, whereas Morty was funny, outgoing and warm. He was going to have a hard job proving himself and winning people around as the sacking of Mortensen had been roundly condemned by players and supporters alike.

I was interested to see what innovations, if any, he would bring. I was pleased with some of the changes. Les brought in a running coach and under his guidance we now had sessions on the track in Stanley Park. Training I felt was more purposeful and more enjoyable. For the first time we were doing positional stuff, working on our shape and practising free kicks. Things were looking promising.

There was a real blow to the club before the season started. Tony Green, twisting on the ball during training, finally, as predicted by Mr Barnes, snapped his Achilles tendon. He would be out for at least a year. Mr Barnes was the surgeon who operated on Tony. He was quite a famous chap as he was one of the doctors who appeared on the TV programme *Your Life in Their Hands*. This was bad news for us. Before a ball had been kicked competitively, we had lost our best player. A poor start to the season, only three wins in the first ten games, put further pressure on the new manager. Gradually, however, results started to improve.

From a personal point of view, one game really stands out for me in that season. Blackburn had an excellent right-back, Keith Newton, who was an England international. As a winger, there are some players that you really enjoy playing against and others that you can never seem to get the better of. Unfortunately for Keith, he came into the former category as far as I was concerned and I usually played well against him. Also, after my failed trial when I was at the Bluebell, I really enjoyed showing the people at Blackburn what they had missed out on.

That day, everything I did turned to gold. It doesn't happen very often in a football career. I could do no wrong, everything I tried came off and poor old Keith just could not get near me. It was well known that he was being watched by Everton and that a bid for his services was imminent. But I just felt so good. I knew from the first whistle that this was my day and that Keith was in for a torrid time. As it happened, it was one of his last games for Blackburn and a few weeks later he did indeed sign for Everton.

I had always wondered what the scout wrote in his report on him that day for Everton manager Harry Catterick! When I joined Coventry, my new coach, Tommy Casey, told me that he had scouted Keith for Everton, that his report was less than flattering and that he had actually mentioned me as a possible signing. But Everton were in the market for a right-back, not a left-winger, and so it was Keith that they pursued and signed! That night, after the Blackburn game, I took our dog Dusty for a walk in Stanley Park and I stood looking up at the full moon feeling I could achieve anything I wanted to.

Off the field, Irene and I were very happy and settled in Blackpool. It was a very lively place to live in the 60s. There were lots of things to do and see for a young couple with no children. The town's theatres thrived because they showcased the popular acts of the day and locals and holidaymakers ensured that 'house full' notices were a frequent occurrence. Irene and I often went to shows. My parents too would go and see their favourite acts when they came to visit.

Their improving financial situation meant that Dad was able to give the Honda 50 bike to my Uncle Will after he had passed his driving test. He was now the proud owner of a green Reliant Robin, the same three-wheel type of car that Del Boy had, only my dad's was an earlier model. Mum and Dad would travel the 230 miles from Dundonald to Blackpool in their Robin. A journey of that length in that car could not have been easy, but they didn't seem to mind. The next time I came home to Fife I was able to go to the car dealer and pay off the balance that they owed.

Many of the acts that appeared in town were football fans and some of them would turn up at our club. Freddie Starr trained with us one day.

He was a manic character who was never serious for a second. When training finished, he joined in our penalty shoot-out competition insisting he would score ten out of ten. As a footballer, he was absolutely useless and I don't think he made the goalkeeper work on any of his pens. As we were getting changed, he asked if I fancied playing badminton later in the afternoon. I had nothing on, so agreed. He picked me up from home in his little green sports car and we headed to a racquet centre out towards Lytham that was owned by the club chairman.

On the way he said he didn't fancy playing unless we made it interesting. I asked what he meant and he said how about putting £20 on a best-of-five games match. That was a big sum to me and I couldn't really afford to lose it. I looked across at him as we drove along, weighing him up. He didn't look like a badminton player, while in my youth I had been very good at the sport, so I took him up on his bet.

When we walked into the hall, we had to walk past the Irish singing group, The Bachelors, who were already playing on the court next to ours. Freddie obviously didn't think much of them as he called them all sorts of names, but under his breath so they couldn't hear. We started our game and I realised that I would soon be £20 richer. He was an even worse badminton player than he was a footballer. When we finished, I asked him why he would want to play badminton and make such a daft bet when he couldn't play. His answer was that he was bored. He just did not want to spend hours alone in a hotel room, probably drinking too much.

In the late 60s, Britain had a number of top heavyweight boxers. Henry Cooper, Joe Erskine, Dick Richardson, Jack Bodell, Billy Walker and Brian London were all contenders for the British heavyweight championship. They were all household names as their fights were regularly televised on the BBC. London lived in Blackpool and owned a number of nightclubs, the most prominent of which was the 007 club. Freddie Starr, along with a host of TV and sports celebrities, was a frequent visitor.

On his nights off from his own Blackpool show he would often turn up at Brian's club, get up on the small corner stage and do an Elvis impersonation, singing his best-known songs. He was top notch and had a great voice. Once again, he did it unpaid and without prompting because he was lonely in his hotel.

He was lucky that Brian was an easy-going friendly bloke, particularly when he joked about Brian's frequent visits to the canvas floor of the boxing ring by asking him how long he had carried adverts on the soles of his boots! I got to know Brian very well. After training, a lot of us players would gather for lunch at a little café near the stadium. The talk would always be about football, how we were doing, how we could improve. Gordon Milne was often manipulating the salt cellar and pepper pot, showing where players should be.

Brian would often drop in and come and sit with us. He had fought for the world title twice, losing first time to Floyd Patterson and then to Muhammad Ali, both by knockout. He told us that he took the Ali fight purely for the purse, £4,000, a lot of money in 1966. He admitted to us that it was the only fight when he didn't give of his best and his sole motivation was to get out of the ring without getting hurt. He said that Ali's punching wasn't particularly hard, but that he hit a lot!

Sitting next to him, having a sandwich in the café, Henry Mowbray once asked Brian if the seat of his boxing shorts were padded, an extension of Freddie Starr's joke. Brian just stared at him deadpan for a second or two, before landing a punch on the muscle on Henry's arm. This left Henry rolling around holding his arm, the rest of us rolling around laughing at him, and Brian sitting there with a big grin on his face. I think Henry would have agreed that Ali might not have hit hard, but to a non-boxer, Brian certainly did! Seeing Henry wandering around with his dead arm for the next few days brought a smile to the face of all who knew how he got it!

Back in Scotland, my family tried as best they could to follow mine and the team's progress. They could always find out Blackpool's result by listening to the BBC on a Saturday evening or by looking at the Sunday papers, but match reports of our games were scarce in Scotland. My mum was thrilled when the teleprinter typing out the results at the end of the old Saturday afternoon sports programme *Grandstand* printed that Blackpool had drawn 1-1 with Arsenal at Highbury in the cup and that her son had scored the equalising goal! There was great excitement in the Hutchison household that night apparently.

There was also excitement in Blackpool, and not only because of our FA Cup exploits. We had improved in the league and were starting to mount a challenge for promotion. In January, however, it was the cup replay against Arsenal that was capturing people's imagination. The *Blackpool Gazette* sent myself and Micky Burns down to the promenade with one of their photographers. We were pictured with Gypsy Rose

Lee gazing into her crystal ball. She didn't tell us the score, but she did tell us we would win. She was right too as we came from two down to beat Arsenal 3-2. The fact that we went out in the next round to Fourth Division Mansfield didn't really upset too many people as the push for promotion was on.

Our good form continued through the last four months of the season where we lost only one more game before promotion was clinched in our penultimate game. Preston were our fiercest rivals and were staring relegation in the face. If we won at their Deepdale home we would be up and they would almost certainly be down. The ground was packed to the rafters with more than 34,000 Lancastrians inside the famous old stadium, an estimated 20,000 of them from Blackpool.

We were tremendous that night and the result was never in doubt. We were 2-0 up at the break and 3-0 up when the game finished, all three goals scored by Fred Pickering, our centre-forward, with me having a hand in two of them. As at Huddersfield two years previously, our fans invaded the pitch in celebration. This time there would be no sting in the tail. We were up! Ironically, we actually finished with five fewer points than we had in missing out on promotion two years previously.

I would finally have my chance to play against the best players in the country. Along with the manager and my team-mates, I felt that we would do well, that our side was good enough to hold our own with the country's elite clubs. I didn't know it on that Monday night in Preston but in a year's time I would be celebrating winning the most prestigious trophy of my career so far, but also lamenting the biggest disappointment.

Chapter 11

A Sinking Feeling

THERE ARE few things more exciting for a footballer than to be a member of a trophy-winning team. I was certainly on a high from the fact that we had achieved promotion. However, in June of summer 1970 an event happened to me and to Irene that no amount of football glory could ever rival. On that day our daughter and first child Lynn was born, in the Royal Victoria Hospital in Blackpool.

Unfortunately for me, as Lynn said hello to the world, I was over 1,500 miles away in Spain on a club tour with Blackpool. I am sure that today a club would give compassionate leave for a player to be at the birth of a child. In those days that didn't happen so it was a while before I could get back home and say hello to Lynn in person.

Most teams getting promoted to the top league really need to strengthen significantly if they are to survive and thrive. Unfortunately Blackpool, in my time, were not a wealthy club and didn't really have the money to sign the players needed. In fact, never mind new players, there were times that we couldn't even afford a few turkeys. Every year the club would give each player a turkey for Christmas. However, funds were tight and we were told that if we wanted some poultry for the festive dinner then we would have to buy it ourselves.

This caused a mini revolt among the players, who informed the club that if we were to be denied our turkey, then we would no longer be prepared to use our own cars to drive from Bloomfield Road to the training ground. The word came back from the boardroom that this was no problem, we could jog there as part of our fitness training.

Well, on the first morning of 'our work to rule' some bright spark borrowed a flatbed lorry and informed the local paper that we would be travelling to training in an unusual fashion that day. The *Gazette* back-page headline was 'Pool Players do the Turkey Trot' with a photo of us all on the back of the lorry off to training. I can't remember how the issue was resolved but I can't imagine any of today's players taking industrial action for that type of fowl!

We started the season in reasonable fashion with a draw against Liverpool and two wins in our first five games. We also had the good news that Tony Green was almost fit enough to play again. He would be like a new player for us. I remember Jimmy Armfield saying to me that the Second Division was a hard league, the First Division even harder, and international football the hardest of all. I didn't feel it was true for me. I felt at home from the off in the top league with the greater time and space I was given, making my footballing life easier. However, for the team as a whole, it wasn't true. Those two early wins were the only ones we would achieve until we beat Coventry in mid-December.

The board did sanction a new signing early in the season, an interesting one from my perspective, as my new team-mate was to be Tony Coleman – the last time we had met he had given me the old Glasgow kiss! Tony was one hard lad, a tough, tough boy who had a tough Liverpool upbringing with a dad, a docker, who didn't believe in sparing the rod. He had been shown the door by his first two clubs, Stoke and Preston, who thought he was unmanageable.

With shades of my Uncle Brickie, he was also very fortunate that he didn't receive a lifetime ban from the game for assaulting a referee. His career was rescued by non-league Bangor and lower-league Doncaster before he landed a dream move to Manchester City where the combination of Joe Mercer and Malcolm Allison got the best out of him and City won the league, the cup and the Cup Winners' Cup in the space of two years. He seemed like a great signing for us.

When we met up at his first training session, things were a bit embarrassing for us both, but we said hello, shook hands and had a silent understanding that we didn't need to mention our previous encounter and would simply forget it. Our training ground out at Squires Gate was very close to the Irish Sea and in winter the bitter wind that blew across our pitches could cut you in two; all the boys would be wrapped up in tracksuits and woollen hats. Tony would be there in his T-shirt and shorts. He never even had a pair of socks on. It was almost as if him wearing warm clothes would have been seen as a sign of weakness.

When he was introduced to Brian London, he seemed fascinated by him. Brian was six-feet-plus and built like a bulldozer, Tony was a good six inches shorter and had a slight build. Despite this, whenever we met Brian in the 007 club, Tony would pester him for a fight. Brian had a boxing gym in the basement of the club and Tony was forever asking him to go downstairs and do a few rounds with him. Tony wasn't joking and I genuinely think that he felt he could take Brian out. He certainly saw him as a challenge. Brian humoured him and never took him up on the offer but he did say, 'Tony, if we went downstairs I wouldn't raise a glove, but it would still be you that would end up on the canvas.' I think he was saying that Tony would punch himself to a standstill, but it still sounded strangely menacing the way that London said it.

Tony certainly wasn't afraid of using his fists. A young chap standing next to a pillar in the club rather foolishly told Tony that he thought he was crap in that afternoon's game against West Brom. Without answering him, Tony punched him straight in the face, causing the fellow's head to bounce off the pillar. As the young chap slid to the floor, Tony thumped his pint class down on a shelf and announced he was going home. For obvious reasons, he reminded me of Billy Johnston.

Luckily for me, considering he had such a violent temper, Tony seemed to like me and we got on well. He had recently got married and bought a new house in Lytham St Annes. He was having wardrobes fitted in the bedroom of the new house which had louvre doors and I offered to come over and paint them. 'That'll be smashing,' he said. When I turned up at his house with my brushes and dressed in my dungarees, the wardrobes were still being fitted. Tony's wife was out and he was somewhere else in the house, so I had a chat with the fitter. He knew Tony from his young days in Liverpool and it was him who told me about Tony's tough upbringing.

As soon as he finished the wardrobes, I started painting the doors, which didn't take me too long. As I was standing back to admire my handiwork, Tony's wife arrived home and they both came up to the bedroom to see how I was getting on. 'They look lovely, thanks very much for painting them, Tommy,' said Tony's wife. 'Tha's nae problem, dear,' I replied. She looked at me for the first time and then turning to Tony said, 'Hey, Tony, isn't this the lad you headbutted when you played for Man City?' Well, Tony was so embarrassed, he blushed bright red and didn't know where to look or what to say! I just found it funny. It would have been interesting to hear the conversation he had with his wife after I collected my brushes and left!

Neither Tony Coleman nor the returning Tony Green could change our disastrous run of results. Despite winning promotion only months before, Les Shannon was coming under increasing pressure as we slumped to the bottom of the league. Matters came to a head after a home game against Chelsea at the end of October. At last, everything came together and in a superb first half we raced into a three-goal lead against a team tipped for the title. We simply took them apart.

In the second half they came right back into the game. However, we still led 3-1 with only 15 minutes to go. Unfortunately, we completely collapsed after Les Shannon substituted Fred Pickering, who had scored twice in the first half. Chelsea added three more goals to win 4-3. Their final goal was an own goal by Dave Hatton in the final minutes. Shannon faced a barrage of criticism for taking off Pickering. He said that Pickering was carrying an injury. Pickering could have supported his manager but instead, for whatever reason, he said that he was perfectly fit. Three days after the game the board acted and Shannon was sacked. However, there is a story behind that game that isn't widely known.

We had an excellent Scottish keeper, Harry Thomson, who, unfortunately, liked a drink. An affable, friendly character in normal circumstances, he could become aggressive and unpleasant when drunk, so much so that when in this state his team-mates would leave him well alone. He lived in a club house next door to the recently married Tony Green and his wife Trisha.

The night before the Chelsea game, Harry had a row with his wife, went out and came back drunk. Finding the doors locked, he put his fist through the window on one of his doors causing a huge cut on his hand. Les Shannon was contacted and stopped Harry from going to A&E, presumably to avoid the story getting to the press, and instead took him around to the club doctor who cleaned and stitched him up. However, this fellow wasn't impressed by Harry – perhaps he displayed his usual aggressive, post-drink behaviour – and told Shannon never to bring him to him again.

Thomson played the next day and wasn't really in action until the second half. We were still leading 3-2 when Thomson went for a cross but, on the point of catching the ball, pulled back his injured hand and

Weller tapped home the fumbled ball for Chelsea. Seeing that Harry was injured, we dropped back to try and protect his goal, unfortunately in vain. It was perhaps when the directors found out about Harry Thomson and the fact that Shannon had picked him despite the Friday night shenanigans that the manager's fate was sealed. Whatever the reasons, Les Shannon was gone. Our new manager would be one of the most influential I had in my career.

Bob Stokoe is probably best remembered for charging onto the Wembley pitch to embrace his goalkeeper Jim Montgomery after guiding Sunderland to one of the biggest cup final upsets when they beat Leeds in 1972. I will remember him as the first manager I had who looked at me as an individual player and worked on improving my game. He also impressed me with his no-nonsense approach, his insistence that everything be done properly. As well as working hard in training and in games and following his instructions, he expected us to dress smartly and to always be on time.

The professional values that he instilled in us stayed with me throughout my working life. While there was no miraculous change in our fortunes in league games, he was in charge for a memorable FA Cup tie. We beat West Ham 4-0 in a game that Tony Green ran from start to finish, scoring two goals in the process. We just thought that we had been very good for once, and that they had been very poor.

It came out in the press a day or two later that four West Ham players – Bobby Moore, Jimmy Greaves, Clyde Best and Brian Dear – had spent the Friday night before the game in Brian London's 007 nightclub, returning to their hotel at 2am. London and Bobby Moore were pals. Had they beaten us the next day, the outcry that happened would probably have been a lot more muted. However, to go on a night out and then to be part of a team that got thumped by the worst team in the division was asking for trouble. The storm went on for several days in the national press with the players concerned fined and dropped from the team.

It was in the same nightclub, the 007, that I met Malcolm Allison, assistant to Joe Mercer, on the evening after we played out a storming 3-3 draw with his club Manchester City. City had an outstanding team at the time, so when Malcolm, making what I am sure was an illegal approach, told me that he wanted me to sign for his club, I was thrilled. He explained that he just needed to talk Joe around to the signing and he would be back in for me. I never heard any more about it, much to my disappointment.

However, one big thrill was just around the corner for me. I found out that I had been picked to play for the Scotland under-23 team in an international against Wales at the Vetch Field in Swansea. This was the first hint I had that the Scotland selectors had me on their radar. In our team that night were Quintin Young (he had joined the squad a few days earlier after a shift down the pit, since he was still playing part-time football for Ayr at the time of his call-up), who would leave Coventry on the day I joined that club and who I have got to know from Sky Blue legend days, and also Willie Carr, my future Coventry team-mate. The game itself ended in a disappointing 1-0 defeat. I got a lift back to Blackpool with Bob Stokoe, who was at the game. I hadn't played well and was probably feeling a bit sorry for myself when I said to Bob that I felt as though the level of the players in the game was far above what I could achieve. I quite rightly got no sympathy from him and he told me that if I felt like that, I had no business playing the game, another statement of his that has stuck with me and inspired me when I have needed to shake off moments of self-doubt.

I scored my first goal in the First Division away at Stoke in April in a 1-1 draw. It was made all the more memorable as it was against the great Gordon Banks. I also remember the game for receiving the biggest bollocking that I ever had from a manager. We were under pressure and were defending when the ball came to me on the edge of our own box. I saw a chance to go past the player in front of me and carry the ball to the halfway line. All of the managers that I played for saw me as an outlet to relieve pressure on the team by carrying the ball as far up the pitch as I could go.

Unfortunately for me on this occasion, my opponent nicked the ball off me and had a shot on goal that, luckily, fizzed over the bar. In the dressing room after the game Bob let me have it with both barrels, calling me all of the bad names he could think of. He asked me why I had been so stupid to try and dribble out from so deep a position. I lamely said, 'Boss, it looked easy to go past him.' 'And did you go past him?' was his question. 'No, but–' I tried to explain. 'Then it wasn't easy, was it?' Bob had the checkmate reply. The lesson, I suppose, was that if you are going to take a chance, you had better make sure that it comes off.

Bob certainly couldn't save us from relegation and we finished the season with only four wins. This was a sad way for a Blackpool legend to finish his playing career, but Jimmy Armfield decided that a home 1-1 draw with Manchester United in front of nearly 30,000 spectators would be his final game. Jimmy was a fine player and a lovely man. He told me that when he first broke into the Blackpool team, the only instruction he received from his manager, Joe Smith, was that whenever he had the ball he was to look where Stanley Matthews was and give him it.

Jimmy was one of the first full-backs who posed an attacking threat by overlapping his wing partner if they had cut inside with the ball. In his first game with Matthews, Jimmy gave him the ball as instructed and, when Stan cut inside, Jimmy went marauding past him down the wing calling for a return pass. Stan looked up, saw him in an unmarked position, but passed the ball on to someone else.

The next time there was a break in play, Stan called Jimmy over. Pointing towards his own goal, he said, 'Jimmy, you see that half of the pitch there?' Jimmy nodded. 'Well, that's your half.' He pointed at the other end. 'And that half's mine, okay?' There was to be no more overlapping by Jimmy with Matthews in the team. It was a shame that Jimmy didn't stay on for a few weeks as he would have finished his Blackpool career in a more glorious fashion.

We had been invited to play in the Anglo-Italian tournament at the end of the season along with a few other less-than-glamorous English teams, but with some quite well-known Italian clubs. Teams were placed into mini leagues with two English and two Italian clubs in each league. Each team would play the two foreign teams home and away. Points were given for winning and drawing but also for each goal scored. The final would be contested in Italy between the English and Italian teams who had most points in their mini league. We played Verona, a 3-3 draw at home and a 4-1 win away, and Roma, a 1-3 defeat at Bloomfield Road but a 2-1 win (in which I scored) at the Olympic Stadium in Rome.

The trip to Rome was a big event for all of us, but an even bigger one for Tony Green and his family who were Catholic. His mum, dad and his brother, who was a priest, all came to Rome. His parents had decided on very different ways as to how they were going to spend their time before the game. While his mum was visiting churches and various holy places, his dad was on a tour of Rome's finest bars and tavernas. They would meet up for lunch and continue on their different cultural routes for the rest of the afternoon. It could be claimed that by the time the evening came they were both full of the spirit!

Tony's brother came to our hotel to have dinner with him and with us. Tony, knowing what Henry Mowbray was like, had warned him to behave himself when we sat down with his brother to eat. Well, Father Green arrived, and everything seemed to be going well until Henry decided to talk about what he and Tony might get up to that evening. 'Great night in that little bar last night, eh Tone? And those girls, eh weren't they fantastic, cheeky little things, eh? We going down there again tonight? Sink another two or three bottles of wine, lovely stuff.'

I think Tony's brother saw the joke as he was smiling at Henry's mischief-making. I'm not sure the same could be said of Tony himself who glared at his mate! I did suggest to Tony that he could get his brother to contact the top man in the Vatican to say he was leaving a couple of tickets at the gate if he was free the following evening and wanted to watch some top Tangerine football. Maybe he didn't fancy watching some 'Orange Men' playing the beautiful game, because I don't think he turned up!

We finished top of our group and would play Bologna in their stadium, the Stadium Comunale, in the final. A crowd of about 40,000 turned up for the game and saw their team take a 1-0 half-time lead, a goal scored from my mistake. There were only a small number of Blackpool fans watching in the stadium, but back in Britain we had an audience of millions as the game was, unusually for the time, shown live on TV.

Bob Stokoe really fired us up for the second half and a goal from John Craven, our captain due to Armfield's retirement, took the game to extra time. Back home, the BBC had not banked on the game going beyond 90 minutes, so Blackpool fans were not able to endure the rigours of extra time on their TV, but instead had to endure David Jacobs presenting *Juke Box Jury* or something similar. A super goal from Micky Burns won us the game and meant I had my first piece of reasonably serious silverware. The next day in Blackpool was fantastic as 50,000 people lined the promenade for our open-top bus tour. What had in all honesty been a disaster of a season was finishing on a high.

But our success could not disguise the disappointment of relegation. I had hoped that my performances against the Italian teams might reignite Manchester City's interest in me, but I was to hear nothing more from them for the next ten years. I felt I had performed well in the First Division and I didn't feel out of place. However, as no club came in for me, I knew that next season it would be back to the slog of Second Division football.

Chapter 12

My Michelangelo Phase

AMONG THE many memorable characters that I met during my time in Blackpool, perhaps Derek Fontane is the one who stands out the most for me, not least because we forged a friendship that lasted a lifetime. I met him first at our lunchtime café, just up the road from the stadium. Derek, although a native of Dundee, had become a Blackpool fan since moving to the town. He would come in for his bacon butty dressed in his dungarees as he had his own painting and decorating business.

Derek was a very kind man and he rivalled my mum in his willingness to part with whatever he had. However, he also had the ability to convince potential clients that he was an expert in whatever his current chosen occupation happened to be, none of which he was skilled in at all. I knew him as a carpet cleaner, a London taxi driver, a chauffeur, a wedding photographer and a street trader as well as a painter and decorator. Derek could be whatever he wanted to be, even if he had no expertise in the job.

He could also gain entry into any event, even where security was so tight a mouse wouldn't have got in. There is a picture of the victorious Blackpool team, John Craven lofted on shoulders, after we beat Bologna to win the Anglo-Italian Cup. The pitch was surrounded by a high fence with security men strategically placed.

Derek, one of the few Pool fans in the stadium, decided he had to join in our celebration on the pitch. He rushed the fence and had almost scaled it when one of the security men grabbed his foot. However, Derek was determined and pulled his foot free leaving the security guy holding his shoe. If you look at the photo mentioned above, looking over my shoulder, there is Derek's grinning face, happy to be with the team and not worried about only having one shoe or the security guys who were closing in on him.

When Derek found out that I was a painter and decorator too, he started to put some jobs my way. Many of the Blackpool players had summer jobs, working on the prom or at the Pleasure Beach, so my picking up my paintbrushes again wasn't looked on as unusual. To drum up business, Derek leafletted many of the town's bed and breakfasts, betting shops and hairdressing salons. The former, he would work on in the winter, the latter two he targeted with the promise of overnight decorating so that they didn't lose a day's business.

I helped him out with the B&Bs during my free time after training in the winter. The bookies and barbers I worked on in the close season. The extra cash this generated was a welcome addition to my football wages. At times, we were decorating up to three bookies a night at £45 a shot, from which Derek would pay me a percentage. One thing that I quickly discovered was that Derek could not paint or decorate for toffee. We came to the agreement that he would sheet up the room and clean up behind me as I did the technical stuff.

One of the most memorable jobs he got me doing was in a hairdressing salon on Talbot Square. It was another night-time assignment. The salon required a complete painting makeover of skirting boards, walls and ceiling. The ceiling was ornate, having plaster fruits, leaves and flowers decorating the entire surface. The owner wanted all these items picked out in sky blue on a white background. Because this was going to be a painstaking job, I roped Henry Mowbray in to help with the more mundane aspects of the job.

As he had been drinking that evening, I had to nudge him occasionally to wake him up. None of the brushes I had with me were small enough to pick out the plaster work patterns without smudging the previously painted white background. I was stumped until I noticed an eyebrow brush on one of the counters. This proved to be ideal. However, by the time I had finished, I fully appreciated Michelangelo's efforts in the Sistine Chapel. At least he was able to lie on his back and paint. I had to bend backwards at the top of a set of steps and as dawn was breaking so were my back and neck!

Thinking back to those Blackpool days, there was a difference between the standard of living that footballers achieved and those of ordinary working-class people (who made up the vast majority of the crowd on a Saturday afternoon), but not the huge chasm that there is today. I think that this made the bond between player and supporter closer. We were certainly paid above-average wages, but even those at the top of the profession would need to find some form of employment to support themselves and their families once their playing days were done. My bit of decorating helped us out financially, but there were other ways to help make ends meet, sometimes through payment in kind.

We were given a number of complimentary tickets for each game. Some would be given out before matchday to family and friends. However, it was quite common for tickets to be collected almost immediately before the game in a rather unusual way. Our dressing room at Bloomfield Road was next to the footpath outside. It was common for us to be getting ready for a game when a knock would come on the window and the person outside would ask for a certain player, a couple of tickets would go out of the opening and some form of produce would come back in.

For example, Jimmy the Fish who lived in Fleetwood was a big supporter of ours and a mate of Greeny. So, when he knocked on the window, Tony would hand him out the tickets and in would come a huge parcel of fish. Tickets would be exchanged for anything: a string of sausages, a few steaks, a bag of home-grown veg, all sorts of stuff. This all seems innocent in these days of megabucks wages, but the stuff we received was really appreciated by the players.

Another small bit of help we had was with our footwear. There were no boot sponsorship deals in those days but at Blackpool you were given £5 towards a new pair which you could buy from the chairman's shop in town. I would sit with my new boots on, my feet in a bath of hot water, stretching them to the shape of my feet. Some of the players gave their new boots to the apprentices to wear, to break them in, but I never let anyone have my boots. They were the tools of my trade. I have lost count of the number of toenails that turned black and dropped off when breaking in a new pair of boots. I still felt it was worth doing this myself rather than getting a youngster to do it, as the boots in the end were moulded only to my foot shape.

On the pitch, a winning end to the season came too late to secure a return to the First Division, with a sixth-place finish a disappointment. However, I was pleased that Stokoe didn't suffer the same fate as Morty for this failure. He was the best manager I had worked with, both from a team perspective and on an individual level too. He spoke to me once about my game and said, 'You know why Tony Green got his big move and you are still here?' Green had moved to Newcastle. 'It's because despite all of your good work, you have no end product. You need to work on your final shot, pass or cross. Do that and you'll be gone within the year.'

This was a remarkably accurate prediction and with his help I worked on improving these aspects of my game. Stokoe was relentless in his expectations. Every training session had to be done right, every game plan that he put in place followed to the letter. Making a mistake in a game was fine the first time. Doing the same thing again after he had pointed out your faults would result in a major bollocking.

He was a tough taskmaster who the players respected and did their best for. We had a really skilful midfielder, County Durham-born Alan Suddick, who was my partner on the left-hand side of the pitch. He once did three full circuits of the track around the Bloomfield Road pitch, juggling the ball for a full 20 minutes without it coming to ground at all. When preparing for a game, Alan would put big wads of cotton wool under his shin pads to protect his legs from the type of tackles we faced in those days. This annoyed both our physio, who saw his meagre medical resources depleted, and Stokoe too. He confronted him once as he was wrapping his shins, 'Are you sure you're a Geordie? I think you're a big soft bastard with your cotton wool. You need to stick that stuff in your ears and then you wouldn't hear anyone coming to clatter you.' No more cotton wool was wasted!

Despite his hard, unrelenting nature, Stokoe did have a soft side. The mother of our goalkeeper John Burridge came to see Bob to ask him for a pay rise on behalf of her son. She explained that she was a widow still living in John's hometown of Workington while John was in digs in Blackpool. John was the breadwinner for both households and his wages barely covered what was needed to live on. Bob showed his soft side and gave John his pay rise.

Now Burridge was mad in lots of ways. The extra cash obviously went to his head rather than to his mum and within a week of his pay rise he was the proud owner of a Lotus Elan. The only problem was that after paying for his digs and the payments on the car, he was left with only 50p for the week. He had the sense to park it around the corner from the club car park but, inevitably, Stokoe eventually found out about the car. His message to Burridge was brief, to the point and left no doubt that he had to be obeyed. 'Get rid of it!' said Bob as he stomped past John and his car, having discovered his secret parking spot. The car disappeared and hopefully Mrs Burridge had a few more quid from her son.

As holders, we again ended our season playing in the Anglo-Italian Cup. Our opponents in the group stages were Sampdoria and Vicenza, who we beat both home and away. The home tie against Vicenza was memorable as it was another of those games where I could do no wrong and I felt almost invincible. As a team we were pretty invincible too and we won 10-0, helped by the fact that the Italian team's goalkeeper had a strop during the game and stomped off the field. We were again through to the final. This time we would meet Roma.

However, we could not reproduce the heroics of the previous year and despite a good performance we were beaten 3-1. I stayed on in Italy with Irene for a holiday. I am not at all religious but I have to say that the atmosphere in the Vatican really impressed me. It seemed such a calm yet purposeful place. I told Irene that if we stayed there, I could see myself developing a faith. This feeling has been there whenever I have been in Italy.

I started my fifth season at Blackpool, once more hoping for another promotion. However, at the age of 25, I knew that I was approaching my peak years and I desperately wanted to spend them in the top division. My international ambitions burned as brightly as ever, but I knew that to achieve these I needed to be playing First Division football. Thankfully for me, an old team-mate of mine had just been appointed as team manager at a top-flight club, and they had a vacancy for a left-winger who, thanks to Bob Stokoe, had a polished end product.

Chapter 13

The 'M' Men

GORDON MILNE left Blackpool in 1970 and had a successful two-year spell as player-manager at non-league Wigan Athletic. When First Division Coventry were looking for a new managerial team, at the start of the 1972/73 season, they appointed Gordon as team manager to work alongside Joe Mercer as general manager. Despite leading Manchester City to four major trophies in six years with his teams playing exhilarating football, Mercer had been shunted into a backroom role at Maine Road, with his coach Malcolm Allison assuming control of all matters regarding the team. Allison, it seemed, had 'stabbed' the popular Mercer in the back, conspiring with the board to take his friend's job. Joe wasn't going to put up with that and he applied for and landed the Coventry job.

Mercer and Milne were christened the 'M' Men by the *Coventry Evening Telegraph*. It was hoped that they would produce an attacking and winning team that would encourage some of the fans that had drifted away over the previous years to return to Highfield Road. I didn't know it at the time, but Gordon had taken the job on condition that, when finances allowed, Coventry would buy me from Blackpool. However, after 11 games with the new regime, things weren't going well and the Sky Blues were bottom of the league.

The first inkling I had that I might be on the move was when my Blackpool team-mate, Tom White, told me that Milne had phoned him and that I was to call him back as soon as possible. Irene and I didn't have a phone, hence Tom White's involvement in Gordon's illegal approach. I spoke to Gordon after training from the phone box next to Stanley Park. He asked me if, providing the clubs could agree terms, I would like to join Coventry. I told him I would jump at the chance. In that case, he said, an official offer would be made. I was thrilled.

A day or two later, Bob Stokoe took me to one side and told me that Coventry were in for me and that Blackpool had accepted their offer. It was up to me to decide if I wanted to go. He did tell me that he would be on the move himself soon (another illegal approach!) to one of the big clubs in his native North East and that if I wanted to wait, when he moved, he would take me with him. I liked working with Bob, but I was well aware by this stage of my career that you had to take the chances when they came along, so I told him that I wanted to join Coventry.

Centre-half Jeff Blockley had recently left Coventry for Arsenal for a fee of £200,000 which gave Mercer and Milne the money to revamp the team. They brought in Colin Stein from Rangers and they came in for me. My transfer wasn't straightforward. It was dependent on another Scot, Billy Rafferty, agreeing to a move in the opposite direction. Billy had come through the youth system at Coventry and had played several first-team games without really establishing himself. A centre-forward, his first-team chances had taken a big hit with the signing of Stein.

I was desperate for the deal to go through and only half-jokingly said to Gordon that if money was the stumbling block in Rafferty's part of the deal, then I would willingly slip him a few quid to get things over the line! Fortunately for me (and, as it turned out, for Billy too, who went on to have a long career with several clubs), terms were agreed and I became a Coventry player for a club-record fee worth £140,000.

I signed for the club at a hotel in Stone in Staffordshire although I also had to do a staged signing with Joe Mercer in the Hotel Leofric in Coventry city centre so the local paper could photograph the event. I had seen Joe on the TV a few times, where he always came across well. He was a genuinely nice chap, a fatherly figure that you couldn't help but like. You knew instantly that here was a man who would never let you down. The fact that Gordon Milne would be my team manager was a big factor in my desire to move to the Midlands. I trusted him in the way that I later trusted John Bond and Ron Wylie. These were men who I believed had my best interests at heart. Gordon was a good man and I felt that he wouldn't have brought me to a club that wasn't right for me.

My transfer came just as Irene was near her time for giving birth to our second child. I was in a quandary as to the best thing to do. I had missed out on being present at Lynn's birth and now the likelihood was I would be 150 miles away when Baby Hutchison Two arrived. At this point my sister Lizabeth stepped in to help. She had moved from Cambridge with her husband Danny to get into the hotel trade and had bought a guest house in Blackpool, across from Bloomfield Road, by coincidence. She told me not to worry. Irene would move in with her until we were sorted in Coventry and she would look after her until the baby was born. As it happens, due to football commitments I did miss birth number two when our first son, John, arrived on the scene. Irene's mum Betty came down from Fife to help and so I knew that my family back in the north were being well looked after.

We had another new arrival at this time, our first car! After five years at Blackpool, the players would receive a little bonus. I had confirmed with Stokoe that mine was on the way and I told him I had my eye on a second-hand car. 'Hutchie,' he advised, 'don't waste your money on a second-hand motor. You never know what you're getting. Buy new.' I followed his advice and got myself a new Triumph. Bob's guidance to me on football matters was always spot on, but he proved to be a bit more fallible when it came to matters of personal transportation!

Within a few weeks of my purchase, I was in Coventry, the place that my new car had started its life. I wasn't too worried when I noticed that the engine had sprung an oil leak. 'No problem,' I thought to myself, 'I'll take it straight back to the factory.' Colin Stein was at a loose end that afternoon, so he came along for the ride to the Standard-Triumph factory. We were directed to a workshop where one of the mechanics put my car up on the ramps and located the fault. After examining it for a while, he came over to tell us, shaking his head. 'Sorry, mate, can't really do anything about that. You'll just have to put up with it I'm afraid. It's more weeping than leaking.' Well, Steiny's response was incredulous. 'Weepin' ye say son, only weepin'? Well, we play th' Arsenal next week. Ah think it might be ye bosses tha' are weepin' when we put it in th' programme tha' their ain mechanics cannae fix a leak in your own car.' Despite Colin's threat we got nowhere and the car continued to 'weep' until I sold it.

Despite the shortcomings of the local factories, I loved it at Coventry. The players were looked after incredibly well. The Leofric was a five-star luxury hotel and to put new players up there must have cost the club a bit. The facilities for the players were top notch too. The training ground at Ryton was a paradise to me. The pitches were bowling-green perfect with each pitch surrounded by a high grass bank providing shelter from the wind. The whole complex was state of the art with first-class changing facilities and even a players' canteen on site where we would sit down to eat together after training.

Highfield Road was also one of the most modern and up-to-date stadiums in the country. It had three new stands, all built in the previous eight years. In a stadium with a capacity of 50,000, over 13,000 spectators could be seated. The Main Stand even had a Michelin-starred restaurant. All of this was the legacy of Jimmy Hill, who had transformed the club in the 1960s and whose influence could still be felt at the club when I arrived, five years after he had departed to work in television.

My debut for Coventry came after only one training session for my new club. I barely knew the names of my new team-mates as we took to the Highfield Road pitch for a game against Manchester City. The match was being billed as Mercer v Allison. It was the first time that the two had faced each other since Allison's acrimonious rise to the Maine Road hot seat. Mercer, a humble and kindly figure, was a popular character with both his old fans at Manchester City and with people nationally.

Allison, by contrast, was seen as brash, opinionated and a bit big-headed. It felt that a lot of people outside of Coventry as well as in the city wanted to see us win and Big Mal get his comeuppance. I had already met Allison in Blackpool and I got on okay with him. However, his son Dave, a nice lad, was an apprentice at Blackpool when I was there and he would have nothing to do with his dad. It did seem as if he had a way of rubbing people up the wrong way. This turned out to be Mercer's day as, despite Man City coming back from two goals down, we put on a sparkling performance to win 3-2. The 'M' Men were finally up and running.

I settled in quickly at my new club. I was helped by playing with a number of my fellow countrymen. As well as Stein and myself, Coventry had three other Scots who were first-team regulars: Willie Carr, Brian Alderson and Roy Barry. I knew very little about the team before I joined but I quickly realised we had some high-quality players. It would have been hard to find a better midfield pairing than Carr and Dennis Mortimer. They were tremendously skilful attacking footballers.

I had wondered if selling a quality defender like Blockley and using the money on two attackers, Stein and myself, might come back to bite the managers on the bum. I quickly understood that with this team and with these managers our attack was going to be our best form of defence. It was an idea that suited me down to the ground. Over the next few games, I would play the best football of my career so far and even score a goal that would be the subject of a chapter in a bestselling novel.

Chapter 14

Fever Pitch

I WOULD never claim to have turned any team's season around simply because they had me out there on the pitch. However, there was a pattern emerging! When I joined Alloa and when I joined Blackpool, both teams went on tremendous winning runs. The same thing happened when I joined Coventry. A team that had struggled to find any sort of form and who had hit the bottom of the First Division table was suddenly transformed. New players can give a team a lift. If those players are capable of scoring and creating goals as Colin Stein and myself were, then belief that had been missing can flood back into a team. Colin and me were perhaps the catalyst that allowed the many good players in our team to regain confidence in themselves again and allow them to play to the level of which they were capable. Whatever the reasons, things really took off for my new team!

We were unbeaten in the first eight games I played in sky blue. Indeed, that run should have been longer. In the ninth game we were beating a very good Ipswich team at Portman Road and dominating proceedings, until the game was abandoned due to the failure of the floodlights. We were playing amazing attacking football and were blowing other teams out of the water, and we started to rocket up the table. I was loving it, our fans were loving it and so was everyone connected to the club.

Derrick Robins was the long-standing chairman of Coventry, the man responsible for the appointment of Jimmy Hill and who, in partnership with Hill, had overseen the club's transformation in the 60s from a rundown lower-league club to a trailblazing top-flight outfit. He must have enjoyed my performances as he nicknamed me 'Mr Magic'. In those first few games for Coventry, I felt so good in myself, so confident that I just knew that I was going to give my opposing full-back a chasing.

By the time we went to Highbury in my fourth game for the club, I had already scored my first Coventry goal, a 25-yarder in a 3-1 win against West Ham. I didn't think I would score a better goal that season. I was wrong! We were already winning 1-0 against Arsenal and were cutting them to pieces when, in the second period, I picked the ball up just inside our half and set off towards their goal. In my mind's eye, I can remember beating Alan Ball about three times on that run. Funny how your memory plays tricks, as match reports reveal that I beat him only the once, although he did try to bring me down. I dribbled past McLintock and Rice and then rounded the goalkeeper Barnett before slipping the ball between two defenders on the line and into the net.

As I ran away celebrating, Colin Stein caught me up and shouted, 'Why did you go and panic?' It was an ironic comment as my finish was so cool! A goal like that is pure instinct. When I set off on the run, I wasn't thinking I would score. The goal simply happened because I beat so many opponents and had no team-mate better placed for me to pass to. Steiny said to me later, 'If the goal hadn't been there, you'd have carried on with the ball into the crowd and up the terrace at the Clock End.' I didn't even realise that it was such a special goal until I saw the reaction later. In fact, one minute after my goal, I almost repeated the feat but Barnett saved after a long mazy dribble. There are a few grainy seconds of the goal available to see on YouTube and I think that the London Weekend Television cameras were there to cover the game, but for some reason they didn't release footage of the complete move, which is a shame.

Joe Mercer described the goal as the best he had ever seen. Considering Joe's longevity and his standing within the game, this was a lovely compliment. Derek Henderson, chief football writer for the *Coventry Evening Telegraph*, said that it was a goal of 'sheer poetry'. Perhaps the most unusual recognition came a good few years after the event. A young Nick Hornby was at the game and he wrote about the goal and the emotions that it aroused within him in his book (later turned into a film) *Fever Pitch*.

Nick describes my goal quite well, but he is really looking back at his 15-year-old self and is a bit ashamed at his anger with, and desire to do violence to, the Coventry fans celebrating at the Clock End while he watched on from the North Bank. Also watching on was Scotland manager Tommy Docherty. As well as the goal, I had played really well that day, so I certainly hadn't done my international chances any harm. Unfortunately, within a few weeks, Docherty left his Scotland role to take over as manager of Manchester United and never picked another international squad. I felt that if I continued to play the way I was then, whoever the new Scotland manager was, he couldn't ignore me.

Without wishing to appear as if I am blowing my own trumpet too much, I think that it is a measure of how well I was playing that in my first nine Coventry games, my opposing right-back was booked on each occasion. Remember this was in an era when bookings and sending offs were reluctantly given by referees. One or two of my opponents claimed that I was a diver. Tommy Smith of Liverpool felt that I went over too easily. He told me, 'You've gone down this time and are able to get up. The next time I put you down you'll be staying there!' I think he was a bit annoyed that he had only tripped me and hadn't studded me!

The fact is that I never dived in any game that I played. That is something that I wouldn't do. I took pride in the fact that I never allowed a full-back to easily put me on my backside. If I was on my feet and had the ball, I had confidence that I could go past anybody. If I did go down it was because I had been put there by my opponent. There was never any of this 'felt a touch so I went over' excuse for going down that you hear today. I was honest in the way that I played. I did develop the technique of beating a player and then moving into his path. This left him with the choice of chasing tight on me with the risk of bringing me down or giving me a bit of space while he tried to come alongside me. If I was caught, I think my gangly physique made it look a lot worse as I crashed to the ground in a tangle of arms and legs. However, I never voluntarily went to ground.

Since my Bluebell days I had been up against opponents who had no qualms about setting out to hurt me. Unless I was badly hurt, I would do my best to stay on my feet or get up as quickly as I could in defiance of what they were trying to do to me. Strangely, the rough treatment rarely got me riled or had me losing my temper. I took it as a compliment in a way, that these were the tactics that they had to resort to in order to stop me. What did make me mad and would have me swinging an elbow was any sort of shirt-pulling. I can remember giving David O'Leary of

Arsenal a haymaker once when he pulled me back. I felt it was laziness by a defender, that they couldn't be bothered to chase me and so would pull my shirt.

That first season at Coventry continued to go well for me and the team. By March we had reached the quarter-finals of the FA Cup and were pushing high in the league for a place in Europe. Early in that month we completed the double over Manchester City by winning at Maine Road. The highlight of the game was the tremendous reception given to Joe Mercer by the Manchester fans. We were out on the pitch warming up when a hell of a cheer went around the ground as Joe emerged from the dressing room to take his seat in the stand before the game. There was no doubting who they saw as the architect of the tremendous success that they had enjoyed in the previous few years. To them he was still the number one.

In the cup we were drawn away against Wolves and excitement in the city was bubbling over. Coventry had never been to Wembley, had never even reached a semi-final of a major competition. Both team and fans were convinced that this was about to change. The way we were playing we could beat anyone on our day. Unfortunately, when we turned up at Molineux it certainly wasn't our day. Despite being backed by over 15,000 Sky Blues packed onto the South Bank, we never got going. Derek Dougan (who had been knocked out in the warm-up to the game) and John Richards, Wolves' twin strikers, were too good for us on the day and we were easily beaten. That cup defeat affected us badly. Our season collapsed and we won only one of our remaining ten games, finishing fourth from bottom of the league.

To me and to most Coventry fans, this was a false position. I looked forward to the new season with optimism. I had won the club's player of the season award and I felt that there was a lot more to come both from myself and from the team. I was also aware that at the end of the forthcoming season, the World Cup would be taking place in West Germany. Scotland had started their qualification campaign with two winning games against Denmark. The two upcoming games in the new season against Czechoslovakia would decide the country's World Cup fate. A new manager, Willie Ormond, had been appointed and I was aware that time was running out for me to have a chance of making the international squad. I would need to repeat, or even better, my performances from the season just ending, and to do it right from the start of the new campaign. There was fierce competition for the left-wing position in that Scotland team that I was challenging for. I felt I was worthy, of not only a place in the squad, but in the starting 11 itself. The question was, did Willie Ormond agree with me?

Chapter 15

Heroes and Villains

BACK IN the early 1970s, long before the Premier League era, it was possible for more clubs to believe that they were capable of winning trophies, even the ultimate prize of the First Division title. In the 20 years from 1960 to 1980, the title was won by clubs such as Burnley, Ipswich, Leeds (twice), Everton, Derby (twice), Nottingham Forest and Aston Villa. Given the unfortunate closed-shop nature of the Premier League these days and despite Leicester's surprise title win, it is unlikely that any of these clubs, or any others outside of the elite top six, will challenge for the top prize anytime soon.

Back at the start of the 1973/74 season, players and fans of clubs such as Coventry would see no reason why they couldn't challenge for honours. Indeed, as recently as 1970, Coventry had finished in sixth place in the First Division. While most of us would have thought it unlikely we would challenge for the title, a European place or a cup win was certainly well within the realms of possibility.

Our optimism looked well founded when in the first game of the new season, I crossed the ball for Mick Coop to head the winner against fancied Spurs and even more so after the second game when I scored an absolute cracker of a goal to defeat the even more fancied Liverpool, the current league champions. I had started the new campaign in excellent form and so had the team. Unbeknownst to me at the time, a Scottish selector had watched the Liverpool game. I think my performance was the clincher regarding my international selection.

Later on, when I found out that I had been watched that evening, it made me think how much of a role luck can play in a footballer's career. If a selector hadn't attended that game, would I have ever had my chance? I was lucky that I was playing alongside Stein as it meant the Scots had another contender to watch as well. For years, a photo hung in the corridor at Highfield Road of my goal in that game. Every time I saw it, I thanked my lucky stars that on that night, in front of that man (whoever he was), for me it all came together.

We lost to Manchester City at Maine Road in early September with Willie Ormond in attendance. The disappointment of our defeat was eased a little by what Joe Mercer had to say after the game. He had spoken to Ormond and it seemed that both Colin Stein and myself would be in the next Scottish squad. Joe went on to say, 'If Tommy makes the Scottish team, it could be the start of a highly spectacular international career. He has it in him to become one of the greatest stars in the four home countries international scene.' I was thrilled by what he had to say but I was taking nothing for granted until the official announcement of the squad to face Czechoslovakia in the forthcoming World Cup qualifier was made. I was aware that injury, loss of form or even a change of mind by the manager could cost me my place.

I heard nothing more for a week or two until one day Gordon Milne asked to see me in his office after training. I didn't know why he wanted to see me. Could it be a pay rise or interest in me by another club? It turned out that Gordon had one of the best pieces of news I was ever to receive. I was in the Scottish squad! Gordon congratulated me on my selection, saying it was well deserved. He told me that he thought that I had completed the step to being an international, getting that initial call-up. He felt it was a lot harder, once you were in the squad, to lose your place. Once you are in the team, if you play the way you can, you would stay there. I knew what he meant and I think, in a roundabout way, he was telling me that he thought I had the ability to have a long international career.

For me, at the age of 26, an international call-up had been a long time in coming. It had been a long, hard road. Leaving Gordon's office, I was totally elated. I couldn't wait to tell Irene and my family back in Fife that I had made it to the Scottish national squad. The news was even better because Colin Stein, who had become a great mate during our first year together at Coventry and who was already a full international, was in the squad too.

The precarious nature of a footballer's life was something I was aware of. We all knew that we were only an injury away from losing our place in a team. Colin Stein was as thrilled as myself to be selected. We made arrangements to travel north together after our home match against Newcastle. Unfortunately for Colin he injured his ankle in the first half. He stayed on the pitch hobbling about until half-time and managed to score a great headed goal, leaping off his 'good' leg to put us in front. However, he wasn't fit enough to come out for the second half and he wasn't fit enough to join up with the Scotland squad the next day. He was bitterly disappointed to miss out and, despite my growing excitement at meeting up with my new Scottish team-mates, I was really sorry for him.

The Scotland team always met up at the North British Hotel in Glasgow before moving on together to our Largs training camp. I was directed to the lounge to meet up with the rest of the players. Now, I was a 26-year-old experienced footballer and had played for three senior clubs. All of that was fine, but it didn't stop me from feeling nervous walking into that room. I had played against many of these lads for Blackpool and Coventry, but I didn't know any of them well. I was very much the new boy.

Billy Bremner was the first of my new team-mates that I came across. Billy was a wonderful player, truly world class, and was the team's captain. He spotted me wandering in and you might have thought that as captain he would have seen it as part of his role to introduce me to the other players and to put me at my ease. That wasn't Billy's way, as I was to find out. He enjoyed being the top dog in the squad and he made sure that he put other players, those not in his inner circle, in their place. I was dressed as instructed in my collar and tie and blazer, so it was a bit of a surprise to see Bremner sat there in jeans and T-shirt.

Billy knew who I was. I had played against Leeds several times and had played very well. However, he looked at me quizzically from the depths of his big comfy armchair, as if he couldn't quite place me. He said, 'Noo tell me son, who is it ye play for?' Denis Law was watching this pantomime. When I was a teenager and as a young player, Denis had always been my hero. Although I think there is a saying that states you should always view your heroes from afar, I very much looked at it that one of the privileges of playing for Scotland would be that I would get to at least train, and hopefully play, with Law.

Denis called me over, 'Hello there, big man. Pull up tha' chair 'n' sit wi' me.' He turned to the waitress walking past, 'Excuse me, hen, can ye git this man a cuppa tae when ye hae a minute?' He couldn't have been nicer and he introduced me to any of the players that came past. Denis was one person who lived up to his hero billing as far as I was concerned, he was everything that I had hoped he would be.

I hadn't really thought about accommodation or equipment when the international call-up came through. I was a bit surprised therefore when we arrived as a squad at our hotel, the Queens Hotel in Largs. It was run by two elderly sisters and it certainly looked as though it had seen better days. Perhaps I had become a bit spoilt during my year at Coventry. Any hotel that we stayed in or went into for a meal was top of the range, we were treated very well with the rooms well equipped with all mod cons. By contrast, I was going to have a spartan stay in Largs. The rooms were big and cold with nothing but a bit of old furniture in them, not even a kettle to make a cup of tea. However, the food was good and there was always plenty of it.

Denis Law, like me, could never sleep in the afternoons. On the Monday of that week, who should turn up at the hotel but Rod Stewart with a huge TV for Denis to have in his room so he had something to do if he couldn't sleep. Denis was certainly well looked after. He was rooming with Donald Ford from Hearts. Now, Donald was a good lad with a good sense of humour. He was soon catering to Denis's every need. Denis wanted a cup of tea? Donald would fetch it. Denis in need of an extra blanket? Donald would go and ask for one. As he was effectively acting as Law's butler, he earned the obvious nickname of Jeeves, which he then played up to. I remember one of the boys saying jokingly that he was just a crawler. His response was, 'Denis is getting auld, someone has tae tak' care o' him!'

I had settled in well and, apart from the frosty reception from Bremner, all the other boys had been welcoming. I knocked about with some of the lads who were newer to the international scene: Kenny Dalglish, John Blackley and Danny McGrain. I was rooming with an interesting boy from Celtic, George Connelly. He was a quiet lad and we hardly had a conversation during our few days together. Like me, he was from the Fife coalfield, although his home place of Valleyfield was a real tough place to grow up in. He was a talented player and as a youngster Celtic had him out on the pitch at half-time during a European match against Dynamo Kiev doing keepy-ups to entertain the crowd.

He came through at the club with Dalglish, McGrain, Lou Macari and David Hay, a talented group of young boys nicknamed the Quality

Street Gang. George only played on for a couple more years after his international call-up. Unhappy in his life as a footballer, he gave it all up to become a taxi driver.

We were meant to sleep in the afternoons, which I found impossible. Even at night, sleep was hard to come by as the wind howled around the old hotel constantly rattling doors and windows. It wouldn't have been so bad if I could have chatted to George but he was such a quiet chap that I would lie there bored.

We were taken from the hotel by bus to the training ground, a 15-minute drive away. Coventry's training ground at Ryton was much more impressive than the fields that we trained on with Scotland. The same comparison could be made with our training gear. My club side would always provide you with a full set of new training kit at the start of each season. It was freshly laundered before each session. The stuff we were given by Scotland was years old and was minging. It was a mishmash of washed-out old tracksuits, shirts, shorts and socks often ill-fitting. It seemed to me that if this was the provision the FSA made for its elite players, looking at the hotel, the pitches and the kit, then they didn't value us very highly.

I had a couple of conversations with Willie Ormond and he came across as a nice man, very warm and friendly. He did seem to be a bit on the soft side and was not much of a disciplinarian. He was the guy that I needed to impress in those few days together if, on the Wednesday of that week, I was to make my debut.

I was now within touching distance of realising the dream that I had carried around with me for most of my life. Being part of this squad was great, but without that next step into the team it would all be pretty meaningless. Would Willie trust me to play in such an important game? We had won our opening two qualifiers against the Danes while our opponents that week, Czechoslovakia, had dropped a point in their game against Denmark. We knew that a win would take us to the World Cup finals whatever the result when we played the return game against the Czechs in Bratislava. It would be a brave decision by Ormond to play me, an international novice in a game of this importance. I found out what his decision was to be in our final practice session the day before the game.

Chapter 16

Fulfilment of a Dream?

I HAD been told by the other players that the Tuesday training session would more or less tell us who was in the team for the following day's game. There was always a full-scale training match between those who would be in the starting 11 and those who, on this occasion, hadn't made the team. Bearing in mind that in those days the manager could only name and use one substitute, it meant that in our 22-man squad there would be ten very disappointed players. I knew that if I was on the same team as Bremner in the practice match then I would almost certainly have made the team.

I watched on with dry mouth and loose bowels as the two differing sets of bibs were handed out. Bremner was one of the first picked and given a blue bib. Those who were handed a red bib now must have known their fate for this match was sealed, the best that they could hope for was a place on the bench.

I kept my head down, eyes to the floor, not daring to look, just saying silently to myself, 'Let it be blue, let it be blue.' I heard my name. 'Tam, here ye go, big man.' One of the trainers, Ronnie McKenzie, was looking at me, holding out the bib. I took it from him. My legs were barely able to carry me, I had been so nervous waiting for the decision. I slipped the bib over my head and wandered over to the rest of the boys wearing blue, gathered around Bremner. I had done it! I was in!

When the team lined up tomorrow night, I would be one of those 11 players. I quickly got control of myself again, focused on the job in hand and listened to Willie Ormond's talk before we started the session. I was determined to make no last-minute slip-up that might make Willie change his mind. Indeed, the players hadn't been quite accurate enough when telling me about what happened in this session as two or three changes were made in the course of the game where someone initially blue swapped sides with someone initially red. Thank goodness this didn't happen to me as I think I may have been in tears at that point.

We were therefore not completely sure of the final make-up of the team until that afternoon when a meeting was held and the final 12 were announced. I was officially in! George Connelly, my almost silent room-mate, was also in the starting line-up with the two of us making our international debuts. Was the inclusion of two novices brave or foolhardy from Ormond? The result of the game would provide the answer to that, but the often-harsh Scottish press would have Willie's guts for garters if we lost and he had played two rookies in such a vital match.

I couldn't tell any of my family the good news about my selection personally as none of us owned a telephone. But I knew that they would be glued to the radio waiting for the squad to be announced. Each player was given four complimentary tickets for the game. More were available if we wanted them, which was good as the match was a sell-out, but these we would have to pay for. Mum and Dad were going to come across from Fife along with a large contingent from Irene's family. Irene herself was being chauffeured from Coventry to the game by my decorating pal from Blackpool, Derek Fontane.

The match had generated huge interest throughout Scotland and would be televised live, the first time that this had happened for a Scotland match outside of the Home Internationals. With the tickets sorted out, the only thing for me to concentrate on now was the game itself. I slept badly that night and the next day seemed to crawl until finally we boarded the coach to Glasgow.

Since I had last played at the ground for Alloa, Hampden – or at least the dressing-room area – had had a makeover. Underfloor heating had been installed and the dressing room had been refurbished with each player having their own little open cubicle to get changed in. When we went into the dressing room, all the shirts were hung up and the rest of the kit for each player laid out in their cubbyhole. In those days there were no squad numbers or names on the shirts and the number 11 shirt belonged to whoever was playing on the left wing in that match. Tonight, that shirt would be mine. I stared at it, just revelling in the fact that I would wear that jersey.

Some of the boys settled down into their own little cubicle, reading the programme or chatting to their neighbours. I didn't want to do that just yet, I didn't want to spoil the perfection of that space, my kit neatly laid out and that dark-blue Scotland shirt emblazoned with the white number 11, just hanging there, waiting for me to put it on. I delayed as long as I could. I always liked a warm bath before I played, particularly on cold evenings. My skinny frame with knobbly knees and elbows has always been susceptible to the cold. I liked to be warmed up in a physical sense before taking the field. I changed in a spare cubicle, leaving my clothes there so as not to disturb the shrine where hung that blue shirt.

Having bathed and dried myself, I returned to the cubicle for one last look at that shirt, the rest of my kit laid out, as if in homage, below it. It is a memory I will never forget and it still brings me out in goosebumps as I describe it now. I finally put the kit on and looked around the dressing room at my team-mates. With the calibre of player I had alongside me that night, I knew that we were going to win. I had no doubts at all. As well as the world-class Bremner, there were Dalglish, Law, Sandy Jardine, David Hay and Danny McGrain in our team. There was no way that we were going to fail.

As we came out onto the pitch the noise of the crowd really did hit me. The Hampden roar was something that I had heard about but to experience it first-hand that night was really special. Close to 100,000 Scots bellowing at full volume made the whole stadium shake. There were a few pipe bands on the pitch with countless sets of pipes and drums all adding to the cacophony. God knows what the Czechs made of it all, but it certainly wasn't a place for the faint-hearted.

If I look at the picture of myself before that game, I am unsmiling and I look really tense. That may have been the case before the game, but not once we got underway. There are a lot of players who are good on a Friday but not so good on a Saturday, maybe not being able to handle the pressure of playing in front of a crowd. Once the game started, I was oblivious to the crowd, I never really heard them. I had also developed a confidence, a faith in my own ability that allowed me to push any nerves that I had before a game, even one as big as this, into the background.

I was really able to turn Bob Stokoe's words to me after my under-23s game into a reality. Him telling me that if I didn't think I was good enough I should have stayed at home were put to good use several times in my career but particularly on this night. I knew I was good enough.

I knew I wasn't here under false pretences. I intended to show anyone watching that this was where I belonged. I was supremely confident that I would do well and that the team would win. The way that both myself and my team-mates began, it seemed as though I was right to feel like that.

We were expecting the Czechs to be very cagey and to limit the number of players that they would commit to the attack. The Leeds and England coach Les Cocker had passed on a dossier he had compiled on each Czech player to Ormond via Billy Bremner, so we had a good idea what to expect. We thought that we would be in a very physical battle, and that is certainly the way that the game started. I had the ball on the run twice in the opening minutes and on each occasion midfielder Antonin Panenka scythed me down. Panenka, later in his career, scored the winning penalty in the shoot-out against West Germany in the final of the European Championships, a cheeky chip that led to this style of penalty being named after him. We were on top and playing well and they were struggling to contain us.

And then disaster struck in a typically Scottish style. The Czech player Nehoda hit a shot from outside the box. He caught it nicely but it still only required a routine save from our keeper, Ally Hunter of Celtic. He somehow managed to get both his hands to the ball while still allowing it through them and into the net. There were a few moments of stunned silence in the stadium before a huge wave of encouragement came rolling down off the terraces. 'We'll Support You Ever More' was the chant, and it was clear that the 100k watching on hadn't given up on us.

In truth, although falling behind was a setback, I don't think it affected us too much and we were back on our game almost straight away. Before half-time we were level when my future Coventry team-mate Jim Holton scored with a great header from a corner. However, we knew that a draw would leave qualification in the balance, with the Czechs as probable group favourites with the return game in Bratislava to come.

Willie Ormond had told us that he felt we would be the superior team in the air, and this proved to be a prophetic comment. In the second half, Joe Jordan came on as sub for Dalglish and netted our second headed goal of the night to put us ahead. We were almost there! The last 15 minutes of the match dragged and dragged but the whistle to end the game finally came and we knew we were on the way to the finals. For me now, the question was had I done enough to keep my place in the squad and in the team?

Chapter 17

The Aftermath

THE SENSE of relief mixed with euphoria was overwhelming. I may have been the new boy in the squad but I felt as much a part of that occasion as any of the other Scottish players. This was my team, my country and I was one of the 12 who had, on that night at a packed Hampden Park, ensured that we qualified for our first World Cup finals for 16 years. I felt that I had played well, and had made significant contributions to our win, but it's always reassuring to hear that other people watching on, people who you respect, had felt the same way. Willie Ormond, when he spoke to me later, told me he was delighted by my performance. Bill Shankly was quoted in the papers next day saying that mine was the best international debut he had ever seen. When someone like Shanks pays a compliment like that it makes you feel ten feet tall.

An equally respected football character, my manager back at Coventry, Joe Mercer, was also very kind when speaking of me. He said, 'It was the most complete international debut performance that I have ever seen. He was superb. He didn't put a foot wrong. His passing was immaculate and the way that he teased and tormented the Czech defence was a sheer joy. The crowd loved him and chanted his name every time he had the ball. After the evidence of his first performance, he will be around the Scottish side for a long time.'

The Czech full-back who had marked me, Jan Pivarnik, wanted me to swap jerseys with him at the end but I had had to tell him, 'No,' as the new home for that shirt was already well and truly earmarked. I wouldn't have given him my shirt in any case. After the return game in Bratislava, he asked me again to swap shirts. This time the reason for my refusal was definitely because of the way he had played. He had kicked lumps out of me for 180 minutes over the two games and I didn't feel very friendly towards him as we walked off the pitch.

At Hampden, Billy Bremner had been getting 'the treatment' from the Czech midfielder Kuna. Billy was a fiery character who believed in giving back what he received (in truth he believed in giving it out before he had received it as well – Billy was no shrinking violet). A clash between the two saw Kuna having to leave the field with blood pouring from a broken nose. Bremner wasn't the only Scot who had looked after himself on the night. After one of our corners, there was a melee and the ball was cleared up to the halfway line. Left behind in the Czech penalty box in a crumpled heap was one of the Czech centre-halves, who also had a facial injury.

Any doubts as to who was responsible disappeared when, at the end of the game, the defender came up to Denis Law pointing and said, 'Bratislava, I have you.' Well, Denis laughed and said, 'Bratislava? Ye'r jokin' man, Ah won't be goin' tae Bratislava. We've qualified.' As it happened, Denis was wrong, he was picked for the squad and did indeed play, needing games to prove his fitness. Bremner, however, was left out of that squad as it was felt that he would be the target of some intimidation with the potential risk of injury.

We lapped the pitch at the end of the game celebrating with the fans who were in no hurry to leave Hampden. Bremner was carried around shoulder-high in recognition of his outstanding performance. Billy ran down the tunnel and returned with a reluctant Willie Ormond. This time it was our manager who was hoisted onto shoulders so that he could take the cheers of the crowd.

After getting changed, I had a chance to meet up with my family and friends in the players' bar. It was there that I was able to give my dad my shirt. That was a special moment for me and another small way of saying thank you for everything he had done for me. I could tell that he was touched by the gesture. When we all emerged from the stadium, I headed for the coach with the rest of the players to be taken back to the hotel in Largs to collect our stuff. My mum and dad went and stood on the Hampden steps to wave us off. There were what seemed like thousands of fans there still milling about and cheering us.

My dad had draped my shirt around his shoulders. Kenny Dalglish saw him and said to me, 'Tell him he's got yer shirt ower his shoulders.

They'll hae it. It'll be gone, tell him. They'll murder him fur it.' Trying to tell my dad to secure the shirt through a coach window at night was never going to be easy and, not surprisingly, he didn't understand. Luckily, no one swiped it and the shirt had pride of place in the Dundonald Park house until he died. As the coach pulled away from Hampden, I looked back one last time at Mum and Dad. Dad had now pulled the shirt on over his head and over his coat and was dancing something akin to a Highland fling. It was great to see him so happy and so proud.

In those days there was no international break. Having played against Newcastle on the Saturday for Coventry and Czechoslovakia for Scotland on the Wednesday, it was now back to the First Division on the following Saturday and a game at previously unbeaten Leicester. A 2-0 win and our rise to second place in the league showed how well we were doing. However, that was as good as it got in the league as a series of injuries helped to scupper our season, this despite the signing of my old Blackpool mate John Craven and striker David Cross from Norwich.

Our best chance of success was in the cup competitions and we had good runs in both the League and FA Cups. We were unlucky to lose in both competitions, going out in the fifth round of the FA Cup to QPR after a replay, and to Manchester City, also after a replay, in the quarter-finals of the League Cup – my Scotland mate Denis Law scored one of the goals that helped put us out. We were playing games without floodlights, starting games early on a Saturday afternoon and on weekdays so that matches were completed in daylight hours. This was due to power-saving measures introduced by the government during the miners' strike. Crowds at the midweek games were well down on what they would normally be as a lot of people couldn't get time off during their working day to go to games. It was a strange time.

I won my second Scottish cap when we played the Czechs in the return in Bratislava. We lost a low-key, dead-rubber match 1-0 in front of only 13,000 spectators, a complete contrast to the packed-out, rip-roaring Hampden event. The only thing of note that I remember from the game was that again I got a good kicking from an assortment of Czech players.

Unfortunately Colin Stein, again selected for this game, was still injured and unable to play. It also meant that he wasn't available for two high-profile friendly games against West Germany, the first of which was in November 1973. They were the hosts for the upcoming finals and were the favourites too. With players like Beckenbauer, Muller, Hoeness and

Netzer, they were the very definition of a world-class team. However, in the first game at Hampden, in particular, we played them off the park. I think this shows just what a good team we had in those days.

We outplayed the team that in only nine months' time would be crowned world champions. I was up against perhaps the best full-back that I ever faced in Berti Vogts. He marked me really tightly, so much so that at the end of the game I didn't swap shirts with Berti as I felt I would only be getting my own shirt back! (I did in fact swap shirts with Netzer who, despite being a gifted, creative player, had also kicked lumps out of me that night.) Vogts was a real speed merchant and I had no chance of outrunning him from a standing start. He could really time a tackle too.

Despite all of this, again I felt I had played well. The Mercer/Milne tactical change to my game, where I tended to drift both deeper and away from the touchline, meant I could collect the ball in midfield and have built up a head of steam by the time Vogts engaged me from the right-back position. We had a good battle and he would have known that he had been in a game.

Berti, like all of the Germans in those games, was very comfortable on the ball. All their defenders could play and pass. They were more like a modern-day team. We were happy for the centre-halves of most teams we played in that era to have the ball. Generally, they were stoppers who would lump the ball forward when they got it, often gifting us possession. Not so the Germans, who had players who could hurt you with a pass or a run from deep. It was unusual to have games like these against a fellow qualifier so close to the finals. These two games had been arranged as part of a series of matches to celebrate the centenary of the SFA.

Both teams used the games as full-scale practice matches and there was very little experimentation from either manager. We were within five minutes of a memorable win in the game at Hampden. Jim Holton scored again for us to put us ahead and, when we were awarded a penalty ten minutes from the end, it seemed certain we would win. I didn't know it at the time but Bremner's miss from the spot that night would ultimately have long-term consequences for my international future. Hoeness then scored an undeserved equaliser for a very lucky German team, minutes from the final whistle.

The fickleness of fate was brought home to me a week after the German game. I had been to see my family in Fife and was returning to

Coventry by train. I had to change at New Street station in Birmingham to complete the last leg of my journey. By the time I got home, the news was filtering through of explosions in two pubs resulting in a huge loss of life. The pubs that were bombed were only a few yards from the station, but I had been totally unaware of the mayhem happening above my head as I waited for my train on the station concourse.

That news certainly put into context the importance or otherwise of the results of any football match. It also made me think of how lucky I was to be completely safe, when someone who was just as blissfully innocent as I was, but who was 50 yards up the road in the wrong direction, had their life ended in a brutal manner. Two innocent people in virtually the same location: one carries on with his life unaltered, the other had his life violently curtailed. These events certainly made me stop and think.

The return match in March was in Frankfurt. My room-mate for this occasion was Martin Buchan, who had brought his guitar with him. Martin was someone who liked to be different. If there was an order for 12 teas and one coffee you can guess who was on the coffee. When travelling abroad, all of us players would surrender our passports to a team official and go through customs as a group. Martin insisted on keeping his own passport and going through on his own. I was curious as to why he had his guitar with him. I was surprised by his answer. He said that he thought that this was the last time he would be selected for Scotland so he thought he might as well enjoy himself.

Martin was a classy player who played for Manchester United. My thoughts that he was perhaps underestimating both his ability and his chances of remaining in the international squad were proved correct as Martin went on to play in the next two World Cup finals. Martin may have found playing the guitar relaxing, but I didn't, as he insisted on playing it while I was trying to get to sleep. However, his enquiry to me as to whether I had any requests did give me the chance to say, 'Aye Martin, cann ye go doonstairs 'n' play in th' garden?'

I didn't have to put up with Martin and his guitar for long as he was unhappy with the fact that our room had no bath. He complained to Willie Ormond, who managed to turf out one of the SFA officials from his room so Martin could have a bath. I was quite happy with the extra space and peace this gave me. When word went around that the SFA official had a room with better facilities than ours, it added fuel to the fire that these guys were on a jolly and were being treated better than the players.

The game itself was in the stadium in which we would play both Brazil and Yugoslavia in the finals. This time the West Germans dominated the majority of the match and going into the last 15 minutes could have considered themselves unlucky to only be leading 2-0. However, a goal in the 75th minute set up a grandstand finish in which we had chances to equalise. Despite the 2-1 defeat, we had still done reasonably well and caused the Germans problems. On a personal note, I had another good game against Berti Vogts. These two games didn't do our world standing any harm and at this stage we were 16/1 to win the World Cup.

As the season drew to a close, my Coventry team-mates were looking forward to a close-season tour of Singapore. Even though this was an exotic trip that I would in normal circumstances want to go on, this time I would be glad to miss out due to being otherwise engaged. My summer would hopefully be spent abroad too, but in Europe rather than Asia. I had played four consecutive matches for Scotland and had done well.

A 40-man provisional squad for the World Cup and a 22-man squad to play in the Home International Championship had been announced and I was included in both. Had I done enough to convince Willie Ormond to pick me for the final 22-man squad that would head to Germany, and was now being talked about as one of the outside favourites to win the competition? I would soon find out.

Chapter 18

Lady Luck Bites Me on the Bum

YOU DON'T have a professional playing career spanning close to 28 years as I did and be prone to injury. Some players seemed to be dogged by injuries and have considerably shorter careers as their bodies don't seem able to stand up to the rigours of so many very competitive matches. My Coventry mate Colin Stein played only a few games after the age of 28 and was completely finished as a league player by his 31st birthday. I was very lucky and seldom missed games. However, as the biggest footballing occasion of my life was appearing just over the horizon, a Welshman and a fellow Scot were about to unwittingly conspire to drastically alter my World Cup destiny.

I was picked to play for my fifth consecutive Scotland game for our opening match of the now-defunct Home International Championship when we were to play Northern Ireland at Hampden Park. This was technically a home game for the Irish but because of the Troubles across the water they were having to play all their fixtures away from Windsor Park.

The game was played on an early summer day but in wintery weather, with Glasgow being the centre of a torrential downpour. This was another one of my special days when I felt on top of the world and capable of achieving anything. I played what I think was my best game for Scotland. I was helped by the pitch, which was slippery and slick, conditions made for me and in which I loved to play. Tommy Cassidy scored the only goal of the game, for the Northern Irish, in what was a very lack lustre performance by us. I say 'us', but my own individual performance I felt was very good and I gave the Northern Irish right-back, Pat Rice of Arsenal, a torrid time.

Several of my team-mates congratulated me at the end of the game with a 'Well done, big man.' I can remember both John Blackley and Kenny Dalglish saying this to me. No praise from Billy Bremner, although to be fair to him, he probably never congratulated anyone else either. It wasn't his way, but, as captain, perhaps should have been.

It was my third Hampden performance for Scotland and I just loved the experience of playing in that stadium for my country. I have thought about it often, but I don't have the words to describe just what a special event each Hampden international occasion was. It has something to do with the fans and the way that they were willing us to do well. I knew that they could turn on the team if they weren't happy but, as an individual, I felt nothing but their support.

The same could not be said of the Scottish press, who we felt certainly did not have our best interests at heart and were looking as hard as they could to find any juicy bit of salacious gossip they could print about us to sell a few more of their rags. After the Northern Ireland defeat they were sharpening their knives for Willie Ormond. While his overall record of something like two wins in 11 wasn't very impressive, he had won the game that really mattered, against Czechoslovakia, and many of our performances were good even if we didn't actually win those games. I was not on the receiving end of any of their criticism but I was aware that a dip in performance would leave me open to their vitriol.

I always felt that the football writers had a knee-jerk reaction to each game. If you played poorly in a particular match then you should be dropped. There was no context, no looking at the bigger picture of performance over several games. It was something that I would learn and have first-hand experience of in a few months' time. As we prepared to face Wales in our next Home International, we knew the pressure that Willie was under. I think most of the squad liked and respected him and wanted to perform in such a way that the words of the press would be rammed back down their collective throat.

Knowing the player that he was at that time, and the world-class player he was to become, it's hard to believe that, in those days leading up to the World Cup, Kenny Dalglish was having major doubts about his ability. I sat next to him on the bus taking us back to the hotel after training one day. I could see he was down and asked him what was wrong. He told me he wasn't enjoying the matches and he wasn't enjoying the training. He felt inhibited in what he could do as everything had to go through Billy Bremner.

I always felt that Bremner only loaned you the ball. Any time he passed to you he wanted it back as soon as possible. To an extent, I ignored it. My game was running at people, so if Billy gave me the ball I was always going to run at the opposition if the opportunity was there. I told him to forget about looking for Billy every time he had the ball and to do what he did so brilliantly for Celtic, to move the ball into areas that would hurt the team we were playing. Whether my advice made any difference or not I would doubt, but Kenny went on to prove what a wonderful player he was both for club and country.

Because of Billy Bremner's penalty miss against West Germany, Willie Ormond had decided a new penalty-taker was needed. We had a shoot-out contest in training before the Welsh match, won by Rangers Sandy Jardine and myself. Sandy was Rangers' recognised penalty-taker whereas I had never taken a spot kick in a competitive game. Sandy was therefore named as the designated penalty-taker with me to step in if he wasn't playing. Back on the minibus, I sat in front of Bremner and Peter Lorimer. They hadn't bothered watching the final stages of the competition and they didn't know that Sandy had been nominated for any penalties due to his greater experience.

Peter commented first, 'So ye'll be takin any pens tha' morrow then?' I said, 'Aye tha's right.' Billy then joined in, 'Well ther'll be 80,000 there. Ye sure ye can handle tha?' Peter agreed, 'Aye tha won't be easy, a crood like tha watchin oon.' 'Well,' I said, 'Ah cannae dae ony worse then tha las' boy who took one,' and that shut them up. It wasn't good-natured banter. It was as if they were trying to sow a seed of doubt in my mind, maybe because they were miffed that Billy wasn't taking them anymore. I also felt that showing any sign of weakness to Billy would leave me open to more of his jibes. Better to show that I wasn't going to back down just because it was him.

I was really starting to believe that not only would I make the squad for the World Cup but that I would be in the team for the start of the tournament. It was my sixth consecutive start and, without bigging myself up too much, I had played well in all of my Scotland games so far. You're probably thinking of that phrase that involves maths and newborn chicks, and you would be right. The Welsh game was only six minutes old when John Roberts brought me down with an over-the-top tackle.

These days it would be an instant red card; in that game I am not even sure he was booked. He had caught my shin with his studs and made a sizable gash down my leg. I have no doubt that Roberts meant to hurt me and was probably trying a little bit of intimidation. However, it was not him that I was subsequently to feel angry with, even though an interview I gave after the game has me saying that I will sort him out later. Roberts was a bruiser of a player and in a game between Birmingham and Coventry he committed a really bad foul on my Coventry team-mate Ian Wallace. Wally had the same eye-for-an-eye philosophy as Denis Law. When the opportunity for retribution presented itself, Wally gleefully took it. Roberts was left writhing in pain on the turf. I can't say I was sorry for him.

Anyway, the physio took one look at my leg and said that it needed stitching so I limped off to the dressing room, thinking I would be back on as soon as the wound was treated. I had received a much longer and deeper wound while playing for Coventry which needed nine stiches and I played on after having these inserted. I was angry and disappointed therefore when our team doctor, a Dr Fitzsimons from Celtic, told me that I needed three stitches in my leg and that was my game finished. I argued with him but got nowhere and he sent a message to the manager that a sub would be needed.

That was me done for the day. I wasn't happy. Fitzsimons got one of his assistants to make me a cup of tea while he sorted my leg out. Denis Law wandered into the dressing room to see how I was doing. He wasn't in the team that day but was watching the match with the rest of the squad. Like me he felt that football was for playing the game, not watching, so he took the opportunity to take a break from the match, 'Och, how are ye daein big man?' he said, and then looked at my leg. 'Well, tha' doesnae look tae bad.' At that point the guy with my tea turned up and Denis helped himself. 'Och, cheers son, naethin lik' a wee cuppa tae.' He then proceeded to drink the tea as I told him, 'Denis, Ah think tha tae was meant for me!' 'Och, sorry big man,' he said with a laugh and handed me the cup! Meanwhile the doctor had my wound stitched in record time, without bothering to disinfect it. His priority was to be done with me as quick as possible so that he could go back out and watch the game.

The team played well that night, putting on an impressive performance to beat the Welsh 2-0 with the second goal a Jardine penalty, to take the pressure off Willie Ormond. As we left Hampden for our Largs base none of us would have known that the pressure on Willie Ormond from the press would, in the next few hours, be ramped up yet again, or that one of our players would be the subject of a life-saving operation carried out by the emergency services.

I was disappointed that my latest Scottish appearance had been cut so short. However, the injury was a minor one and I was certain I would be fit for the weekend game, the big one against England at Hampden. I didn't know that the treatment that I had received that night would not only keep me out of the game against the auld enemy but would also threaten my appearance at the World Cup itself.

Chapter 19

Gone Fishing

WHEN WE got back to Largs after the Wales game, everyone was in a buoyant mood, including the manager, who gave us some time off to go for a few drinks at a club in the town. Me and a few others left the place after a couple of hours to go back to the hotel. The first I knew that anything was amiss was when I heard one of the elderly ladies who owned the place shouting at someone. I looked out of the window and there she was outside the front entrance, several police officers looking on, giving out to several members of the squad, 'Ye'v let me doon and taken awa th' good name o' mah hoose. Ye's will nae be welcome back here agin.'

The story of that night is well known. Briefly, what happened was this. After the early leavers had gone back to the hotel, the rest of the squad had stayed drinking at the club until about five in the morning. They then strolled back towards the hotel along the shore. They came across an oarless rowing boat pulled up on the sand and Jimmy Johnstone decided to get into the boat and serenade the rest of the boys stood on the side with a song. His choice of tune was 'Michael Row the Boat Ashore', quite funny considering the boat had no oars.

As a joke, Sandy Jardine pushed the boat into the water, thinking it would stay within wading distance of the beach, but it was immediately taken by the tide, and with Johnstone, a non-swimmer, still standing and singing (his song choice now apparently Lulu's 'The Man Who Sold the World'). Oblivious to the danger he was in, the boat slowly drifted away into the Firth of Clyde. A second rowing boat was launched by David Hay and Erich Schaedler to rescue Jimmy but they had to quickly return to shore when they discovered the boat had a leak. One of the players came back into our hotel and phoned 999 for the coastguard, who launched and brought back a cold, shivering and by now non-singing Johnstone back to shore.

We were ordered to attend a team meeting in the hotel's TV room at ten o'clock that morning. The squad gathered, sitting around on the comfy chairs, some still hungover from the night's events, waiting for Willie Ormond to arrive. Jimmy, who it has to be said didn't look at his best, had seated himself out of the way by the wall. A few of the boys were enjoying his discomfort.

Earlier in the season Jimmy had fallen out with his Celtic manager Jock Stein and been banned from the club for two weeks for some misdemeanour. Jock was a big man in both stature and personality and Jimmy was afraid of him. Denis Law looked across at him and said, 'Ah can see th' headlines noo.' He raised his eyes to his hand which punched out his words, 'How I Saved Ace Scottish Winger'. He continued tormenting Jimmy: 'Aye, n' thay will hae a picture if one o' th' coastguard boys sat on his creel, arms folded an a smile on his face.' Jimmy scowled back at him and then Bremner started, 'Aye, A'hm fairly sure tha' big Jock will be wantin' a word with ye aboot thi' Jimmy.' Lorimer piped up too, 'Aye n' your wife will nae be tae pleased either.' By the time Willie Ormond appeared, Jimmy was about ready to throw himself out of the window!

Willie scanned the room, looking for Jimmy, and stared at him for a few seconds when he found him behind the door against the wall. This was too much for Jimmy, who complains, 'Eh ye'r throwing me some awful dirty looks there ye know.' Well, this was too much for Willie who launched into a tirade, 'Dinnae ye think Ah've every riht tae. Oot in a boat on th' Firth o' Clyde at five in th' mornin'. Ye'r an international!' And so, his rant went on until it eventually blew itself out.

The press were onto the story straight away and they relished ripping into Willie and the players. Denis had been amazingly accurate; one of the papers did indeed have a picture of the coastguard boy who had brought Jimmy home. The official story from the Scottish camp that the boys were on an early morning fishing trip fooled no one, but it did mean that several fishing books arrived at the hotel over the next couple of days with the request for Jimmy to sign them.

The outrage in the press continued unabated to the Saturday when we were to play England. Vitriolic comments were made about the whole squad, but they were particularly pointed about Ormond and Johnstone.

They only served to bond us together and gave the squad an 'us against the world' (or at least the press) attitude.

From the morning after the Wales game, it had become clear to me that I would be taking no part in the upcoming game, the match every Scot wants to play in, the one against the English at Hampden. My leg was badly swollen, the wound had festered and I could barely walk thanks to, in my opinion, the shoddy job done by the team doctor. I was concerned, not only to be missing this game, but the effects the injury and my absence from the team would have on my long-term international prospects. I was managing to do the hard task that Gordon Milne had mentioned to me – losing my international place – even though it would be through no fault of my own.

The Friday night before the England game we had been given an 11 o'clock curfew to be in our rooms which, after the shenanigans earlier in the week, was fair enough. Willie Ormond came along to the hotel lounge and said, 'Right there boys, away tae yer beds.' We all got up to go and Willie went over to the bar where Billy Bremner was sitting with a pint talking to a guy called Jim Ferris, a representative from Adidas, about our boot deal. Why Billy was responsible for this deal rather than an agent or a representative from the SFA, I don't know. Why he was conducting negotiations such as these, late at night before a crucial game, also calls into question his judgement. Anyway, Willie says to him, 'Ye tae now Billy, away tae yer bed.' Billy turned on him and with a lot of the lads watching snapped back, 'Can ye nay see Ah'm talking tae this man n' have mah pint tae finish. Ah well go when Ah'm done.' Willie was embarrassed and backed down with, 'Well, aye. Make tha' yer last pint then,' and off he went, leaving Billy there.

I think that this was one of Willie's failings. He was too nice, too soft. However, he was in a difficult position with Bremner as, without a doubt, he was our best player. Deprived of him, we would have been a considerably weaker team. Yet Billy was a law unto himself. In training, he was the one player who did not put in the work in the way that the rest of us did. While we were going flat out, he would be trying fancy flicks and tricks and generally strolling through sessions. He could do this because he knew that he was going to be picked whatever he did. It could be argued that he was at a stage in his career where he was having to manage his body, perhaps conserve his energy for games, but his lifestyle didn't really indicate that looking after his body was a major concern of Billy's. Rules on curfew, drinking and smoking did not apply to him.

I remember on one occasion he was sat in his usual position at the back of the team bus and called loudly to one of the physios to come from the front and give him a light for his cigarette. I know that some of my team-mates think that he was a great player and a great captain. To me, he was certainly a great player and a good captain in games that mattered, in that he led by example with his attitude and application. However, in all other aspects of captaincy I thought he was poor. He had his own agenda and certainly wasn't a team player. His old colleague at Leeds, Terry Yorath, was my skipper at Coventry for a while. He could have shown him a thing or two about captaincy.

Peter Lorimer took my place in the game against the English, who were now under the temporary control of my Coventry manager Joe Mercer following the sacking of Alf Ramsey. I watched, frustrated, from the stands as my fired-up team-mates set about them with relish and convincingly beat them 2-0. The game was a personal triumph for Ormond and for Jimmy Johnstone. Both relished proving their journalistic tormentors wrong. Jimmy, who had a good game, swapped shirts with Peter Shilton at the end of the game and danced around the Hampden Pitch in the huge yellow shirt.

After a word on the pitch from Ormond, Jimmy took great delight in flicking 'V' signs at the press box. I tried my best to be as euphoric about the performance and the result as the rest of the squad but in truth I was feeling deflated about missing out on such a great occasion. It was probably the worst that I ever felt about missing a game.

The announcement of the final squad for the World Cup cheered me up. I was now confirmed as one of the 22 players who would shortly be travelling to West Germany. I was now caught up in all the paraphernalia that goes along with World Cup qualification. We had been measured up for our World Cup suits. These were supplied to us by C&A and had huge lapels and a huge Scottish badge. They were beezer, a Scottish word meaning 'could certainly have been better' or, in other words, crap! We were also issued with trench coats and, when these arrived, we were asked to assemble on the hotel lawn for a photo shoot.

We were all gathered there except for the extremely tall Jim Holton and the extremely small Jimmy Johnstone. Ormond noticed their absence and asked, 'Where's Holton and Wee Jimmy?', just as they arrived on the scene. They had swapped trench coats, Holton looking like he had been sewn into his while Jimmy looked like Dopey from the seven dwarfs with his hands hidden by the sleeves of what should have been Holton's coat and the hem trailing along the floor. As we fell about laughing at them, Jimmy said to the gaffer, 'Hey, Donny [his nickname for the boss, Ormond being close to Osmond], who measured these?'

We had a guy called Bob Bain who was in charge of putting together the commercial deals that would see the squad rewarded for our World Cup qualification. He assured us that we would do better than the lucrative deal that the English squad had had for the Mexican World Cup in 1970. We had visions of our pictures appearing on boxes of Rice Krispies and all sorts of similar deals. He assured us that each player would be at least £5,000 better off as a result of the deals he would do. Ormond wasn't impressed with him and said that he was, 'All promises.' His ability to go missing when certain questions needed answering earned him the nickname of the 'Tartan Pimpernel' among the squad.

An indication that things might not go as well as the smooth-talking Bains had suggested was the deal done with Vauxhall for the players' World Cup cars. An agreement had been made with the company to supply all the players and staff who featured in any of the qualifying games with a new car. This meant my Coventry team-mate Willie Carr, who had played against Denmark, would get one too. Each car had a stereo radio and had the players' initials stencilled on the driver's door and dashboard. We were under the impression from Bob Bain that these cars were ours to keep while Vauxhall insisted that the cars were on loan for a year, after which we would be able to buy our model if we wanted.

Bain insisted that he would challenge this ruling, but after much bluster in the papers, the decision remained the same. The cars were great. Mine was painted a very bright yellow. At the end of the year I would have handed mine back but my Coventry team-mate David Cross asked if he could buy it, which was fine by me. Afterwards, DC could be seen on the roads of Coventry and Warwickshire driving a car the colour of a banana with TH on his door!

To be fair to Bob, some of his promises did come true. He had said that he would get us a record deal for our World Cup song, although his claims of a number one in the record charts and an appearance on *Top of the Pops* never happened. Its highest place in the charts was 20. The song itself, 'Easy', has been widely acknowledged as one of the worst football songs ever, something that I would have to agree with, this despite it being co-written by Phil Coulter and Bill Martin and that we recorded it with Rod Stewart helping out on vocals. I think the opening lyrics 'Yabba dabba do, we support the boys in blue, and it's easy, easy' tell you all you need to know as to why it wasn't a bestseller! I remember travelling to Old Trafford and meeting up with the Scottish boys there to do the publicity pictures for the song, running up and down the pitch. I still have the piece of vinyl containing the song. It is an LP which features genuine Scottish singers and groups such as Stealers Wheel and includes some good songs and music. And then there is us!

We finished our preparation in Largs on a high as we had a visit from Billy Connolly. At that stage I had never heard of him, but Kenny Dalglish and John Blackley knew who he was and told me that I would need to listen to him and that I wouldn't believe how funny he was. We were all assembled in the sports hall at the hotel and this fellow comes onto the stage, long straggly hair, beard to match and strange set of clothing. To be honest, I thought, 'This boy could dae with a good wash.'

When he started, well, he had us falling off our seats with laughing. There was only the squad and the staff present so it was an informal thing. After half an hour or so he came down off the stage and sat with us and had a cup of tea. That's where he stayed for the next hour and a half, telling us his stories. It was brilliant! He actually said that performing in front of us was the most nervous he'd been as he'd look one way and there was Denis Law and he'd look the other way and there was Billy Bremner, real heroes of his. We couldn't have had a better send-off.

Willie Ormond did worry that all the peripheral stuff might distract us from the task in hand. I can only speak for myself and say that none of the commercial stuff made me lose sight of what we were trying to achieve. My sole focus was in getting back into the team as soon as possible. We had two warm-up games before the tournament started, playing first in Belgium and then in Norway. I was now back to full fitness with the infection in my leg gone. I was hoping that my previous good performances for Scotland might mean that I was straight back in the team.

The good performance against England and the fact that my replacement Peter Lorimer was an established player made this unlikely. It was still a big disappointment to me though that, when the team was named for Belgium, I was one of two substitutes. I did get on in the 80th minute of a poor 2-1 defeat. Sometimes when you come on in that way you think that it might be because the guy you are replacing has played badly, and that this might provide an opening for you to get back in the team. In my case, I came on for Kenny Dalglish and I knew that there was no way he was being left out once the World Cup started.

We moved on to Norway for our final friendly. We were billeted in the halls of residence of a university campus for a week. Nowadays there is no way that an international football team would stay in a place like that. Even in 1974 it was really unacceptable, but it shows the mindset and penny-pinching nature of the SFA at the time. At club level we would never have had accommodation as poor as this. Even though Coventry were not a wealthy club, they ensured that the players always had first-class places to stay when away from home. When playing in London, for example, we would always stay at the Russell Hotel. We made our feelings known but it was too late at that stage to change anything.

An incident happened while we were in Norway that has always stayed with me. We were on the fourth floor of a block in the university's halls of residence. In the squad was a full-back from Hibs, Erich Schaedler. Erich was a character who would do some very strange things. He was born in Scotland but was the son of a German POW who had stayed in the country when the war ended. Ironically, his one and only international game had been in one of the friendlies with West Germany. Billy Bremner was the cards man of the squad and, as usual, he kept the card game going. He said to Schaedler, 'Erich, go and fetch us some beers.'

I would have told Bremner to fetch his own beer, but Erich was more amenable than me. However, instead of walking down the corridor to the fridge in the kitchen, Erich climbed out of the window onto the narrow ledge that extended around each floor. Despite being about 70 or 80 feet above the ground, he shimmied, James Bond-like, along the ledge to the window of the kitchen, where he climbed in to get the beer. While some of the boys knew Erich and knew he was a bit strange, Bremner couldn't believe what he was seeing. 'Is he alright?' Well, things clearly weren't alright for Erich. A few years later, at the age of 36 and still a player at Dumbarton, he sadly killed himself in Cardrona Forest.

Things weren't alright in the squad either. On the pitch, we weren't playing that well. I was back in the team for our last game before the World Cup, but the performance in our 2-1 win wasn't good. It certainly wasn't a lack of effort that was at fault. Every one of us was going at full tilt to try and claim a place in the starting line-up for our first World Cup match against Zaire. However, off the pitch, problems caused by alcohol were threatening to derail our chances. Bremner and Johnstone were absent from a team dinner held in the campus after a late-night drinking session.

Although Willie Ormond wasn't pleased that the two had missed the dinner, he could hardly complain about the late-night session as he had been there himself. Officials from the FSA made their feeling of displeasure known to Billy and to Jimmy. At that stage it wasn't clear whether they would walk out, unhappy with the dressing-down that had been delivered, or be sent home by an equally unhappy SFA. In the end both players were 'severely reprimanded' and were allowed to stay on after they had apologised, but also only after Ormond had intervened on their behalf.

We flew into Germany and were taken to our training camp at Erbismuhle, located in beautiful countryside 30 miles outside Frankfurt, on a fantastic coach decked out in the colours of the Scottish flag. Needless to say, this had been provided by our German hosts, not the SFA! As we settled into the complex, my mind was on that first game against Zaire. I was thinking about what I could do to ensure I was in that opening 11. Despite starting the last friendly against Norway and again playing well, I had the nagging feeling that this time I wasn't going to make it. The next few days of training would be make or break and would tell me if I was in or not.

Chapter 20

Will We Stay or Will We Go?

IN 1972, West Germany staged the Olympics, but the event was overshadowed when a Palestinian group stormed the complex where the Israeli team were staying and took several members hostage. A failed rescue attempt by the authorities saw both the hostages and the people holding them killed. The Germans were determined that there would be no repeat of those terrible events at this World Cup. As soon as we got off the plane, we were surrounded by soldiers carrying guns. When we boarded that very posh bus of ours, we were accompanied by three heavily armed guards. They told us that if any incident occurred on any of our trips on the bus in Germany, we would be instructed to get on the floor, and we were to do it quickly.

As we set off to Erbismuhle, we were followed all the way by a helicopter flying just above and beside the bus. The side door of the helicopter was open and a lad was sitting there, legs dangling, a gun across his lap. More guards awaited us when we got to the complex. They patrolled outside and in the corridors inside. If we went downstairs in the hotel for a game of table tennis, a guard would be there as well. I remember David Hay telling me that he went out on a sunny day, up onto a little hill beside the complex, to sit and read his book. He was advised not to do this again as they were concerned that snipers might be on the lookout and a little trigger-happy. Although it was a little unsettling at first, we were young lads on an adventure and we quickly accepted this level of security as the norm.

We trained every day and the level at which we worked was ferocious. It wasn't directed by Willie Ormond, but he was aware of it and he didn't try to pull us back. This was 22 footballers with the chance of a lifetime.

Each one of us wanted to be in the starting 11. Tackles were flying and the risk of injury was high. Inevitably, tempers were close to being frayed in such a highly charged atmosphere and players did come near to blows on several occasions.

I can remember Bremner having to step in between Joe Jordan and Martin Buchan to stop them knocking lumps out of each other. Squad numbers had been issued and a huge disappointment for me was to be allocated the number 18 shirt, with Peter Lorimer wearing the number 11. This was a clear indication that when the team lined up against Zaire, I would not be there. Still, in training I did everything that I could to impress and make the manager aware that I wanted my place back in the team.

Billy Bremner's negotiations with Adidas could not have gone well as an agreement wasn't reached on a footwear deal. Whether Billy had asked for too much money, I don't know, but the fact was that we were going to get no reward for showcasing the company's product on the world stage. This did seem unfair to us: we would be wearing Adidas boots but have no reward for doing so. The boots and training shoes had been stored in a basement room at the complex in anticipation of a deal being done. We managed to acquire the key to this room one evening and helped ourselves to what was there. The Adidas boots and trainers all had the trademark white stripes. Now we had them in our possession, each of us carefully unstitched the stripes and polished over the place where they had been, leaving us with boots that were all black and with no obvious indication that they had been designed by Adidas. We at least had the satisfaction of knowing that, while we may not have been making any money out of wearing their stuff, neither were Adidas.

We travelled from our camp at Erbismuhle to our hotel in Dortmund where our first game would take place. By this time I knew my fate. Willie had picked the team and, as expected, Peter Lorimer was in, but at least I was on the bench with a chance of coming on. We watched the opening match of the World Cup, a game that was of particular interest to us as it was between the other two teams in our group, the reigning world champions, Brazil, and Yugoslavia. Both were very strong teams and by common consensus the two teams to qualify from our group would come from ourselves, Brazil or Yugoslavia. Zaire, even though they were the African champions, were thought to be considerably weaker than the other three countries in the group. The match between Brazil and the

Yugoslavs was a dreadful game which ended in a boring 0-0 draw. We saw nothing in that match that would frighten us.

We knew very little about Zaire or the way that they would play. Willie had been to watch them and hadn't been very impressed. All we knew was that we should win. Watching on from the sidelines, I could see that they were big and quick but that they were also very naïve in the way that they played. They were also very physical, but their tackles were clumsy rather than cynical; they just hadn't been coached how to do it properly. We raced into a 2-0 lead and could have had more, hitting the woodwork twice and missing other good chances. We knew, and Willie had drilled it into us, that goal difference could be crucial in this group. We needed to beat Zaire by a big score.

The game wore on and we couldn't score again. I came on for Dalglish with about 15 minutes to go and I did create a chance for Denis. He fired goalwards only for the goalkeeper to push the ball around the post. If he had looked inside, he would have seen that I had continued my run and was free and unmarked in the box. However, Denis was a striker and his first instinct was to go for goal, which I understood. The score stayed at 2-0, which was a disappointment for us. On chances made, it could have conceivably been about 8-3. I did try and swap shirts at the end with the Zairian full-back, but he made it known that they couldn't swap, they only had one set of shirts with them and would be needed for the next game.

We were back to Erbismuhle to prepare for our next game, a match against the world champions, Brazil. I was desperate to play but I realised that my chances weren't looking too good. Peter Lorimer had scored the opening goal, hit the bar and had generally played well. Something out of the ordinary would have to happen for me to displace him. Someone else who was concerned that he might not play was Willie Morgan. We had been told that we were not to have any contact with the press during the World Cup. However, Willie managed to have an article published in which he had said that if he wasn't picked for the Brazil game, he would walk out of the camp and come home. As Willie had broken the disciplinary code, it might have been expected that Ormond would have something to say about it but no action was taken, again showing the manager's tendency to be too soft.

The final training session before the game had the usual probables v possibles game. As expected, I was on the possibles team, meaning that I was unlikely to start. What I found surprising and disappointing was that Willie Morgan was in the probables team, meaning he would likely start. I started to think that the way to get into the team was maybe to kick up a stink rather than to impress in practice games like the one we were about to play. I was frustrated before we started and that feeling only intensified as the practice went on. Denis Law was on the possible team too and late in the practice I laid a ball through for him to run onto. It wasn't a good pass, but Denis didn't even try to get on the end of it. Well, that was too much for me and my frustration turned into anger and I had a real go at him. 'Oh, so you're so good yer cannae be bothered tae move yer arse 'n try 'n get the ball. Ye wannae make me look bad, eh?'

As far as I was concerned, I was busting a gut trying to impress Ormond and get myself in the team and he couldn't be bothered to try and turn my bad pass into a reasonable one. As we trudged off at the end, Denis came over to me and asked what was wrong. I told him that I'd had enough. If I wasn't going to play, I felt as though I might as well go home. He stopped me and said, 'Tam, yer one of only 22 players oot here from the whole o' Scotland. How many players dae ye know that would give up everything tae be in this squad?' He carried on in the same vein until he had calmed me down and got me to agree that I would be going nowhere. I apologised to him for bawling him out and he just laughed it off. It says much for the mark of the man that Denis was willing to spend that time with me when he would also be disappointed that he was unlikely to play.

One of the reasons for my frustration that day was that I didn't feel selection for Scotland was on a level playing field. In some ways I was at the bottom of the pile when it came to be considered for the international team. I felt that home-based players who played for the Old Firm, Celtic and Rangers, would always take precedence. Next in line was any other player who might be playing well for another Scottish club. The Scottish press would certainly be pushing the claims of any of these players over the 'Anglos', Scottish players playing south of the border. I had heard Bremner and Law describe how they had been on the team bus heading out of Glasgow on a couple of occasions when it had been stoned by 'fans' after heavy defeats. The windows they aimed at usually had an England-based player sitting behind them. The selectors and the manager shouldn't have been affected by all of this, but I think they were.

The selection pyramid had other levels too, I think and the next group would have been players who played for the glamorous English teams like Manchester United, Liverpool and Leeds. My clubs, Coventry and Blackpool, certainly weren't in the glamorous category, so I was down in the basement of the pyramid. There was also the Tommy Docherty factor. The former Scotland boss was managing several Scots at United, including one of my winger rivals Willie Morgan, and had no hesitation in pushing their international claims in the press and no doubt in Willie Ormond's ear. I felt that for me to be picked, not only did I have to be better than the players in my position, I had to be considerably better. My failure to regain my place in the team, I felt, was partly a symptom of this unfair system.

I was on the bench again for the Brazil game, this time alongside Jimmy Johnstone. Willie Morgan, as expected, was in the starting 11 taking the place of Denis Law. If I had been picking the team, I would have started Jimmy Johnstone. He was such a skilful player, so good at going at the opposition and beating a player, that I felt he would have been one of the few players in our squad who could make the most out of the limited possession we were likely to have. There are only two players that I have played against where I felt I had them cornered with no way of them coming past me, yet with the minimum of space and time they were able to beat me. One was Jimmy, the other was Franz Beckenbauer, an indication of how highly I rated my team-mate.

As it happened, we had an increasing amount of possession in the game. Brazil may have been world champions but they were not the fantastic team of 1970, even though they still had players like Rivelino, Jairzinho and Paulo Cesar. They started on top but, as the game went on, we increasingly came to grips with them and started creating chances. Willie Morgan, I had to admit, was having a great game. We knew that if we beat Brazil, we would be through to the knockout stage. Any other result would leave us vulnerable to both Brazil and Yugoslavia running up a big score against Zaire and having a superior goal difference. Both sides created and missed chances but undoubtedly the best chance fell to Bremner, who followed up on a save by the Brazilian keeper but was unfortunate as he didn't have time to react. The ball hit him on the shin and trickled agonisingly inches wide.

With a few minutes left, Willie Ormond told Jimmy Johnstone to warm up, but Jimmy refused, saying, 'Ah'm no going on there.' I don't know why he refused. Perhaps he thought that the game, with both teams going hammer and tongs at each other even in the final minutes, was too fast for him. Maybe he felt that with only two or three minutes left, he wasn't going to have time to do anything. Whatever the reason, that was his last chance to appear at a World Cup finals gone. If it had been me being asked to go on, I certainly would have. Even with only a few minutes left I would have fancied my chances of creating a chance. The game ended goalless, in reality a good result for us, but one which left us slightly disappointed considering the chances we missed. We were also a bit deflated when we heard that the Yugoslavs had beaten Zaire 9-0 which put our meagre two-goal win in the shade. The likelihood was that the Brazilians would also put an avalanche of goals in the African's net when they met in a few days. All of this meant that we would almost certainly have to beat Yugoslavia to progress.

We went back to our training complex for the final few days of preparation for our last group match. One afternoon, I was in bed trying to get to sleep and failing as usual when I had a message from reception. They told me that my brother had arrived to see me. This was a real surprise for me as I didn't have a brother. When I got downstairs, my 'brother' turned out to be my Blackpool mate Derek Fontane. That man would have been able to talk himself into teatime with the Pope if he had wanted too. The level of security at the complex was intense with anyone trying to enter having to provide evidence of who they were and of the permission they had to enter. God knows what Derek said to the guards but, as was his way, he was able to blag his way in. We had a good chat and I introduced him to a few of my team-mates. I was able to give him a ticket for the upcoming game, but I have no doubt that, if I hadn't, he would still have got in somehow.

As if the security around us wasn't tight enough, we had it ramped up another notch when a threat was received by the authorities, supposedly from the IRA, that they were targeting our players. Considering the number of Celtic players and Catholics in the squad, the validity of the warning had to be questioned. No chances could be taken, however, and we were warned to be on our guard. This was all too much for Jimmy Johnstone, who walked from the hotel entrance to the coach taking us to our final game holding a Celtic bag above his head while shouting to any potential sniper, 'Ah'm a Catholic, Ah'm a Catholic.' He wasn't joking either – Jimmy was a funny guy but he was genuinely scared. He was still wandering around telling anyone who would listen what his religion was while we were all on the coach waiting for him. Ormond had to come down the steps and order him to get on or we'd go without him. Jimmy climbed on still with the Celtic bag 'protecting' his head.

I was again on the bench for the Yugoslavia match, again very disappointed as I really felt I could help us get over the line. We simply had to win as we were fairly sure that Brazil would beat Zaire by more than the two goals we did. Our opponents were a good side but we were confident that we could get the result we needed. We started well and were on top and creating chances but not converting them. At half-time we heard that Brazil were beating Zaire 2-0. They would surely score more in the second half so we knew that we would have to score at least once in the coming 45 minutes.

We continued to dominate in our game but again with nothing to show for it. In the 65th minute I got my chance, coming on for Dalglish. Nine minutes from the end we fell to a sucker punch when, out of nowhere, Yugoslavia scored. That perhaps should have been the cue for us to give up as we now needed two goals to go through. The spirit in that team was great though, and we still went looking for the goals we needed. In my 20-odd minutes on the pitch, I had already gone past the full-back twice and put dangerous crosses into the box. Two minutes from the end I received the ball on the left and did it again. This time I got to the goal line and pulled the ball back for Joe Jordan to score. Try as we might, we couldn't score again. We needed a miracle from the Brazil v Zaire match but unfortunately we didn't get it. At the final whistle we were told the score. The South Americans had scored a late and lucky goal, a terrible mistake by the keeper, to win 3-0. In effect, we had been knocked out of the World Cup by one goal.

We went over to the corner of the stadium to say thank you to the Scottish fans who had supported us so well. If we were sad, well, some of them were in bits. It shows the power of football and the effect it can have on human emotions when the result of a game reduces people to tears. We were able to have a chat with a few and to try to console them. They had been great and had been welcomed wherever they went in Germany because, although they were raucous, they were good-humoured too. The only place I could ever remember our fans not being welcome was at Wembley, but maybe that was because they sometimes brought some of the pitch home with them!

Back at the hotel that night there were plenty of discussions on how we had performed and on what might have been. We all felt that we had been the better team in all three games, possibly just shading the match against Brazil. Looking back, it was our game against Zaire that cost us. We could and should have beaten them by more. We were perhaps unlucky to play them first when they were at their freshest and most resilient. However, despite being unbeaten, we really only had ourselves to blame for not progressing. We didn't take the many chances that we created in all three games.

We were entertained that night by Lonnie Donegan, Billy Connolly and Rod Stewart, and it was a bleary-eyed bunch of Scots that headed off to the airport next day. We were in for one more surprise, and a very pleasant one. The scenes when we arrived back in Glasgow were unbelievable. The airport was rammed with fans who had come to cheer us home. Estimates put the crowd there at 50,000 people, cheering, singing and waving flags and banners. We hadn't even reached the second stage and yet this was our reception. Imagine what the scenes would have been like had we won the thing!

From a personal point of view, I was £500 and two pairs of boots better off because of the World Cup, a long way from Bob Bain's promised £5,000. Although I had spent only 36 minutes on the pitch, it was an experience that I will always treasure. My fond memories are tinged with a little bit of bitterness as, but for an over-the-top tackle and some medical incompetence, I think I would have started every game. I also think I showed in my brief time on the pitch that I was a threat and capable of hurting teams. Had I played, would we have got through? Well, that's a difficult query and one that's impossible to answer. The players I was competing with, Peter Lorimer and Willie Morgan, both had a good World Cup, so I would have to have produced something very special to have improved on what they did.

Now I needed a break after a long season and I was looking forward to spending a few weeks with friends and family back in Fife. When we got home, however, the news wasn't good.

Chapter 21

It's Farewell to Scotland

WE HAD very few opportunities during the football season to see our families. Because of this, the few weeks of the close season were always spent back in Fife with the Hutchison and the Adair clans and our extended families. During our few weeks at home, we would be visiting aunts, uncles, cousins and friends, which was lovely, but busy too. The summer of 1974 was a particularly memorable one as everyone in Dundonald wanted to say well done on being the first native of our village to play in a World Cup (Willie Johnston achieved the same feat four years later in Argentina). My friends and neighbours seemed genuinely proud that a boy from the raws had done so well. However, that visit home was tinged with sadness and worry.

My dad's health had always been up and down. He was never a truly well man, but there were times when his respiratory problems really laid him low and left him bed-bound. These spells would usually coincide with the cold, damp months of the year. Unbeknownst to me, while the World Cup had been taking place that summer, my dad had been very ill and had taken to his bed. My mum and uncles gathered around the TV with my bed-bound dad to watch our games, but apparently my dad was really out of things, sleeping most of the time. According to my mum, the only occasions during the football when my dad stirred or showed any interest was when the commentator said my name. Then his eyes would open and for a few minutes he would take note of what was going on.

As he always did, my dad recovered enough from this latest bout to return to work at the pit, but it was obvious that his spells of poor health were more frequent and more serious and that his recoveries were longer and more laboured. His later years in the mines were spent on the surface, operating the winding gear, his body no longer able to cope with the physical demands of working underground. He took a cut in his wages, but he had no choice.

I returned to Coventry for pre-season still worried about things at home but with no choice but to carry on earning a living a long way from family. Things at club level weren't great either. Although my own form continued to be good, Coventry City were about to enter a period of financial difficulty. Gordon Milne had spent big money on bringing Liverpool centre-half Larry Lloyd to the club. The mammoth fee, £250,000, was to be recouped by the imminent sale of two of our good young lads, Mick McGuire and Jimmy Holmes, to Spurs.

That transfer had been agreed but the day before it was to be completed the Tottenham manager, Bill Nicholson, was sacked. The deal was scrapped and it left Coventry with a big hole in their finances. We started the season as relegation favourites and, as we didn't win any of the first nine games, the prediction looked accurate. But as so often happened in my time at the club, when things looked really bleak we suddenly found some form, and eventually finished the season in 14th place.

Despite the often-precarious league positions we occupied, the Coventry squads I was in always had a good team spirit, helped by some of the characters we had. Ernie Hunt was a very funny boy. He didn't look in the least athletic, his unique physique helped no doubt by his ability to drink for England (and Scotland and Wales), but he could play and was a very clever footballer. He had developed a technique where, when he was on a run, he would catch his foot on the back of his own heel and trip himself up. In the penalty area, he would feel contact and go down – the only problem was it was contact from himself. Ernie conned many referees into awarding us penalties with his trick.

Another funny boy was the goalkeeper, Bill Glazier. He had suffered a broken leg earlier in his career and whatever way they had set his leg, it had left him with a misshapen shin bone which had a huge bump sticking out halfway down. It was amazing he was able to play again. Bill had an incredibly posh voice which really stood out in our working-class dressing room. This only added to his ability to make people laugh.

On one occasion we were on an overseas trip in an airport lounge. Bill was sitting smoking his pipe next to the immaculately dressed Wilf Smith, resplendent in white trousers. Someone cracked a joke, making Bill laugh and he blew ash from the pipe all over Wilf's pristine slacks.

To make matters worse, before Smith could stop him, he was saying, 'Terribly sorry, dear boy. Here, let me help.' He proceeded to attempt to brush the ash off Wilf's trousers, leaving long smears of grey down each leg, much to the amusement of those of us watching on.

The mid-70s was a time of turmoil with players sold at bargain prices to keep the wolf from the door. Colin Stein and Willie Carr left the club; so did McGuire, who went to Norwich. Holmes did go to Spurs eventually, but for much less than the original fee. Jimmy Hill returned to Coventry, this time in the role of managing director. He is a legend at the club and has a statue at the ground in his honour but he was someone I didn't really trust after a disagreement about his involvement in a newspaper article about me. I will mention that later.

Despite Coventry's poor start to the season, I was delighted to be back in the starting line-up for Scotland when we played East Germany in a friendly at Hampden Park in October 1974. It was a particularly significant game as I scored my one and only international goal. Early in the game, Sandy Jardine took and missed a penalty. After 35 minutes we were awarded a second spot kick. I collected the ball. Jardine came up to me and said, 'Ye'll put this away nae problem, big man.' Despite it being my first senior penalty, I wasn't nervous. I made up my mind to hit the ball hard with my laces rather than side-foot it, and go to the keeper's right. The keeper went the wrong way and I had reached another milestone, scoring for my country.

We went on to win the game 3-0. The East German lads arrived only a few hours before the game in their tracksuits and left for the airport straight after to return home, probably a feature of the Cold War times we were living in with the East German authorities fearful of defections to the west. I know that because of thick fog shrouding Glasgow that day that there was real concern that the German plane might not be able to land and the game would be off. Luckily for me, that didn't happen.

A month later I was back in the Scotland team to play against Spain in a qualifying game for the 1976 European Championship. It was to be a turning point in my international career. The pitch that night was not one that I liked playing on. It was freezing and the ground was really hard. The ball bobbled about on the tufty surface and because of the hard frost, you could actually hear the ball as it travelled through the rime. It was probably my worst performance in a Scotland jersey, though things started brightly for the team when Bremner scored in the opening few minutes. They seemed to be getting even better when, on 20 minutes, we were awarded a penalty and I stepped up to take it.

A 2-0 lead at that stage would probably have knocked the stuffing out of our opponents. I was confident when I picked up the ball. The penalty was at the same end as my previous one and I intended to do exactly the same thing again, putting the ball to the keeper's right. Unfortunately he had done his homework, anticipated which way the ball would go and dived to make the save. He did only parry the ball back out, however, and my biggest regret is that I was caught flat-footed. If I had been sharper, I could have got to the rebound before him.

Also, taking the kick, I was a bit wary about whether my studded standing foot would slip on the icy surface or not, so unlike the last time, I side-footed it rather than putting my laces through it. None of my team-mates followed up on it either. I took that as a sign that they were so confident I would score that they were all back in our half waiting for the restart! No excuses, however. From 12 yards out the advantage is always with the attacker and I should have buried the penalty. The miss was pivotal for the outcome of the game, which Spain came back to win 2-1, and for our chances of qualifying for the finals, as Spain were now in the driving seat. I was subbed off in the second half and had no complaints. I was playing poorly.

My team-mates were fine and there were no recriminations from that quarter. The Scottish press were less kind, citing me as the villain of the piece for my miss and my poor performance. However, the reaction of the SFA was perhaps the most damning. A report on our performance stated: 'It appears that in the early stages that we had the ability and the spirit to win. A missed penalty by Hutchison wrecked the team's composure and their will to win. Scotland have now missed five of the last seven penalties with Hutchison's the most crucial of all.' While I accepted responsibility for the penalty miss, it did seem that it was being used as a bit of a stick to beat me with. The whole team were surely responsible for letting our one-goal lead slip.

Although I continued to play for Scotland, I do feel that my miss was there in the background, not forgotten by the people who made the decisions. Certainly, many Scotland fans never forgot. A few years later I was playing in a pre-season tournament for Coventry against Man City, Hearts and Hibs. I went out before the game at Easter Road to warm up with my team-mate Barry Powell.

One of the Hibs fans leant over the perimeter wall a few yards from us and yelled, 'Ah ye big mug tell him aboot yer penalties.' Barry said to me, 'What's he on about?' 'Ignore them.' The Hibs fan yelled again, 'Tell him how good ye are at tha' penalty kicks.' Powell raised his eyebrows at me so I told him that he was talking about my miss at Hampden. 'But that was about five years ago,' said Barry. 'Aye. They hae long memories up here!' I told him.

The return against Spain was in Valencia in February 1975. Willie Ormond still had enough faith in me to pick me in the starting 11. We played well, took the lead on two minutes through Joe Jordan, missed loads of chances and conceded the inevitable equaliser with 20 minutes to go, leaving Spain as the favourites to qualify. In April we played a friendly against Sweden in Stockholm. On that occasion, I didn't even make the bench. However, in an end-of-season friendly against Portugal I was back in the starting line-up. I remember the half-time 'entertainment' was provided by the Wombles. After the 'warm' reception they received from the Hampden crowd, I think it's safe to say that they wouldn't have ventured out onto the streets of Glasgow that weekend for any Wombling activities!

Although in the squad, I wasn't picked at all for the first two Home International matches against Wales or Ireland, but I was back on the bench for the big one against the English at Wembley. The match was a disaster, particularly for our goalkeeper, Rangers' Stuart Kennedy. His performance led to a joke being circulated north of the border, with typical dark Scottish humour, that the boy a few years before had shot the wrong Kennedy! Stuart had an absolute howler that day, a performance that left him being compared to Frank Haffey, the Scottish goalkeeper in the infamous 9-3 defeat to England at Wembley.

Our 5-1 defeat wasn't that bad. Indeed, our performance, hard to believe with that scoreline, wasn't that bad either. It was simply one of those days when every shot England had at goal went in while Ray Clemence at the other end played a blinder. I came on with half an hour to go and hit a 25-yarder that I thought was in from the second it left my foot. At the last second, Clemence reached it with his 'wrong' right hand and flicked it over the bar. Wembley, as usual, was full of Scots and it was a cruel result for such fanatical support.

Bruce Rioch scored for us from the spot that day and I later played with him in Seattle. He was a boy who could really hit a ball hard. I remember him talking to us about his free kicks. He said to watch out for the rebounds from the first free kick he had, as they wouldn't be standing for his second one! It reminds me of a similar session we had at Coventry with our coach, Tommy Casey, in preparation to play Leeds and in particular to face a Peter Lorimer free kick. Casey put the ball down in a likely position on the edge of the box and told Glazier to line the wall up.

Everyone was ready. Ernie Hunt, who could also hit a ball, prepared to imitate Lorimer. He was waiting on Gordon Milne to blow his whistle to take it. As he was about to run up to the ball, Casey halted him and said to the five of us in the wall, 'Oh, by the way, if it is Lorimer on free-kick duty tomorrow, my advice would be to duck, cos if that ball hits you, it will kill you!' I said to him, 'Why have ye prepared a wall for? Ah ye telling us tae duck?' He said, 'I'm telling you, if he hits it, get out of the way.' None of this putting your body on the line malarkey when Lorimer was around, obviously!

I played twice more for Scotland, in qualifiers for the Euros. Firstly, as a sub in a 1-1 draw in Romania when I came on for Rioch, and then as a starter in Denmark. We won the game 1-0 with John Duncan coming on for me with 20 minutes left. That trip was another that ended in controversy due to off-field events. There was a club, Bonapartes, downstairs from our hotel in Copenhagen. After the game, we went in for a few drinks. Lads from the Scottish under-21 team were also in Denmark and there were one or two headcases in that group. The bar was illuminated with upturned coloured light bulbs and when a couple of the younger boys were refused drinks, they retaliated by smashing the light bulbs. Billy Bremner got involved and ended up throwing a drink up the back of one of the waiters.

All of this was a cue for some of us to leave, not wanting to be involved in any of the nonsense. Apparently the police were called, fights broke out and one of the younger lads was arrested when running up and down the street outside, unfortunately using parked cars as the pavement. After investigation, five Scottish players received lifetime bans, including Billy Bremner. It was a sad end to an international career for a truly great player. Unfortunately, his off-field behaviour finally caught up with him.

At the time, I didn't realise that it was the end for me and Scotland, too. I was 28 years old and as far as I was concerned, I was just coming into the prime years of my career. When I was left out of the next couple of squads, I was disappointed but I still felt I was playing well enough for Coventry to earn a recall. It was only during the following years that I really felt disadvantaged that I wasn't playing for one of the elite clubs. The exposure other players had made international call-ups far more likely.

My mate Colin Stein was not in the least arrogant, but if there was a bit of teasing going on about our respective abilities, he would slap the table and say, 'Well, show us yer caps then.' In other words, how many times have you played for Scotland? When we first came down to the Midlands together, my cap count was zero. I told him many times that he was going to find it a lot harder adding to his cap collection now he was at Coventry rather than scoring with ease for Rangers, and I was proved to be right. I was happy at Coventry, liked the club and the people I worked with. I knew, however, that my chances of winning things and of playing in another World Cup would be greatly increased by playing for one of the glamour sides. I didn't know at the time, but one of the historic giants of the English game were watching me and were preparing a bid for my services.

Chapter 22

Money, Money, Money
(or the Lack of It!)

LACK OF money was an ongoing problem at Coventry and it produced a downward spiral effect. Limited cash meant that good players were sold. Supporters seeing this became disillusioned, and some stopped coming to games. Decreasing numbers at the turnstile meant that even less money came into the club. It did have an effect on me, and I am sure on others too. I wanted to play for a club capable of challenging for trophies.

During these years, the aim of the club and the remit given to Gordon Milne was to try to balance the financial books while keeping the team as competitive as possible. It was a difficult task. He was now installed as general manager, looking after both club and team affairs, as Joe Mercer had accepted a directorship and joined the board. Over the next two seasons we lost Brian Alderson to Leicester and Dennis Mortimer to Villa for fairly meagre fees. Mortimer was a great player who was going to be sorely missed. The fans knew it and so did his former team-mates. Milne was being asked to work miracles in keeping us afloat.

Even though he was a senior professional when I knew Gordon at Blackpool, he was never standoffish with us younger lads as some of the older pros could be. We had a players' social most Monday evenings during my Bloomfield Road days and Gordon would always come from his home in Preston and mix with everyone. He was an even-tempered man. During our nine years together at Coventry, I can't remember him ever losing his temper or becoming flustered. This says a lot about him considering the pressure he was under many times during those years. I can remember occasions when Highfield Road would echo with the chant of 'Milne Out, Milne Out' from fans dissatisfied from what they were seeing on the pitch. Credit to Jimmy Hill and the board, where Joe Mercer would have been a staunch ally of Gordon's, for resisting fan pressure.

Credit too goes to Gordon himself. Despite the pressures exerted on him by the board and by the fans on a Saturday, he stuck to his footballing principles and tried to produce teams that played open, attacking football. Being a forward-thinking and creative player, this was something that I very much appreciated. His even temperament was perhaps a double-edged sword as he disliked confrontation. There were times I felt that the odd player needed to be told in no uncertain terms to up their game and to sort themselves out. Gordon would raise these issues with the players concerned but they were never given the good old-fashioned bollocking that on occasions were needed. The manager I most enjoyed working for, John Bond, would certainly do it, as would Bob Stokoe. Some players needed it before they would conform and do their best for the team.

I knew that Gordon rated me as a player. He had signed me after seeing me play at Blackpool. He consistently picked me in the team, never leaving me out until my final season at the club. He would often say nice things about me in the press and has since said that I was the best signing ever made by Coventry City. However, in all those nine years together, he never called me into the office and said 'well done', which is something I would really have appreciated. I genuinely think that such was the precarious financial situation at the club, he thought that if he praised me then I might come back to him asking for a pay rise.

My nine years at Coventry was a stable period for me and Irene and our children, who now numbered three: David, a real 'Cov kid', arrived at Walsgrave Hospital in February 1976. But I never made the sort of money that would give us any sort of security once my football career was over. When I got back from the World Cup, I was on £90 a week. I knew from chatting to the other Scotland boys that most of them were on considerably more. Gordon did offer me a rise of £15 a week which I was never going to accept. I knew I was worth more. Yes, I was on more than the average wage, but if my career had ended then in the mid-70s, I was looking at a very uncertain future, being unqualified in anything but professional football, since I hadn't finished my painting and decorating apprenticeship. In the end, I was given a rise of £50 a week, which I was happy with. Putting the issue of money aside, I would have liked that bit of confirmation that I was doing alright for him.

Just mentioning David there, a lot of new fathers are walking on air for a few days after the birth of their child. I was actually sent up into the air the day after he was born. My old adversary from my first reserve game at Blackpool, John Craggs, launched me skywards after I had pushed the ball past him at Middlesbrough. Unfortunately for me, his method of propulsion resulted in me being stretchered off the pitch with a match-ending dead leg. His challenge, which had happened right in front of the dugouts, must have been particularly robust. Jack Charlton, the Middlesbrough manager and no shrinking violet himself when it came to a tough tackle, apologised to me, said the tackle was out of order and gave Craggs, his own player, a right old bollocking.

David was the only one of my children that I came close to seeing be born. On the Monday he arrived, I took Irene into the hospital and sat by her bed. The midwife asked me at one point to step outside, I don't know why, and when I was called back in two minutes later, there was David in Irene's arms. So in reality I missed all three of my children's births. I stayed with Irene and David for a while but I was addicted to football and to training, so I decided to go over to Ryton and do a couple of hours on my own. When I got there, I went to tell Joyce the cook about our big event. 'Irene had a boy, Joyce,' I told her proudly. She scowled at me and proceeded to give me a good telling-off, asking me what in the world I was doing at Ryton when my wife had just had a baby. Joyce often told me off, as you will see!

Ron Wylie had replaced Tommy Casey as coach and I really liked working with him. He had my sort of attitude to the way things should be. Despite the club's financial difficulties, everything had to be done in the proper way. I remember the first day he took training. He emptied the practice balls out of their sack. Even after years in England, he still had a broad Glaswegian accent and he said, 'Whit ur these?' The balls were in a ragtag state, some peeling, some misshapen.

He left the field and was straight on the phone to secretary Eddie Plumley. He told me later that Eddie had asked what the problem was, as the balls were only to be used in training. Ron had asked Eddie what type of ball was used in games. When the reply came back that a new ball would always be used, Ron replied, 'Well, that's the type o' ball we need in training too.' The next day we had a set of new balls and they were replenished regularly during the season.

One of the reasons that we survived and on occasions thrived in the old First Division was down to the detail that Ron and Gordon insisted upon. Equipment, kit, travel and accommodation all had to be spot on. When Ron took training, as he did on most days, there was an attention to detail that meant we all knew exactly what our jobs were and exactly what was expected of us in games. Ron was much more likely to call a player out if he felt he wasn't doing what was asked of him.

He was also the first coach that I worked with who made use of the new-fangled video technology. When full-back Bobby McDonald joined the club later on, he hated the sessions where video was played back as it would inevitably show him out of position and make him the target of Ron's team talk and of his team-mates' humour. Together, Gordon and Ron made a good team.

I hadn't had too much to do with Jimmy Hill since he had returned to the club, as managing director. However, I did have a conversation with him about his supposed involvement in the failure of a possible transfer taking me to Arsenal. Rumours had started to circulate that they were looking to come in for me. Most of the time I never paid any attention to what was written in the papers. I had learned from experience that a lot of what you found there was made up and half-truths at best. With the club's constant need to generate funds, however, it wouldn't have surprised me if they decided to cash in on me. Perhaps the main reason why this hadn't happened was because of the likely reaction of our fans. There had been a huge furore when Dennis Mortimer had been sold to Villa, and the same thing would happen if I left the club.

A story appeared in the *Daily Mirror* stating that Arsenal were preparing to make a bid for me. What I really found annoying was a quote from Jimmy stating that he didn't think I would suit Arsenal as I was a 'luxury' player. I think that he was inferring that I was a showy footballer with no end product, something that I would have disputed greatly. I was angry with him. Firstly, because a statement like this from such a senior and respected figure as Hill could have made Arsenal think again about signing me. Secondly, I would have expected much more support from someone within my club. If he had a problem with my performance, he should have raised it directly with me or used Gordon as an intermediary.

I had my chance to bring this up with him when I was in the reception at Highfield Road before a game. Jimmy came in and I asked if I could have a word with him. He denied making any such comment about me and said that, as he had been in Spain and out of contact with anyone for the previous two weeks, the comments attributed to him were obviously false. I left it there with Jimmy. However, I knew the boy at the *Mirror* who wrote the story. When I spoke to him, he confirmed that Arsenal's interest in me was serious and that the quote had indeed come from Jimmy Hill. He said he had spoken to him before his trip to Spain. As far as I am aware, there was no bid from Arsenal (although Coventry wouldn't necessarily have told me if there was) so that was the end of the matter.

The transfer dealings of this period couldn't all be one-way traffic. We needed bodies in the door and indeed we did sign some useful if slightly cut-price players. I was delighted when another Scottish international, Celtic's Jim Brogan, arrived on a free. Brogey was a funny boy, full of life and laughter. He caused a stir at Ryton when he arrived for training on his first day in a Rolls-Royce which contained a telephone, very cutting edge for those days. He had made his money from the motor trade, not from football, but he didn't like us talking about how wealthy he was.

He also had a strong dislike for Celtic's legendary captain Billy McNeill, known at that club as Big Caesar. The policy at Celtic was that if the players wanted a rise, it would be discussed with Billy first who would then take the request to the manager, Jock Stein. Jim's bad feelings for Billy McNeill came from one particular occasion when McNeill had taken the players' appeal to Stein, but after a few weeks nothing had happened. Enquiries led to the discovery that although the rest of the team had got nothing, Billy McNeill had earned a huge rise for himself! Oh, Brogey was bitter about that!

Brogan was always up to tricks and pranks. He got on well with Joyce, the cook in the players' canteen at Ryton, and he would play her up quite often. Joyce could give it back when she needed to and she and some of the lads started to suggest that, due to his receding hairline, Brogey might think of investing in a wig. 'Don't be startin' any o' that malarkey, son,' he would say to whichever team-mate was suggesting follicle replacement. One day he came in and he says, 'Ah've got a cracker fur Joyce.' After training, he dressed himself up as a Bay City Roller, complete in white shirt with a 70s collar, tartan three-quarter-length trousers and a tartan scarf tied to each wrist, the ensemble being topped off with a black wig.

One of the lads introduced him, 'Hey, Joyce, there's someone here to see you.' He comes in and dances up to the canteen counter, giving it all the Rollers' stage moves and singing 'Shang-a-Lang', with the kitchen staff and players all having a good laugh.

To Brogey's dismay, after his performance, he couldn't find his clothes. John Craven had missed Brogey's routine because he had gone to the dressing room, picked up Brogey's normal clothes and hidden them in the boiler-room cupboard. Mysteriously, all spare kit, tracksuits and the like had also disappeared. Brogey had no choice but to go home in his Roller dressed as a Roller. The best bit wasn't Brogey driving to his Leamington home impersonating Stuart 'Woody' Wood, having to stop at traffic lights beside other cars. It was when he told us the next day that his Rolls was almost out of petrol and he'd had to stop at a garage to fill it up. I don't think there was any Shang-a-Langing going on at the petrol pump!

Talking of Joyce, she was one of a number of people working for Coventry City who made it such a happy club. I would often pop into the boot room for a chat with Bill Trew, an elderly Scot and an avid user of snuff whose jacket would be sprinkled with powdery tobacco. Speaking in broad dialect, most of our conversations were incomprehensible to any non-Scot present. Then there was Jimmy Herbert, the kit man. Like all the kit men I have known, he would guard the club's equipment as if it was his own. I would go and see him, holding up my holey socks and say, 'Herby, any chance of a new pair o' socks?' He'd scowl, examine the socks and then hand them back saying, 'Plenty more life in those yet, son.' In fairness, he knew that if I went out training in a new pair of socks, he would be inundated with players coming to ask for the same.

Joyce herself was a character who loved dogs and who bred miniature poodles. On one occasion, she showed me pictures of a new litter she had just bred. We have always loved dogs so I asked her if I could buy one of them. She went on to give me an interview to make sure we were a fit and proper family, capable of looking after one of her dogs. More or less satisfied, she agreed that she would bring the pup we had chosen into Ryton on Friday and that I could take it home after training, I went training that Friday morning leaving behind three children beside themselves with excitement.

After training, Joyce brought our cute new family member out to my car and then looked on in horror at what was in my boot. I had got a cardboard crisp box from the local shop, cut a hole in it for a door, spread an old towel out in there for the pup to lie on and written the word 'Rover' over the door. 'My dog is not going home in that!' she insisted. My joke had backfired and she marched off with her pup, ignoring my pleas about disappointed children. On Monday, she arrived at Ryton with the pup and a brand-new luxury dog bed. Even then I couldn't take charge of our new pet until I had promised Joyce, on my life, that we would not call him Rover!

I may not have been signing for Arsenal, but later in the season I did nearly join Norwich City. I had no agent then or at any time in my career, but I was accompanied to Carrow Road by Coventry's chief scout Bob Dennison. He advised me to make sure that Norwich were going to look after me, which I took to mean make sure that they were going to pay me a decent amount. I met John Bond and his assistant Ken Brown in his office, but there were no negotiations. They simply asked me what I wanted. Well, I had a figure of £12,500 over the two years of my contract in my mind, so that is what I asked for. It didn't seem excessive.

Nothing was finalised and, when I got back to Coventry, Gordon Milne told me that the deal was off, that I had been asking for too much money. I did feel a little let down by Gordon. He was far more knowledgeable than me when it came to wages and I thought that he may have given me a bit of advice on what to ask for. The whole transfer saga left me baffled. They had never said anything like, 'Don't be daft, Tommy, that's far too much, here's what we can pay you.' As I say, no negotiations took place.

My confusion then turned to anger later that week when I read a newspaper report in which John Bond was quoted as saying, 'He has made excessive financial demands for his services. From what I hear about him he is not the sort of person I want in my football club.' I just could not understand this at all. He had rated me enough to put in a bid for me, there had been no falling-out when we met, I just didn't know what had happened to change his mind.

It was the slur on my character that really stung. I had been at Coventry for four years. I had missed only one game in all that time, been picked for my country and had been voted the Coventry player of the year for three of those four years. Why had he come to these conclusions? There was someone at Norwich who knew me slightly and whose opinions John Bond may have listened to. On one of the Scotland trips, I had roomed with centre-forward Ted MacDougall, who by this stage was at Norwich. We didn't get on very well. As far as I was concerned, he was surly and unfriendly.

Most players that I roomed with were pretty easy-going. Not so with Ted. I had the TV on in the evening when he came into the room and got straight into his bed, even though it was early. With most players, you'd have a bit of a chat, maybe watch the telly together for a while. Not Ted. He'd been there a few minutes when he turned over and says, 'Are you going tae switch that racket off?' Ted was either a model professional or a grumpy old sod! Needless to say, we weren't best buddies. The only thing I can think of that turned John Bond against me would have been listening to a character reference from MacDougall.

Jim Brogan knew I was a genuine lad and when he heard that the deal was off, he told me that he was going to write to John Bond and put him straight on the sort of person I was. While grateful, I told him not to bother as I felt it wouldn't change anything. The move to Norwich would have given a boost to the Hutchison household finances, but I was still perfectly happy at Coventry and so life continued.

Despite the club's precarious financial situation, we managed to stay out of serious relegation trouble throughout the mid-70s, often flirting on the edge of the relegation zone but always having just enough to get out of difficulty. It wasn't great for the fans as we were losing plenty of games and only treading water, never really threatening to mount anything like a challenge for trophies. It is ironic, therefore, that in season 1976/77, when the club was finally able to find some money to bring in new players, circumstances conspired to push us to the very brink. With only one game left, we were in the bottom three and staring relegation in the face.

The final game of the season, a game against Bristol City who were also in grave danger of going down, was one that I made a significant contribution to. The happenings on and off the pitch were controversial at the time and are still debated and argued over even today, several decades after the event.

Chapter 23

Survival

EACH SUMMER we went back home to Fife, I could see the deterioration in my dad's condition. I helped Mum and Dad out financially, but he still needed to work to get by. If it could be proven that he wasn't fit to work due to the coal dust on his lungs, then he would be given monetary help. I was able to accompany my dad when he went before a medical panel set up by the Coal Board to see if he qualified for compensation and an enhanced pension due to his breathing difficulties, caused by the years of working in air full of coal dust.

As we walked along the Edinburgh streets, we had to stop every few steps so he could catch his breath. The consulting rooms were on the first floor of the medical centre and going up the stairs took real effort from my dad, stopping on every other step to gasp for air. I waited while he was looked at by the doctor and sat beside him for the verdict on his examination.

Considering the difficulty he now had in doing simple everyday things, activities that shouldn't have been a problem to a man only in his 50s, I was angered and astounded by what the doctor said. 'Ah'm sorry, Mr Hutchison, but your condition is no' severe enough for you to qualify.' I couldn't believe what I was hearing and said, 'He cannae put more than a few steps together before he's standin' there gasping. How bad does he have tae be?' He turned to me and replied, 'A'hm sorry, Mr Hutchison, but Ah can only allow so many through each year. M'ah hands are tied.' So, in reality, the compensation scheme was based on quotas, not the severity of health.

Years after both my mum and dad had gone, my dad, along with thousands of other miners like him, was awarded several thousand pounds in compensation due to a scheme brought in by the Labour government. As neither of my parents were alive, the money came to the family and was split between myself and my sisters. It made me sad to think of the difference that the money could have made to the lives of my dad and my mum had it been awarded, as it should have, during their lifetimes. It would not have given Dad his health back, but it would certainly have made life easier in his final years.

Season 1976/77 started in depressing fashion with defeats to Middlesbrough and Man United in the opening two games. It was a really bad start for me on a personal level too as I was injured in pre-season training and missed the first seven games. However, for the team at least, reinforcements were on the way with the signings of John Beck, Bobby McDonald, Ian Wallace and particularly Terry Yorath, a member of the great Leeds side of the 60s and 70s. They brought about an immediate upturn in performance and results.

Terry assumed the role of captain and it was a role he fulfilled perfectly. He was a link between management and players, he was a mentor to team-mates young and old, and he was often out and about in the community being the public face of the club. What I thought was an outstanding quality of his captaincy was his willingness to lead the team, even on days when he himself was playing poorly (though this didn't happen often and I think Yorath was a very underrated player). He would organise the team superbly on the pitch and would not stop encouraging, cajoling, bollocking when necessary and instructing throughout the 90 minutes. Ironic that he came from a club where Billy Bremner was his captain. Terry was by far and away the better captain of the two. He was easily the best captain I ever had.

I did wonder if my proposed transfer to Norwich at the end of the previous season had been set up to fund the purchase of these four lads. Despite my deal falling through, the sale of David Cross to West Brom presumably paid for their arrival and their purchase had not left the club with a financial hole. But with no signing-on fee or wage increase, I personally wasn't getting richer. When an opportunity came to make a bit of money on the side, I was keen to take it. I was useless at getting to sleep in the afternoon before a night game. We were under instruction from the club to go home and go to bed, but I never could sleep, my mind was too active. After training on a Tuesday or a Wednesday afternoon, I would go up to the John Reay golf range at Keresley in Coventry and hit a bucket of balls. Through my visits there I got to know John himself.

Every month or so he would head down to Northampton to buy Dunlop golf shoes for his shop and he asked me if I would like to go. We would visit a number of shoemakers, including the Tricker shoe factory. For some reason I have always liked shoes and I could see that those produced by Trickers were of a very good quality. I started to buy a few pairs and would sell them at the training ground. I was making about £2 a pair but the boys buying them were getting them cheaper than shop prices so everyone was happy. It got so popular that I started taking orders and Friday at Ryton, after training, became shoe day!

John would also go to the British Open every year and I would often go with him. He had a huge Mercedes, no power steering in those days, that was built like something from the Panzer Division. It was ideal for carrying the golfing gear he bought at events like these. He would go around the tented village, chat with manufacturers and retailers and come away with a load of stuff for his shop. I was with him one year at St Andrews and I had bought a nice golf sweater, decorated in sky blue diamonds, ideal for a Coventry player. Jack Nicklaus had worn the same type of jumper at one of his open victories and they were very popular.

I was at a stand, looking at beautiful and very expensive carved wooden maps of famous golf courses, and had taken down the one of St Andrews to buy. A Canadian man came over to me and asked where I'd got the jumper as he wanted one as a present for his son. I told him the stand where I bought it, but he told me that he had tried there and that they were sold out. John Reay comes over to us and says, 'Tommy, take off the jumper and give it to the man; these are Lyle & Scott, I stock those and I can get you one.' So, I gave my jumper away to a grateful guy.

About five years later, when I was playing on loan in America, I had travelled across the Canadian border with Seattle to play against Vancouver Whitecaps. When we arrived, the receptionist stopped our manager, Alan Hinton, and told him that there was a package there for Tommy Hutchison. When I opened it up, inside was a note saying 'Thanks for the jumper' alongside another of the carved wooden maps, this time of Winged Foot, a lovely golf course near New York. I never met the Canadian again but he obviously never forgot my good turn for him.

One of the privileges of being a footballer was the number of places that we got to travel to. Despite the money problems that the club suffered, we still went on tour and played games in exotic places. We once had a fabulous trip to Japan, travelling on the bullet train and appearing in a Japanese TV advert for Tiger boots. We also had several trips to Saudi Arabia. I assume these were paid for by the Saudis themselves and would have been part of a contract that Jimmy Hill had negotiated with the Saudi FA where he would provide coaches to work with local players with the objective of bringing up the overall standard of Saudi football.

I remember one trip there where our flight was delayed. When we arrived, we were taken to a palace where one of the royal family presented each member of our party with a gold watch as an apology for our late arrival. That certainly doesn't happen with Ryanair! Trips to Saudi were ideal from the club's point of view as there was a complete absence of alcohol. When we saw how the Saudis dealt with anything that they deemed as criminal behaviour, it was unlikely that any of us players would have stepped out of line.

We had a guide assigned to us and one day he took us to a local gold market. We were told that any item we bought there would be of good value. The goods on sale may have been expensive, but the market itself was in a really shabby part of town and the stalls themselves, though loaded with gold items for sale, were rough wooden and tin structures. A guy came walking through the crowded street carrying a stack of boxes. Our guide told us that the boxes were full of money from the stalls. One of our players suggested he was taking his life in his hands, walking around with a stash like that in what appeared to be a dodgy area. Our guide assured us that he was perfectly safe. The next place he took us to showed us why. We arrived in a square and he told us that, once a month, executions by beheading were held there in public. An offence such as stealing an item of gold or money would result in the perpetrator having their hand chopped off in the square. It was a chilling place to be. I think most of us were glad to get back to the hotel.

An event looked forward to by everyone at Coventry was the annual Soccer Ball, a swanky affair put on by the football club. Each Soccer Ball had a theme to it. This particular year, presumably due to our Saudi trips, a mural had been painted along the back wall of the ballroom at the Leofric Hotel that featured caricatures of all of the players riding camels. On the lead camel at the front they had Jimmy Hill and Gordon Milne. After training on the day of the ball, players went for a drink before arriving at the Leofric suitably dressed in suits and bow ties. Meanwhile, wives and girlfriends would be out having their hair done and generally being pampered.

Local and national celebrities and sporting stars would be invited along. On this particular occasion, the music for the evening was provided by Kenny Ball and his Jazzmen and among the guests were husband and wife actors John Alderton and Pauline Collins. While Irene had a dance with John, I was dancing with Pauline. Whenever *Shirley Valentine* is shown on TV, I still have to remind Irene or anyone else there that she was once my dance partner! Also present that year, among ex-managers and ex-players, was John Bond with his wife Jan. I couldn't help giving him daggers!

There were various fundraising activities at the Ball. Some of the monies raised went into the pot of any player whose testimonial year it was, some of it would go to various local charities. There was always a tombola draw with some really good prizes and that year I won a ball autographed by all of the Arsenal players from a previous FA Cup Final. As the evening wore on, several times I said to Irene that I was going to go over to Bond and have a word with him. Each time, she said 'No'. I'd had too much to drink and I'd make a show of myself.

At one o'clock we got the call that the taxi to take us home was outside. As we were leaving, I managed to step away from Irene and I headed for Bond. Playing for Norwich at that time was John Bond's son, Kevin, who was a full-back and who I had played against many times. As John turned and saw me coming, I tossed the ball to him and said, 'Here, give that to wee Kevin, cos when he plays against me, he never gets a kick.' And I turned on my heel, never looked back and walked out. I would find out later what he thought of my stunt!

The signings had a dramatic effect on performances and results. We reached tenth in the table by December and even in early February we were in a comfortable 12th place. Then, in typical Coventry fashion, the wheels came right off the Sky Blue Express. Ian Wallace, who had been a revelation as the season progressed, was in a serious car crash which resulted in facial injuries and damage to his eyes, which at one point threatened his sight.

Mick Ferguson had replaced David Cross very effectively and proved to be the perfect goalscoring partner for Wallace, but he was also out injured for several weeks. Fergie was well over six feet tall but by some freak of nature only had size seven feet. We used to say he had Capodimonte ankles because at the slightest knock, like the China figures, they would crack. Jim Blyth, who had taken over from the injured Bryan King in goal and made the position his own, was himself injured at Easter, leaving 17-year-old Les Sealey in goal for the remaining games. Even the weather and the FA Cup conspired against us in the new year. Postponements of league games meant that from the end of December to early April we had no home games, playing ten consecutive games away.

All of this meant that, as we headed for the final games of the season, we were likely to be involved in a fight to stay up. It was my only real relegation battle in my nine years at Coventry. The club built up a reputation over its 34-year top-flight stay for always surviving on the last day of the season. This wasn't the case in my time at the club, and after experiencing what happened at the end of this season, just the one battle was enough for me.

I was delighted in March when my Scottish international team-mate Jim Holton joined us after an unhappy spell at Sunderland. This meant the end of the road at Coventry, and seemingly the end of his First Division career, for Larry Lloyd. His transfer from Liverpool had never really worked out for him. I liked him and got on well with him, but boy did he have a temper. He joined Brian Clough at Second Division Nottingham Forest. None of us would have guessed the heights that Larry and Forest would hit over the next few years. As for Holton, I was quite surprised at how timid he was in training. If you went near him with any sort of challenge, he would put his hands in the air and say, 'Steady on, steady on.' In a game situation he was completely different and he would have tackled a rhino if he thought he could win the ball. He was totally fearless.

We arrived at the last game of the season knowing that to be certain of being safe we had to win. Stoke and Spurs were already relegated and the final spot would go to Bristol City, our opponents at Highfield Road, or Sunderland, who were at Everton, or ourselves. A defeat for us or Bristol meant that team was down. A win or a draw for Sunderland ensured their safety and they would still be safe even if they lost if Bristol or ourselves got beaten. Jimmy Hill decided to try and show us what our First Division status meant to the people of the city. He arranged for us to visit the huge Chrysler car plant at Ryton, round the corner from the training ground.

After our slump in form in the second half of the season, some of the factory boys weren't slow in letting us know their feelings. However, the overwhelming majority of the workers were supportive and urging us on to make sure we won the game. It was obvious to us how much they cared and how much Coventry City meant to them. We had lunch in the directors' dining room and a couple of them spoke to us saying how much our performances affected factory life. When we won, the guys had a spring in their step and production went through the roof. They too were keen for us to know how much preserving our top-flight status meant to them.

Gordon Milne told us later that one of the directors offered to pay the squad a bonus of £4,000 if we stayed up. He turned them down saying that we didn't need money as a motivating factor. We were in fact already on a club bonus of £11 a man! Bristol had brought in Norman Hunter from Leeds during the season and he had spoken to Terry Yorath in the week and told them that each Bristol lad was on £1,500 a man to stay up, an enormous amount in the 70s. While the money would have been nice, I think that Gordon was right, money wouldn't have motivated us to run more or to tackle harder. For me, and I think for all our team, personal pride and the well-being of team-mates and club is what we were playing for.

Highfield Road was packed on that Thursday night with thousands of Bristolians present. Because so many had travelled from the West Country, huge crowds developed at the Kop End of the ground trying to get in. The referee, on police advice, delayed the kick-off by five minutes. When the match started, we were marginally the better team in the first half and we took the lead when I turned the ball home after the keeper dropped a cross. I got my second goal of the game early in the second half. We seemed to be on course for safety and Bristol on course for relegation. However, just a minute later, Gerry Gow pulled a goal back and all of a sudden we were up against it. There were waves of Bristol attacks. They equalised 11 minutes from the end. We were dead on our feet and it was us staring the Second Division in the face.

Bristol were well on top and looking the likely winners when, with a few minutes left, word filtered onto the pitch that Sunderland had lost. If our game ended in a draw, both clubs would be safe. Bristol had the ball and proceeded to play sideways and backwards with no challenge from us. The score from Goodison was flashed up on the screen, to enormous cheers from both sets of fans, we found out later on the instruction of Jimmy Hill. When the referee blew the whistle on what had become a non-game, both sets of players celebrated together. The relief was enormous.

Sunderland, understandably, protested about what had gone on. A winner from either side in the final few minutes would have seen them safe. They were relegated by a result that came from a game lasting 85 not 90 minutes. A hearing later exonerated Coventry from any wrongdoing. While it is true that Jimmy Hill had the Sunderland result displayed on the scoreboard, it had no effect on the game as by that stage both sets of players had downed tools. To my mind, the Bristol players were as much at fault as we were. I believe that some Sunderland supporters still have a downer on Coventry after that night some 50 years ago. This does seem a bit one-sided because it seems to me that both clubs called a truce.

Whatever the rights and wrongs of that occasion, we were safe and would be playing top-flight football once again. I felt that our being at the foot of the table was false and that we were a much better team than our position suggested. My optimism wasn't misplaced, and we were about to embark on one of the most exciting seasons in the club's history. Unfortunately, from a personal point of view, it was to be the saddest of seasons too.

Chapter 24

On Our Way to Europe?

WE WENT on our annual pilgrimage to Fife that summer to see our families. It was obvious that things were becoming more and more of a struggle for my dad. We would descend on the house in Dundonald Park with our three children and sleeping arrangements often required a degree of working out, considering Mum, Dad and my two uncles were in permanent residence. On this occasion I found myself sharing a bed with my dad for a few days. If we were sitting downstairs, perhaps watching the telly, my dad would sit in his chair and often quietly whistle to himself, trying to disguise the way he was gasping for breath.

When he was asleep in the bed beside me, I could see the full extent of his difficulty in pulling oxygen into his body. His breathing was laboured and harsh, his damaged lungs having to work overtime even though he was lying down. For a while I tried to match his pattern of breathing. I found it difficult to do and after a while I was forced to stop as it was making me feel dizzy and short of breath myself. By now he would have an oxygen cylinder and mask by his chair or by his bed and he would put it on if he was particularly short of breath.

One thing that did brighten his life for a bit that summer was the purchase of a little red second-hand Renault. Any time I saw him I would always give him a few quid. Anything left over from this bit of cash after he had made sure that Mum and him were getting by, he would save. And it was these good few years of saving a few quid here and there that meant he could replace the Reliant Robin. It was with sadness and worry that we returned home south of the border that summer. Chances to return to Fife and to see our families were limited due to the nature of a footballer's life. For me, being immersed in training and playing and being around my team-mates took my mind off the situation back in Scotland for a while.

By this time my parents in Fife had a phone in the house. At least we could stay in touch more easily, even if I couldn't get back too often to see them, and I knew that my dad's health was continuing to go downhill. Despite this, it was still a huge shock when my mum phoned me one late August day to say that my dad had died. He had been bed-bound for a few days, something that was a fairly common occurrence for my dad. This time, however, he wouldn't be getting up again. He was 59.

My mum told me that the night before he died he asked her for a glass of brandy. This was something unusual as my dad wasn't a drinker at all. The doctor said, 'Just give it tae him, Liz, get him anything he wants.' My mum knew then he hadn't long left. After his death the doctor told my mum that he was putting 'silicosis due to dust on the lungs' down on the death certificate. He said that if my mum were to request a post-mortem it would be proven and that the Coal Board would have to pay compensation. My mum said no to this, 'He's been through enough, he'll no be going through anymore.'

For me, his death was a real blow, even though I knew that it was coming. He was someone that I had looked up to, respected and loved all of my life and who now was gone. I know Bill Shankly was tongue in cheek when he made his 'matter of life and death' quote about football. At this point, I couldn't have cared less about results, league positions or any of the rest of it. I was hurting, but I knew the one place that the pain would stop for a bit was on the pitch.

The day after I found out about my dad, I was due to play for Coventry in a league match at Old Trafford. I went to see Gordon to say that I wanted to play against Manchester United. That is what I did. For 90 minutes I was able to ease the pain doing something that I loved and which my dad, through all his help, support and advice, had helped me to achieve. My performance that day was very much dedicated to him. After the game, I travelled straight from Manchester to Dundonald to be with my mum and the rest of my family, to remember my dad and to be at his funeral.

We started the 1977/78 season with a radical, some would say reckless, formation. This did result in one or two heavy defeats, but also in some storming victories playing a brand of exhilarating football that was a joy to be a part of. Milne and Wylie set us up in a formation that on paper looked like a 4-4-2. In practice we often played with only the centre-halves as defenders.

Me and right-winger Ray Graydon were told to stay up alongside our striking pair of Ferguson and Wallace, pinning opposition full-backs deep in their own half. Our midfield two of Yorath and Barry Powell were expected to work like Trojans and run their legs off each game, something they willingly did. Full-backs Bobby McDonald and Graham Oakey were skilful attacking players in their own right and would do as much attacking as defending. Our two central defenders, Jim Holton and Mick Coop, were often left on their own when we attacked, as our forwards, midfielders and full-backs swarmed around our opponent's penalty box. Jim Blyth in goal was sometimes left exposed but he had an exceptional season, eventually attracting a world-record bid from Manchester United for his services, a deal which would have gone through had he not failed the medical due to a back problem.

Our fans loved it, attendances at Highfield Road rocketed and the atmosphere was electric as those watching were almost guaranteed to see a thrilling game of attacking football. Star-studded league leaders Manchester City, unbeaten in eight, were crushed 4-2 on a fantastic evening in October. Over the course of the season we inflicted big defeats on QPR, Man United, Chelsea, Birmingham and Wolves. From a personal point of view, I was delighted that we did the double over John Bond's Norwich. The game at Highfield Road at Christmas time was a rip-roaring, rollicking, stonker of a game. We won it 5-4 with Jim Blyth saving a last-minute Norwich penalty that would have made it 5-5.

This game was typical of the excitement our style of football generated. Ferguson and Wallace were an excellent striking combination and scored 47 goals between them that season. It was a typical big man–small man partnership in the Toshack and Keegan mould with their friendship off the pitch complementing the relationship they had on it. Many teams that season just couldn't cope with them. Fergie was tremendous in the air, but for a big man with size seven feet was surprisingly good on the floor too. Wally was a feisty character whose red hair perfectly matched his fiery temper. He was a sharp, skilful forward who was deadly in front of goal.

Another reason for our success was the quality of our two midfielders, Terry Yorath and Barry Powell. Terry was a hugely influential character

A group of miners from the Dundonald colliery. My dad isn't there but the picture reminds me of him and how he would look returning to the raws after a shift.

Mum, dad, Lisabeth and me one Christmas in the raws. The tree was liberated from the Den Woods.

My older sister Lisabeth and me. I would be about six and looking dapper in my bow tie.

Boys from the raws. The very neat haircuts here tell me that this picture was planned. The reason I am front and centre is because it was my ball, nothing to do with ability!

Mum and Dad with the fairly recently arrived Ann. Taken about 1960 in the back garden of our house in Dundonald Park.

Ann and I in the back garden at Dundonald Park. The deckchair shows that the sun does shine sometimes in Scotland! I was trying and failing to get our dog Shandy to look at the camera.

Alloa team picture. I am front row second from the right.

The second of two telegrams that arrived at our house in the space of a few days. The first was from the Alloa secretary, this one was from Stan Mortensen prior to my joining Blackpool.

The best match of my life! Irene and I outside the registry office in Kirkcaldy in 1968

My first taste of Lancashire hotpot served to Irene and me by Kitty, the landlady of my first, 'posh' digs across the street from Bloomfield Road.

Here we are at Irene's brother Joe's wedding along with my mum Liz in 1979.

Promotion for Blackpool sealed at Deepdale. Jimmy Armfield is on my right and the hider of prams, Henry Mowbray on my left. A sign of the times is provided by the smoking Fred Pickering.

I loved running at my opposing full-back. I seem to be getting the better of Dennis Clarke here but he had the last laugh as Huddersfield beat us in one of my first top flight games, 1970.

Chelsea v Coventry 1973. I tried to anticipate when the defender would hit me and jump as the damage to my legs was lessened than if my studs were in the turf.

in the way we played. Yes, he deserved his hard-man reputation as he was not adverse to leaving his foot in a tackle, but he could also play and was far better than many people gave him credit for.

His nickname while he was at Leeds, 'Plank', doesn't do justice to the excellent passer of the ball and reader of the game that he was. His ability to play anywhere meant that Don Revie used him in a variety of positions. Although often deployed in a defensive role, he could always do a job in attack too. If Eddie Gray, Leeds' excellent but injury-prone winger, was out, he might fill in there and provide an outlet for Bremner and Giles to find when they came under pressure. He was expected to take the ball but play it back to them as soon as possible, sometimes with one touch, hence he was 'Plank'.

To be a part of that great Leeds team of the 60s and 70s says more about him as a player than the nickname does. It was a pleasure playing with him in five-a-side games. He simply controlled things with his touch and ability to dictate play. On the field, he was such a great organiser and motivator, it was like playing with the manager in your side. And then there were his shuddering tackles. I became a footballing vulture, feeding off his tackles. When Terry went in to win the ball, even when not the favourite to do so, I knew that something would come loose – sometimes the opponent's leg considering the force he used in the challenge, but often the ball. I learned to hover in the vicinity of these confrontations knowing that the odds were stacked in my favour of picking up the loose ball and then being able to set us on the attack.

For most of the season we were in the top four and, although we never really threatened a challenge for the title, a place in European competition for next season seemed to be in our grasp. I don't know whether it was a lack of self-belief or fatigue due to our style, which required non-stop running in games, but one win in six games meant we arrived at the final home game, against Nottingham Forest, finding ourselves seventh in the table and outside of the European places.

Forest, under Brian Clough, may have only just been promoted, but they arrived at Highfield Road only needing a point to be the new First Division champions. We were on top for most of the match and looked to have won when, late in the game, Mick Ferguson planted a header into the far right-hand corner of the goal. Peter Shilton was the Forest keeper and, with a save reminiscent of Banks from Pelé in Mexico, dived and somehow managed to claw the ball off the line.

Shilton was the best keeper I ever shared a pitch with, better than Banks in my opinion. He had everything you look for in a goalkeeper and had the essential ingredient of consistency. He made very few mistakes. He was a constant talker too, always on to his defenders, cajoling and organising, meaning the amount of saves he had to make was fewer as his defence was so well set up. With that save he ensured Forest earned their title-winning point and denied us the chance to move back into the top six.

Our European dreams were still alive, just. If Arsenal, the favourites, beat Ipswich in the upcoming FA Cup Final, we would still be on course for football nights in Rome, Madrid or Munich. Unfortunately for us, due to Roger Osborne's solitary goal, the Cup ended up in Suffolk, not North London, and we ended up staying at home. We were bitterly disappointed at missing out on our European dream. What had been a brilliant season in terms of the football we played hadn't ended with the reward we felt our exciting style deserved, while still acknowledging that those last few games that cost us dear were down to ourselves.

Any regrets that our goalkeeper Jim Blyth felt were tempered by the knowledge that he would be travelling to Argentina as part of Ally MacLeod's World Cup squad. Blyth had a quality I felt that all good goalkeepers such as himself, Glazier and Corrigan had – the ability to forget a mistake and not let it play on their mind and affect their performance in the rest of the game. He deserved his World Cup call-up. Ian Wallace, however, faced double disappointment as he just failed to make the cut for the Scottish squad.

It was over three years since I had been picked for Scotland, but even at the age of 30 I felt I was playing well enough to get my place back. The season we had just finished was arguably Coventry's best ever in terms of the performance level of the team and the dazzling football that we had played. With other Scots in the team and with us being near the top of the league, there was always a chance of the selectors taking notice of me. Despite all of this, I was never to pull on the blue jersey of Scotland again. Unfortunately, that season was the peak for the team in my time at the club. The following year, although we again played well and on occasions repeated our sparkling football, the consistency wasn't there and we finished tenth. Injuries to Ferguson and the continued absence of Graham Oakey from an injury the previous season (from which he was eventually forced to retire) really didn't help. Garry Thompson had emerged as a rival for Ferguson's number nine shirt and he was a real handful as a centre-forward; strong, mobile and athletic. I would have said that it would have needed someone wielding a scaffold pole to break his leg, but suffer a leg break he did in the most innocuous circumstances, falling awkwardly on the training ground.

Although things had gone downhill slightly on the field, I was still enjoying my time at Coventry with the thought in my mind at that stage that I would finish my career playing in sky blue. I still had one or two money-making schemes in place, but I was to find out to my cost that I was never going to be a billionaire businessman!

Chapter 25

Not Open All Hours

THIS WAS the season of our infamous brown away kit, which I think has been voted the worst kit ever. For me it was the source of a little extra income. I would give each of my mates at the local pub three guesses to identify the colour and style of our new away kit. No one correctly got the colour and each set of wrong guesses earned me a fiver! Mind you, the kit wasn't so lucky for us at the Hawthorns that season as West Brom walloped us 7-1, the heaviest defeat of my career.

We took a few tonkings that season, although in losing 4-0 to Southampton, we did at least have the excuse that half of the team were unnerved before the match when the fire brigade had to rescue six of our players stuck in the hotel lift. As a club, we were still showing ambition, trying to sign England defender Kevin Beattie from Ipswich for £500,000 and Trevor Francis from Birmingham for £1m. The bid for Beattie was rejected by Ipswich and Francis opted to join Brian Clough at Forest in the first million-pound deal in this country. If those two players had signed, I think that we could have been a real force going forward.

I was never a prolific goalscorer but I did score a few corkers. One of these came that season at Wolves where I caught the ball perfectly from outside of the box and watched it fly into the Molineux net. I can remember thinking that my action then in striking the ball was like a perfect stroke in golf. When the timing of striking a football or a golf ball is spot on, you don't feel the weight of the ball, they just fly off your foot or your club with power and direction.

In training, or when warming up before games, when I was practising shooting, my mate Barry Powell would often take the mickey, standing behind me as I lined up to shoot. All I would hear from him was 'Bump, bump, bump', his imitation of one of my typically weak shots trickling to the keeper. After a rare event such as my goal at Wolves, I thought I would have the upper hand for once. Reminding him of the perfection of my strike, he had a perfect comeback with, 'Even a blind squirrel will eventually find the odd nut!'

I had been playing First Division football for several years now and had favourite grounds to play at and favourite teams to play against. I also had favoured individual opponents too. Full-backs I loved playing against were Mick Mills and George Burley, both of Ipswich. Both were good players, both were internationals but, for whatever reason, I just loved them as I felt that I was on for a good game. I think if I had been able to play against George each week, I would have been a fixture in the Scottish team for years.

A player that I always had a running war of words with was Tommy Smith of Liverpool. As well as trying to kick me to bits, he would always try to intimidate me verbally. I remember one game at Anfield where he tried to run me, putting the ball one side of me while he ran around the other. I had read what he was going to do and got back ahead of him and rolled the ball back to Blyth in goal. As we jogged back up to the halfway line I decided to have a go back at him, 'What dae you think you are daein', trying to oot run me? Ah'll tell you what, at the end of the game Ah'll race you for yer wages.' 'That's okay,' he said, 'then we can fight each other, double or quits, okay?' No, it wasn't okay. In a fight between me and Tommy there would only be one winner and the winner wouldn't have been Scottish!

As always, I took the kicking I got from someone like Tommy Smith as a compliment as it was the only way they were stopping me. I have been asked, did any of the defenders of the day tell me that they were going to break my legs if I went past them again. My response is that none of those guys wanted to give prior notice of their intentions, they just went ahead and attempted to do it!

That year, now in my early 30s and with one eye on life after football, I opened a sports shop in Everdon Road in Holbrooks, Coventry with a friend of mine, Alan Kenny. It was called Hutchison and Kenny Enterprises. Alan had married into an Italian family in Coventry who ran two well-known restaurants in the city, Nellos and the Trevi Fountain, so he had some commercial experience. The family already had premises where they made pizza bases, in the block where there was an empty shop front, so Alan suggested opening this to sell sports goods.

I got in contact with Adidas who, presumably not knowing I was part of the Scots gang who defaced their boots at the 1974 World Cup, agreed to supply us with plenty of gear. I also had contacts through John Reay, my golfing friend, who proved useful as they were able to supply me with a lot of stuff, some of it quite exotic for the time, kits from teams such as the New York Cosmos for example.

It wasn't long into our tenure when we had an unwelcome guest. I had a call from the police saying that they had caught someone coming in through the skylight of the shop. I had to laugh when they told me about the guy they had caught and what he had been doing. It explained why the lady who ran the shop would come in some days and find odd items of clothing scattered about on the floor. Apparently, this chap had been pinching stuff for a while by hooking items of clothing on a stick and pulling them out through the letter box on the shop door. However, he had a certain honesty about him as he had posted back anything that didn't fit him! The shop didn't last long, a couple of years perhaps.

Our demise was down to corporate villains rather than the Coventry variety. In the end, companies like Adidas decided they didn't want to be bothered with low-budget orders from shops like ours and would only look at orders over £5,000, too much of a risk for us. We would also have to take some of the more niche market stuff like skiwear. (At least, that's what they told me; maybe they did find out about the defaced boots!) Unfortunately, there aren't too many ski slopes in downtown Holbrooks and so Alan and myself decided to knock our sportswear business on the head.

Season 1979/80 rolled around and there seemed to be a change in policy within the club. The emphasis seemed to be more on youth with players like Thompson, Hateley, English, Gillespie, Blair and Whitton coming into the picture. I wasn't sure if this signalled another downturn in the club's finances or that the management was just confident that, in the long run, these players would be at the heart of a better team. Whatever the reasoning for the change, I was really disappointed to see Terry Yorath depart for Tottenham. It was undoubtedly a good move for him, particularly as Andy Blair was keeping him out of the team, but I doubted that in the long run it would be good for the club.

However, Terry's departure did signal another milestone for me as Gordon Milne asked me to take over from him as captain, something that I was honoured to do. I was never going to be the same type of captain he was and from the outset I felt that my style would be through setting an example on the pitch with my work rate and professional approach in training and in games. I was always pretty involved vocally in encouraging and in directing and I saw my captaincy as a way of extending this.

My big pal Barry Powell also moved on, in his case to Derby. Many footballers don't stay long enough in a town or a city to put down very strong roots. Indeed, nowadays, many footballers live away from the town or city that their club represents. Because I was at Coventry for nine years and we lived in the city, we built up quite a network of friends. Through John Kenny, the father of my sports shop partner, I became a regular darts player at Coundon Social Club, playing with the same circle of lads.

John, who lived just up the road from us in Allesley Village, came around one night and asked if I fancied going down to the club and watching the snooker as the Coundon first team were at home that night, so I agreed and off we went. These matches were keenly contested, often with a bit of needle, and would have a good crowd watching them. All the lights in the hall would be out, with only the floodlight over the snooker table lit, adding to the atmosphere and the importance of the occasion.

When we got to the club, just before the match started, John was asked by a committee man to referee. In reality, all that this meant was handing out the rests when needed and keeping the score. The match proceeded and, in the last frame, Coundon were behind. The opposition lad bent over the table to take his shot when John halted the match with, 'Excuse me, son, I need to clean the ball.' Now, John had lost all of his natural bottom teeth and he took out his set of dentures, fitted them around the white ball as it sat on the table and left them there to mark its position while he cleaned it with his duster. He then replaced the ball and popped his false teeth back in. Well, there was uproar from players and spectators alike. He knew what he was doing and had done it deliberately to put the player off his stride, and everybody in the hall knew it too! I can't remember if his intervention saved the day for Coundon Social or not, but I do remember that not only was John removed as referee from that game, but the committee were forced to ban him from the snooker room at the club!

One of the biggest characters around the club during my time there was George Curtis. He had been Jimmy Hill's centre-half and captain as they rose through the leagues in the 1960s and was the club's record appearance holder. After retirement he held various senior positions around the club, most famously as joint manager with John Sillett when Coventry won the FA Cup in 1987. He was a larger-than-life boisterous character who had his finger on the pulse of every aspect of life at the club. He worked hard and he expected everyone else to give their all too.

Ron Wiley had been asked to bring over a Coventry City team to play in a charity fundraising friendly to be staged at the ground of non-league Lichfield City. We would play against an all-stars team. I was asked to go, along with a variety of first-team and youth players plus some background staff. George was asked to come too. Ron reminded us before the game started to take things easy and make sure that none of us or our opponents got injured. I wasn't ever going to take things easy. As I have mentioned, I have never played a friendly match in my life. If people were paying to watch, then I felt an obligation to do my best. I thought that Ron might also have a problem with George as I doubted that he 'did' friendlies either.

Just before we went out on the pitch before the game, Ron told us that Trevor Francis had turned up to play for the all-stars team and was going off after the game to join up with the England squad. We were to be particularly careful around Trevor as England needed him in one piece.

Well, the game began at the usual slow pace, typical of games like this. When I got the ball, I would take on and try to beat my full-back in just the same way I did in any other game. Trevor Francis was up for taking on our defence too. The first time he got the ball he was racing through when George Curtis tripped him up and brought him down. This brought Ron Wylie to the touchline and he shouted, 'George, remember what we said, take it easy.' George gave him a cheery wave.

Later in the first half, Trevor did it again. He was racing through our backline until he was up against George, who he was going past until he was again dumped on his backside. Ron was out again. 'George. What are you doing man? Remember, go easy.' George stuck up his thumb in agreement and after Trevor got back to his feet the game resumed. A few minutes before half-time, Trevor and George were at it again with Francis once more left sprawled on the turf. This time he got gingerly to his feet and limped to the side. Ron just stood on the touchline this time, hands on hips, glaring at George, who was the picture of innocence. As we came off the pitch at half-time, Ron was waiting for Curtis. 'George, man, did Ah no tell you tae take it easy, Trevor's sitting over there with an ice pack on his ankle.' Curtis was ready with his answer, 'Ron, it's like this. Trevor can go past me, that isn't a problem. The ball can go past me, that's fine too, but Ron, there's no way that Trevor and the ball are going past.' And he strolled off for a well-earned half-time drink!

At various times I was the chauffeur for younger Coventry players since the Ryton training camp was a difficult place to get to without a car. At one stage, Gary Gillespie and Ray Gooding were my passengers. One day I was late going to pick them up before a game and we were in danger of holding up the team bus. I was obviously going too fast to make up the time and I was pulled over by the police. When the boy came to my car window, I was hoping he was a Sky Blues fan and I told him my predicament. He obviously supported Villa or Blues as he was having none of it and told me my excuses made no difference, an offence was an offence! And so, a fine and points on my licence were coming my way.

My two passengers always complained about the musical offering in the car as we travelled through Coventry and Warwickshire. I decided that I would make the journeys to and from training even more of a musical trial for them and have the pleasure of knowing that they were paying for it. I said to them one day, 'Boys, ye have a really good deal here, ferried aboot, picked up, dropped off and it doesnae cost yous a penny. When are you going to give me some petrol money?' They were adamant that church mice had bigger bank accounts than they did and that they would be bankrupt if they had to give me any cash. Well, I was ready for that so I told them that the deal was that once a month they would buy a cassette for the car. They thought about this and then agreed to the deal, but weren't so happy when I told them that I would be choosing the cassette. I'd have had to listen to some real auld headbangers if it was left to them!

Ian Wallace had been trying to get a move away from Coventry for a few months. He could see, the same as the rest of us, that the policy based on youth was going to take some time to come to fruition, if it ever would. Jock Stein, the Scottish manager by this stage, never came to see us play despite half the team being Scottish. Players like Wallace and Gillespie, I felt, should have been regular members of the Scotland squad. Ian felt correctly that a more high-profile club would improve his international prospects as well as give him a chance of winning some trophies, something that was now looking increasingly unlikely at Coventry. He eventually got his big move, joining Brian Clough at Forest.

The huge £1.25m fee was invested by Jimmy Hill in the building of a state-of-the-art sports hall facility, the Sky Blue Connexion, at Ryton. He saw this as being an invaluable aid for training, but also, as it was to be open to the public when not in use by the club, a money-making facility. Unfortunately, it didn't work out that way and a few years later when finances were again squeezed at the club, the facility was sold for around £400,000. When the sports hall was officially opened, the club did attract a high-profile personality to do the honours; the Duke of Edinburgh was helicoptered in to Highfield Road and chauffeured out to Ryton.

As the senior pros at the club, Mick Coop and myself were part of the welcoming party that greeted him for his tour of the Connexion. He was an affable chap but I don't really think football was high on his agenda. The opening of the centre may have been a big deal for us but was all in a day's work for him. I had hoped that he might have gone into the players' canteen for his lunch but the powers that be were keeping him well away from Joyce's cooking.

Towards the end of my final full season at Coventry, I went to Ron Wylie and told him that I would like to go and play in America for a spell. I explained that I wanted to go while I was still a good player and not when I was past it and looking for one last payday. It had become customary for lots of English and Scottish players to go over to the USA in the British close season and play on loan for a NASL team during the summer months. Things had been booming in the US for a few seasons. When a player of Pelé's stature is playing in your league, then it is bound to have a big impact.

I had liked the things that I had heard from my Coventry team-mate, Steve Hunt, who had played at the New York Cosmos alongside Pelé for a couple of years. Players liked going to the USA for a new experience and because the money was good. Clubs liked it because it got players off the wage bill for a few months. The downside for both was that there would be no rest for players, who would be playing continuously for at least two years with all that that entailed for wear and tear on the body.

I trusted Ron because he had good contacts in the game, including America, and I knew that if he was involved, he would do right by me and find me a good club. Jimmy Hill had a big stake in a team called Detroit Express and had invested some of Coventry City's money in the venture. I had heard some not very flattering things about that club though and knew that I would not be going there, not least because of the Jimmy Hill connection. After my chat with Ron, he told me to leave it with him and that he would sort me out. I didn't know it, but myself, Irene and the children were going to have some of the best few months of our lives as Ron found the perfect American club for me.

Chapter 26

Carefree in Seattle

RON WYLIE had worked at Villa with Bruce Rioch who was now playing in the US. I never asked either Ron or Bruce if they arranged my move but, a couple of weeks after my raising the prospect of me playing in America, Ron told me that I would be signing for Seattle Sounders and that everything had been sorted with Gordon Milne and the Coventry board. I would be on double my Coventry wages for my spell abroad. What I earned would also be tax-free, so it was going to be a lucrative trip. I would miss the last game of the English season and the first few games of the following one. By the time I arrived, the NASL season would be a few matches old. From a football point of view, it wasn't ideal missing games in two leagues over what was in effect three seasons. However, all of us as a family were excited at the prospect of living in America for a few months.

As soon as we arrived, we liked the set-up and we liked the city. Everything was sorted by the club. For a couple of weeks, we stayed in a hotel by the stadium, while our club house in the Bellevue district was being freshly furnished. We moved out there alongside most of the Sounders squad and their families. It was a lovely area and we soon got to know the families of my team-mates. Roy Greaves from Bolton, John Ryan from Norwich and the Derby centre-forward Roger Davies were all close by. The accommodation was immaculate, a lovely house. The club also supplied us with a car. My team-mates and I took it in turn driving in to train at the stadium each day.

Irene, too, enjoyed the social life; there was always something going on in someone's house where we lived. Irene had never been a sporty person but Liz Davies, Roger's wife, introduced her to running and she would be out for a two-mile jog every day. The children had a great time too, including David, once he had overcome a bout of measles. After school, there were always some activities or visit to take part in. They might go out on the Sound, go salmon fishing in one of the rivers or visit a Native American village. They loved it too.

Everything seemed to be on a large scale. While we were there, Roger and Liz Davies bought their own house. It needed to be renovated and it had this huge, dusty basement, big enough to play five-a-side football down there. The kids were in there playing all the time. They would emerge sweaty and with faces black enough to rival Jock the chimney sweep back in Dundonald.

We shared the stadium with the local baseball, basketball and NFL teams. Because it had an artificial surface, any amount of activity could take place. Depending on who was playing in there, one type of surface would be rolled out and another one fitted that suited the sport. The stadium, the indoor Kingdome, was a great place for someone like me to play football. The type of AstroTurf was slicker and moister than in some of the other stadiums. Slide tackling by defenders was less likely on AstroTurf as they would lose skin and their legs would be cut to ribbons in much the same way as they would be on the shale-covered side of the Dundonald Bluebell pitch! This was good for an attacker as it made getting the ball off me that bit harder. The moisture in the pitch meant the ball would zip about nicely on the surface and it also meant that the burns from falling on the pitch when tackled were less severe.

Some of the pitches weren't great. In Vancouver the surface was like an old snooker table, all patches everywhere. It was an outdoor pitch too and it had a huge camber because of the amount of rainfall that they got. If I stood on one touchline, I could only see the head and shoulders of a player stood on the far side! We played the Cosmos in New York's Giants Stadium which, because it is an outdoor arena, had a very dry surface. Playing for them that day was the Dutch international Johan Neeskens, a great midfield player who liked a tackle. At half-time, he had to change his shorts as they were soaked in blood from the lacerations on his thighs due to him going to ground in challenges. I remember thinking how much that was going to hurt once he was sat in front of the telly that night.

Everything was done properly at Seattle, which was the way I liked things to be. The Sounders people were lovely and very professional in all that they did. All the players had no-trade contracts. In other MSL clubs, players could be shipped off to another club at very short notice and have no say in the matter. An indication of how Seattle looked after us can be seen in the way that we travelled. Because the country was so vast, most of the travel to away games was by air. If we were playing a club in a different time zone to us, we would arrive two days early so we could acclimatise to both weather and time difference. Jim Holton played for Detroit Express and he told me that their team sometimes flew on standby flights and that they would often be left waiting a long time to get home.

On the pitch, everything was going well and the American fans seemed to like me. After my fourth game, I was being interviewed on the pitch by Canadian TV. The interviewer asked me how I was enjoying myself and I told him that I had settled in well. He said, 'The supporters seem to like you,' and he indicated a huge banner draped along the balconies of one of the stands. It read 'And on the seventh day, God made Hutch'. That someone had gone to the time, trouble and expense to do something like that gave me a great feeling of appreciation.

We had a successful time in the season I was there. We won our regional championship and got through to the play-offs with a record number of wins in the NASL. The play-off game against Vancouver ended in a draw after 90 minutes and, as each game had to have a positive outcome, we had a shoot-out. This required the attacker on one team to run from a 30-yard line marked on the pitch, to try and score against the other team's goalkeeper, within a certain time limit. I was chosen as one of our shoot-out players and I was up against Bruce Grobbelaar in the Vancouver goal. In the shoot-out, I took the ball around him and was about to score when he brought me down. We were now given a conventional penalty. Shades of Scotland against Spain, Grobbelaar saved my penalty and we were eliminated.

The standard of football was below what I had been used to in England. Many of the European players over there were coming to the end of their careers and some had the attitude that it was almost a holiday. That certainly wasn't the way that I saw things and, as usual, I played at full tilt. I remember one game against Minnesota Kicks when Willie Morgan played for them and I upset him. He had the ball on the wing and I chased him back and won a throw-in. He said, 'What are ye doing, no need for all the chasin' we're on holiday here.' I didn't agree at all and told him so, 'Ye might be but A'hm certainly no.' As I went to take the throw-in, I cracked him on the head with my wrist, accidentally, I have to say. Well, he wasn't happy with me. He was throwing a party that night and had invited all the Sounders players as well as his own team-mates. After the game, he let it be known to one or two of our players that I was no longer welcome because of our little fall-out. In a nice show of solidarity, with me now frozen out, the rest of the Sounders party boycotted Willie's shindig.

There was one particular party that I did attend in America. Irene and I organised a get-together to celebrate our 12th wedding anniversary. American friends that Irene invited were impressed by the fact she had managed so many years of marriage with the same man! John Bond was out there for some reason and he came along to the party, probably to see John Ryan, the Norwich full-back and my neighbour. When I saw Bond there, I just blanked him. Irene, however, had been chatting to John Bond's wife Jan. She'd said that she couldn't stop laughing about the ball-throwing incident at the Leofric, she had thought it was fabulous. As far as I was concerned, I was unlikely to be seeing much more of John Bond in the future, so our frosty relationship didn't bother me.

There was a big ex-Derby contingent at Seattle with Bruce Rioch, David Nish, Jeff Bourne and Roger Davies all playing. We were managed by Alan Hinton, the winger with the cannonball shot and the white boots that stood out in the Baseball Ground's ankle-deep mud. He was a good manager too. Training was always skills and tactics. Ally never liked running-based fitness training as a player and he didn't like it as a manager either, so running was off the menu, unless as players we chose to do it ourselves, which sometimes some of us did. He was also reluctant to play too many five-a-sides in training as he felt that they often caused injuries. I trusted and got on well with him.

Roger Davies was an unpredictable joker and you would never be sure what he would get up to. In the NASL, we would have what were called road trips. These could mean up to ten days away from Seattle, when we would play two or three games. On one particular trip we were playing in Tulsa, Washington and New York. The Tulsa game, even though it was in the evening, was played in temperatures of over 40 degrees Celsius. We could only play for ten or 15 minutes at a time before we had to take a drinks break. The dressing room had a fan as big as an aero propeller, trying to keep us cool. On these trips we were given a day off or even two between games and some form of trip or entertainment would often be organised.

After the Tulsa and Washington games, most of us were knackered and turned down a trip to the local horse-racing track to relax by the hotel pool, and it was only management and backroom staff who went racing. Late in the afternoon, Ally Hinton returned to the pool with a wad of dollars in his fist, obviously having had a successful time. Looking at his winnings, we told him that the drinks were on him. Hinton was having none of it, 'I'm not wasting my hard-won cash on drinks for you lot!'

Roger Davies, deciding he needed to be punished for his meanness, picked Hinton up and dropped him in the pool. Hinton went bonkers and called Davies all the names under the sun as he hauled himself from the water, telling him the cost of a new suit would be taken from his wages. As was often the case with incidents like this, the next day everything was forgotten and I doubt that Davies ever did buy Hinton a new suit.

It was in another US pool, this time one in Bellevue Seattle, that I had what could be called my Bert Trautmann moment. I was teaching my youngest son David how to dive. Despite lots of coaxing, he wouldn't go in head first. I got him to agree to go in, head down, if we held hands and went in together. The pool was unusual in that it was bowl-shaped with quite a slow fall to the deepest part of the pool. The surface of the pool bottom wasn't tiled and had a rough, pebbly non-slip finish. We dived in and I felt a sharp pain in the back of my neck as my head caught the bottom of the pool. As I surfaced, I felt strange, not all there and immediately went to the side. As I clambered out, I saw some of my hair floating on the surface of the pool. I felt my head and found that I now had a bald spot.

The next day we had a home game against the Cosmos. I was desperate to play but when I got up the next morning things still weren't right. I told Ally Hinton what had happened and he told me to have a fitness test that evening before the game. I was asked to do a few runs and I was given a few headers and apart from a bit of stiffness when I twisted or turned, I seemed okay.

Half an hour into the game I was brought down outside the box and inevitably landed heavily on my shoulder and neck. I was really out of it and the ref wanted me to be replaced, but our physio who was attending me said, 'Don't worry, ref, he's just got concussion.' I protested that I wanted to stay on too, but I didn't really know what I was doing and was replaced a couple of minutes later. I recovered sufficiently to play in the next game and was prescribed five weeks of traction on my neck that relieved most of my symptoms.

A few months later, now at Man City, I was sent for X-rays on a troublesome pelvis. While there, I asked the doctor if he would X-ray my neck, which now and then gave me pain. As he looked at his screen he asked, 'When did you break your neck, Tommy?' I was shocked, but he reassured me that whatever had happened, the break had now healed.

I think back to that day at the pool on occasion and ponder the possible outcomes for me if I had dived in a fraction more steeply or if I had been a couple of steps closer to the shallow end of the pool. A life spent in a wheelchair would not have been beyond the bounds of possibility. As it is, I have been left with occasional soreness in the neck and a small bald spot on my head where my hair never grew back. I was a lucky man!

I didn't know it at the time, but I had come very close to losing the lifestyle that I loved. Even the travelling involved in being a footballer never bothered me. This was a good thing in the US due to the vastness of the country. For away games or on road trips we were given a monetary allowance for food and for upkeep. The club paid for our hotel bed and breakfast; anything else we had, including our pre-match meal, we paid for from the allowance. Nowadays, diet is a big part of an athlete's preparation and certainly what is eaten before an explosive event like a football match would be specified by the club's backroom and medical staff.

In the US, what we ate before we played was up to us and was based on finance as much as anything. I would always have a bowl of soup, meaning that I made a saving on the allowance. We had a few American boys in our squad, with every team having to have a certain quota of American-born players. These lads were generally less well paid than European imports such as myself and the allowances were a big part of their salaries. They would often bring their own food with them, sandwiches and the like, to eat when they were away from home.

Being away on road trips for nearly two weeks at a time was a possible problem for family life. After all, leaving Irene alone to look after three young children and all that entails was clearly not ideal. However, in reality this was not a difficulty as the community of players' families at Bellevue was close-knit and they all looked after each other when we were away.

There was certainly a difference in the approach, mentality and know-how between the European players and the American boys. They were still a bit naïve in their approach to the game. If you contrast most of the American players' experience to that of someone like Alan Hudson who was playing in the Seattle midfield, the contrast was stark. Hudson's last game in England had been in the FA Cup Final for Arsenal and he had played at the top level for the whole of his career. I got on well with Huddy, but he did have one or two quirks. He would never answer his phone when it rang. He told me if it was bad news then he did not want to know and if it was good news then it would get to him anyway. He was also a man who liked his beer. He could go on an all-night bender and then be in for training and run all day. He was a very fit boy. He played in a similar way to Billy Bremner, he liked to control the game and its tempo. If he played you the ball then he wanted it back as soon as possible. I had to explain to him when we started playing together that when he gave me the ball, if I had the opportunity to run with it then I wouldn't be giving him it back.

The eccentric mentality of some of the American players can be seen through an incident with our keeper Jack Brand who, it has to be said, wasn't the brightest button. Although born in Germany, he had spent most of his life in Canada and had begun his career with clubs in Toronto. On days when we could not train at the Kingdome due to it being occupied by other Seattle sports teams, we would train at an outdoor sports and athletic facility next to the Bowen motor factory in Renton. Times of training could vary day by day. We would use the oval of green inside the athletics track for training at Renton. Some days you couldn't hear yourself think out there as the noise from the factory, where they were testing the engines, was deafening.

At lunchtime the athletics track would be packed with workers from the factory since they were paid by Bowens to do laps of the track in order to improve their health and fitness and presumably cut down on absenteeism. On one particular day at the Bowens' site, it was noticed at the start of a session that Jack Brand hadn't turned in for training, which was unusual. As training started, we were buzzed by a light aircraft that flew low over us a few times before disappearing. About an hour later, Jack turned up flustered and apologetic. He had mixed up the time of training and had been having a flying lesson when he spotted us out on the field below. He'd swooped in a couple of times to make sure it was us and then hot footed it back to the airport, if you can hot foot it in a plane. A mad dash in his car completed his journey. As an excuse for missing training, taking a flying lesson beats having a cold, but you can imagine the lads gave him pelters.

There was a feeling among the players of the teams in the NASL that things were made a lot easier for New York Cosmos than they were for the rest of us. For me, this was proven on our visit to play the Cosmos. We went into the game at Giants Stadium with Roger Davies the leading scorer in the league. This had been the subject of quite a lot of attention in the media leading up to the game. Cosmos centre-forward Giorgio Chinaglia was second in the goalscoring charts, but this wasn't good enough for the Cosmos, who expected to be top dogs in everything. Our game was only a few minutes old when Davies was involved in a tussle with a Cosmos defender. The referee came over and sent him off. I had seen the two players challenging and there had been no violence, not even a foul by either player. To me, Davies was removed as it meant that he wasn't going to score in this game and he wasn't going to score in the games for which he would be suspended.

Obviously, we were incensed at the injustice taking place. Tackles started to fly in from both sides. Later in the first half, I was on the ball and was going past the Iranian Cosmos full-back Andranik Eskandarian when he launched himself at me, went over the ball and caught me on the shins with his studs. (Ironically, Eskandarian had the same number of international goals for Scotland as I did: one. His goal came in the 1978 World Cup when he put through his own goal for the Scots in a 1-1 draw.) I went down in a heap. I didn't see it at the time as I was in agony on the turf, but Bruce Rioch arrived like a train, knocked Eskandarian spark out with a single punch and was walking off the pitch before the referee pulled out his card. Inevitably the game was lost but it illustrated the team spirit we had at Seattle.

One thing I wasn't a fan of was some of the razzamatazz stuff that they had at the US stadiums. For each Sounders home game the club gave out 20,000 kazoos. They made a real racket, but not in a good way as far as I was concerned. As my kids went to all the games, they always came home with these things too, and I had to listen to them all over again both in the car and in the house. Once they were in bed, the kazoos found a final resting place in the Hutchison bin!

Another feature of football in the US was the organ music. The organ would boom out during games with the tempo of the music supposedly matching the action on the pitch. If we were attacking, the music would be exciting and upbeat. If our opponents didn't realise we were threatening their goal by what was happening on the pitch, the organ music would certainly have alerted them!

We had a brilliant time in Seattle. Irene loved it and our kids thought that living there was wonderful. From a footballing point of view, I had really enjoyed myself. I felt I had played well and the positive reaction I had from Sounders fans seemed to confirm this. Ally Hinton was keen for me to return and we came to an agreement that I would be back in Seattle the following year.

My contract situation at Coventry meant that I was entitled to a free transfer at the end of the season. We agreed that I would see out the season in England and that I would return to the USA the following summer. My plans had changed. I no longer intended to end my playing days at Coventry. I saw both my footballing and family future as being in North America. With my levels of fitness and the less-competitive nature of the NASL, I could see myself playing on for many years. The monetary rewards of playing in the US would make us more financially secure. Things often don't work out as planned and as we flew out of Seattle I didn't know that I would never play in the NASL again. For the next 18 months, I would still be playing in sky blue.

Chapter 27

Sky Blue to Sky Blue

I RETURNED to Coventry in time for the eighth game of the season, a home game against Everton. It was a real baptism of fire back into English football for me. Not only did we suffer a record top-flight 5-0 home defeat, but I was carried off the pitch unconscious. I watched the incident that injured me later on TV and saw that as I went up for a header and flicked the ball on, the Everton full-back John Bailey (a player who, when I was later with Man City, would gladly have knocked me out!) headed the back of my skull in trying to get the ball away. I could see I was out of it from the moment of contact and was limp when I hit the ground.

At that stage, I didn't know that I had suffered a broken neck while in Seattle. I would have been reassured that it had stood up to the impact of that collision. I was stretchered off and came to in the treatment room. There were none of the concussion protocols of today in place then, so I was given a couple of paracetamols and sent off to the players' bar for a beer! I think the general consensus was that the club were pleased that it wasn't an important part of my body, my right foot for example, that was damaged. My head was expendable!

A lasting injury from that incident has not been to my head – no sense, no feeling, Irene would say – but to my shoulder and my arm, both of which I hurt in my unconscious fall to the ground. Periodically over the years, even to this day, I have pain from not being able to break my fall and landing heavily. I was back in training the following week and back in the team for the following game during which I scored my last Coventry goal, against Brighton.

I played only two more Coventry games after being concussed against Everton. I was in the squad for a game at Leicester when Gordon Milne told me that he was leaving me out of the team, the first time in nine years that I had been dropped by Coventry and one of the few times it had happened in my career. I didn't take too kindly to it. Gordon took me aside before the game at Filbert Street and, having told me I wasn't playing, said, 'I've told those lads in there [he pointed to the dressing room] that you have run a million miles for this club and that I now want them to do the same.'

I was upset and I told Gordon that what he had said to me meant nothing. I also told him that if he intended for me to now play in the reserves, he had another think coming. If any club came in for me then I would be happy to talk to them, even if they were outside of the First Division. I honestly thought that my time in sky blue had come to an end, possibly along with my First Division career.

In mid-October we played Norwich at Highfield Road and for the second game in a row I wasn't in the team. John Bond had left that club days before to take over at Manchester City, who had just sacked Malcolm Allison. After the game, I saw Kevin Bond in the players' lounge and half-jokingly asked him if his dad might be looking for a new winger. Bobby McDonald, who was standing with us and who was also out of the Coventry team at that time, chipped in with, 'Aye, and Ah new full-back tae.'

Despite this conversation, I was still surprised on the Monday following the Norwich game when Gordon Milne told me that there had been interest from Manchester City. I was taken aback that Gordon would be prepared to sell me to the Manchester club who were perhaps more likely to be their rivals in the league than someone like Norwich. That wasn't really a question for me. All I wanted was regular games.

I travelled to Maine Road and for the second time I was ushered into an office to meet John Bond. He was there with his assistant John Benson. I was much more wary than I had been all those years ago at Norwich. His first question – how much did I want – immediately put me on my guard. I reminded him of our previous transfer dealings. 'No need to worry on that score, Tommy,' he said to me as he gestured with his arm, 'these have loads of money!'

We discussed the financial side of the move, and they were fine by me. Bond thought that I would sign there and then but that was something that I hadn't considered would happen. I had thought that I would be given a bit of time to consider my options. I was concerned that if I didn't sign there and then that I might scupper the deal for Bobby McDonald. I didn't know if he was signing us as a left-side partnership. Bond assured me that Bobby's deal was independent of whatever I did. However, I had also promised Ally Hinton at Seattle that when I left Coventry I would be returning to the US and be signing for him. I wasn't going to break that promise until I had the chance to speak to Ally himself. I didn't want to bring Seattle into the discussions with Bond and so I told him that I couldn't sign until I had gone home and spoken to Irene about it. He said that was no problem. 'Here's the phone,' he said, 'we'll leave the office and you can discuss it with her now, see what she says and then sign.'

I had to come clean and tell him about the promise I had made to Hinton. If he wasn't prepared to release me from that promise, then I wouldn't be joining Man City. Bond was definite that this time I wasn't getting away. He got me to sign the contract. He signed it too. He told me, however, that if I wanted to be released from it, he would rip it up. I think he felt that because my signature was on that form, I was less likely to pull out of the deal. Because of the time difference between the UK and the US West Coast, I wasn't able to speak to Hinton until the next day. Bond told me, 'If you decide that you are coming, phone up reception tomorrow and ask for me. If you decide that you're not coming, then ask for John [Benson], because I won't want to speak to you!'

I spoke to Ally Hinton the next day. He asked me what I wanted to do so I told him that this was my last chance to play for one of the big English clubs. If it was left to me, I would sign for Man City. He was great about it and he told me that if he was in my shoes then he would do the same. I was able to tell John Bond he could register my signature. As it happens, both Roger Davies and I were invited to play in a testimonial match back in Seattle later in the season, so during the week I spent out there I was able to apologise to Ally in person.

I signed for the rather odd fee of £47,000 (why not £45,000 or £50,000?). I was quoted in the papers as saying that I was joining City as I wanted to be at a big club. This was made to look as if it was a slight on Coventry, implying that they were small-time. That was certainly not what I meant. I was and always will be grateful for my time at Coventry. However, I think that in stature, even Coventry fans would agree that City were the bigger club. That said, when I joined them, they were having a terrible time. City were bottom of the league and looking like one of the favourites for relegation.

I never had any qualms about joining them. When I signed for Coventry, they were bottom and then, with the help of two Scottish signings – myself and Colin Stein – we went on a fantastic winning run. The same thing happened this time. Three new Scots in the team – Bobby McDonald, Gerry Gow from Bristol City and me – and City were up and running! We won ten out of the first 15 games and shot up the table. I loved playing at Maine Road. It was great to come out of the tunnel and see the wall of sky blue facing you on the massive Kippax terrace, willing you to win. I was a bit surprised, however, that a club of City's stature didn't have better facilities.

The infrastructure at Coventry was much better. At City, we changed in the Maine Road dressing rooms and then walked through narrow, *Coronation Street*-type terraced roads and alleys to get to the training ground. This consisted of one full-size pitch and a small AstroTurf five-a-side area. The people we passed on the way to and from training would always have a word for us; even elderly ladies who you would think would have no interest in football would tell us to make sure we won that night or the following Saturday, obviously knowing who and when we were playing.

The first game I played was away at Brighton. At the pre-match meal, I was sitting next to the coach driver, Derek, a smashing lad, and Bobby McDonald. Bobby and I were a bit surprised when a few of the players went up to the bar and came back with bottles of wine. We were even more surprised when Derek did too! In fairness, the bottles were shared and amounted to perhaps a glass or two each. Nevertheless, this was certainly different to Coventry.

When we first signed, the three of us were staying in the Boden Hotel in Altrincham. They had events on there and one evening Bill Shankly was a guest speaker. Bobby, Gerry and myself had a chat to him before he went on stage. He asked me about my time in America and I told him how much I had enjoyed it. He thought close-season jaunts like that were a bad idea. He couldn't see how a professional athlete could perform at their maximum when playing for two years without a break. I told him that I disagreed as I had felt re-energised by my time in Seattle and had come back to England ready to play. Because the games over there were much less intense and because I wasn't getting kicked from pillar to post every week (except for the guy in New York), it was more like a competitive way of keeping fit.

I knew Shankly fairly well as, after his retirement, whenever Coventry played at Liverpool or Everton, Bill would always join us for a pre-match meal because of his friendship with Gordon Milne, one of his former players. He was a great man to listen to. He told us the story of a conversation he had with a journalist about Tony Currie (at that time an exciting and very skilful player at Sheffield United who was also playing well for England). Shankly said, 'He had the cheek to ask if Tony Currie was as good a player as Tom Finney [Shankly's old playing colleague at Preston]. I told him that I thought that they were probably on a par, before saying, "Mind you, Tom is nearly 60!"'

After about a month at the club, John Bond called me into his office to ask me how I was getting on. I told him that I was enjoying myself and that things were going well but that I was a bit surprised by some of the players' attitudes to training. I was playing with some big-name internationals, but I didn't think that the squad had the same professional attitude to training as I had. I thought some of the players were a bit slack. He agreed with me and things gradually changed and sharpened up over the season.

If given a drill, I would always try to be spot on, sharp and intense. Bond stopped the group one day and got them to watch Dennis Tueart (also a very professional player) and me doing a passing drill. 'That's the way I want it done, sharp and crisp. No half-hearted stuff while you whine on about playing five-a-side. I want to see you put the effort in. Do your best like these two.' It was good to hear that sort of praise from him.

Another thing at City that surprised me was the salaries that they paid to the younger players. At Coventry, young players coming through had to become established in the first team before they saw their status reflected in a bigger pay packet. Here, players like Ranson, MacKenzie and Reid were on good money at an early age. It seemed that Allison had tried to protect the club from the recently introduced freedom of contract rule where players were now free to go at the end of their agreement with a club. Steve Kinsey, an 18-year-old on the fringes of the first team, had a seven-year contract, something I had never come across before.

I enjoyed the training with Bond. Everything was focused on attacking play, shooting, crossing, creating chances. In my time there, I think we only looked at defensive structure two or three times. He wasn't afraid to let you know his feelings about you, whether that was good or bad, and I liked that. He would praise you or tear strips off you in front of the other players, something I have never had a problem with.

While in general he was very positive in what he said to me, he did have a real go after a game at Arsenal. He loved to win and, being from Essex, he particularly liked to win in London. On this occasion we were badly beaten. He had a go at a few players including his own son, Kevin. Then he turned to me and he says, 'And you, you go past Kenny Sansom two minutes from the end and we're 3-0 down. Where were you for the other 88 minutes?' Well, I wasn't having that and told him that he could criticise me for not playing well, but that he could never call me out for not trying as that would never be the case.

A few days later, Bond's assistant John Benson was chatting to me about the incident and said that Bond had done the same thing to Martin Peters at Norwich. Peters was another player whose effort and attitude was beyond question. Benson told me he did it as a marker to the other players. In other words, if someone like Peters or me who obviously gave our all were getting a tongue-lashing, then no one was safe.

From a supporter's point of view, I was probably an odd signing. I was 34 and so should have been past my best, well on my way down the slippery slope to retirement. Some possibly thought I was there for one last payday. The fact that I got off to a really good start justified my signing for City from both mine and John Bond's point of view. I can remember having a real go at our full-back Nicky Reid for bombing forward in the last few minutes of that first game at Brighton when we held a slender lead. I can remember Bond commenting on this and saying, referring to me, 'That's why we bought him.' The young players were good but naïve and that bit of experience that I brought with me, as well as what I did on the ball, helped to justify my signing.

It was a happy time. The supporters were very good to me and my team-mates seemed to appreciate what I brought to the squad. After a few weeks we were able to buy a house on an estate in Wilmslow. Gerry Gow and his family moved in across the street and Bobby McDonald was just around the corner. We got on well with Gerry and his wife Julie and their kids would play with ours, so as a family we were very content. Gerry couldn't drive so Bobby and I took it in turns to be chauffeurs. Unfortunately, there was no cassette as a reward for our services from Gerry! The fact that the three of us had such a positive impact on performance and on results added to the pleasure of being there. Irene and the kids loved going to the games too as there was such a positive atmosphere about the place.

As well as going great guns in the league, we were also having a good run in both cup competitions, although me and the other two new lads were cup-tied for the League Cup. John Bond, however, commented that his three signings had contributed greatly to the League Cup performances, even though we hadn't kicked a ball in the competition for City. His reasoning was that the three lads who came in were playing out of their skin to try and stay in the team for FA Cup and league games. There was a real buzz about the place. This was added to on a matchday by comedian Eddie Large coming into the dressing room before games. We had a real laugh with him and went out onto the pitch relaxed and with smiles on our faces.

It was frustrating for me and for the other two Scots lads that we missed out on that League Cup run as the team was playing so well and we wanted to be part of every game. The team reached the semi-finals of that cup, the other three teams involved being Liverpool, West Ham and Coventry. The latter were in their first major semi-final and my performance and my goal for them in an earlier round at Brighton had both helped them on their way, but was now preventing me from playing in the competition for City. As it happened, the two clubs avoided each other and unfortunately both went out one step away from Wembley. We lost 1-0 on aggregate to Liverpool but were the better team over the two games. We should have won both legs and weren't helped by some dubious refereeing.

Our disappointment at falling when we were so close to glory in the League Cup was eased by our continued good form in the league and by our progress through each round of the FA Cup. We could sense, and so could the fans, that something special was about to happen. Each round of the FA Cup that we negotiated successfully increased the sense of excitement and anticipation of everyone connected to the club. The series of games that we played that year were among the most memorable of my career, games I would never forget.

Chapter 28

Que Sera Sera

CONSIDERING WE were bottom of the table when John Bond took over from Malcolm Allison in late October, our 12th-place finish in the league was more than satisfactory. We could and should have finished higher, but league results did tend to tail off a bit as we progressed in the FA Cup.

The first game of our cup run was a home third-round tie against Crystal Palace. The draw had set up an interesting managerial clash between Bond and Allison, who was now in charge of Palace. I watched a TV programme on the Friday night before the game that featured a discussion with the two managers. They had been team-mates at West Ham, part of a group that became a football ideas factory in the café where they would meet after training.

Many of the salt-and-pepper-pot tacticians, including these two, went on to be top managers. Allison had a reputation for being loud and brash, but I was struck by how much more confident Bond was in the way that he put over his points of view. Bond himself could come across as a larger-than-life football character, flamboyant and frequently seen on TV. It was only through working with him at City that I began to appreciate that he was a real down-to-earth football man, knowledgeable and astute, who cared deeply about how his teams played.

I think the measure of a manager is whether they can improve the players they work with. I was in my mid-30s and had been a professional player for 16 years when I joined City. I felt that while working with Bond, even at my advanced age, I added to and improved my game. He said to me once, 'I wish I could have got hold of you when you were younger. I would have changed your game for the better.' I believe he would have too.

I remember one training session; forwards against defence. Bond always started the sessions and, on this occasion, he rolled the ball to me. As usual, as soon as I got the ball, I ran at the defenders. On this particular day he stopped the session and he said to me, 'God help you, Hutch, on the day we play a team with the same-coloured socks as us. Get your head up, man.' Over time, he got me to think about and vary my game more so that I would temper my instinct to always run with the ball. I became much more aware if a pass was the better option.

Certainly, Bond's methods had transformed City from the struggling group Big Mal had left behind. The difference in organisation and class between the teams was apparent that day. Allison came out onto the Maine Road pitch before the game and waved to the crowd with his trademark fedora hat, but the reception he got was very mixed, lukewarm at best. The mess the team had been in just a few short months ago was probably still fresh in the minds of many supporters who had seen Big Mal fail in both of his stints as City boss.

We were confident but, in truth, took a while to get going in this game. It was into the second half before we scored, but in the end ran out easy winners by four goals to nil. Allison had the good grace and class to come into our dressing room at the end of the game to say well done and good luck, and to congratulate John Bond. You could see that the manner of the defeat and the fact that it was against us had left him shell-shocked.

We had another quirky draw for the fourth round. This time we were to play Norwich at home, Norwich being Bond's team until a few months previous. It also threw up another intriguing clash of personnel. This time it was to be Bond v Bond as Kevin, the manager's son, was still full-back for his old club. It was the older Bond who was smiling when the final whistle blew as we produced a ruthless display and blew away his old club, beating them by six. The older Bond's good mood didn't last for long, however. He had tried to clamber over the wall from the directors' box into the players' tunnel so he could greet Kevin as he came off the pitch. In preparing to lower himself down, he had slipped and, instead of landing on his feet, he landed on his back. Considering how far he fell, he was lucky that he didn't do himself serious or permanent damage. As it was, he was left shuffling around for a few weeks and moaning about the pain he was in.

If John Benson was in earshot he would roll his eyes and tell his boss to stop complaining. This would set them off on one of their frequent arguments. These were often funny and well worth listening to. The management and coaching team at City consisted of the three Johns, the third one of the trinity being coach John Sainty. They were a close-knit unit who worked well together and who had certainly got us playing exciting and winning football.

The fifth round saw us travel to our only non-First Division tie of our cup run. We were drawn against Fourth Division Peterborough and this proved to be one of the most difficult matches we faced. John Benson was in charge as John Bond was laid low at his home in bed. This wasn't due to his self-inflicted back problems, although he probably would have told you of the pain he was in had you asked, but was down to a heavy cold.

In his pre-match talk, Benson conjured an image of our prone manager glowering at his radio as the commentary was broadcast and of what hell to pay there would be when he met up with us again should we mess things up. Bond in a bad mood wasn't a thing of beauty. London Road was packed and the home side were pumped up and ready for a challenge. They put us under pressure at times and made one or two half-chances, but we generally controlled things well and a solitary goal from Tommy Booth was enough to see us through. Bond would emerge from his sick bed a happy man.

He wasn't so happy after the quarter-final draw meant the blue half of Manchester would have to travel to play the blue half of Merseyside, in other words a very difficult game at Everton. They absolutely battered us in the first half of the game, roared on by the majority of the fans in the sell-out 55,000 crowd. An equaliser from Gerry Gow saw us go in level at half-time but it took another late equaliser from Paul Power to earn us a replay.

What had been a feisty game from the first minute got even feistier towards the end. In the last few minutes, we had the ball deep in the Everton half. Twice in quick succession I played the ball against the Everton defender Kevin Ratcliffe's legs. He didn't take kindly to this and on the second occasion he chopped the legs from under me. He wasn't finished. I got to my feet and he headbutted me, catching me on the cheek. Down I went again and off went Kevin, his moment of madness costing him his place in the replay.

As I left the field, the Everton bench weren't happy with me, accusing me of faking injury to get Ratcliffe sent off. Their sub, John Bailey, came up to me and said, 'I'm disappointed in you. I thought you were better than that.' I said to him, 'What are you on aboot? He's just headbutted me.' 'You're a cheat,' he said to me. 'Anyway,' I said to him, 'I don't know what you're complaining about, you'll be in for Wednesday.' 'Yes,' he said, 'and I'll be looking for you!' By this stage my cheek had started to swell where Ratcliffe had caught me. When Everton captain Roger Kenyon spoke to the media after the game, he apologised for the incident. It was good that someone from Everton acknowledged what had happened.

This didn't seem to matter to my friend Bailey. Early in the replay at Maine Road he caught me high on the knee, bringing me down and then leaning over to tell me, 'There'll be more of that coming your way.' Well, that night was one of my special ones and I ran him ragged. By the end, he didn't know whether he was coming or going. I set up two headed goals for Bobby McDonald, who very nearly had a hat-trick as he had another effort tipped onto the bar. We ran out 3-1 winners in front of an ecstatic 55,000 crowd and were through to the semi-finals.

I was given a huge bottle of brandy for being named man of the match, but I passed it onto McDonald because of his two goals. It was nights like this that I wanted to experience before I finished my career and I was far more likely to get them at a club like City. Bobby McDonald was proving to be a real threat in the opposition penalty area, but he frustrated John Bond who said to him, 'In our box you go hiding, you're like a baby, you never get your head on the ball in there. Up the other end, when there's a bit of glory involved, you get your head to everything, sort yourself out!'

I was now about to play in my first semi-final, but if we were to get to Wembley, we were going to have to beat the favourites, Ipswich. Managed by Bobby Robson, they had a fine team and were on course for a treble of trophies: league, FA Cup and UEFA Cup. In the end, it was only the latter that they won. Ipswich were driven by two Dutch midfield players, Arnold Muhren and Frans Thijssen. It didn't take a genius to know that if we could stop these two from playing then we would curb Ipswich as an attacking force. Nevertheless, I think John Bond showed his tactical know-how in the way he set us up. While Gerry Gow would sit on Muhren, I was detailed to look after Thijssen.

You might be surprised to hear that there was always a big defensive part to my game. I was never given a complete licence to roam free. I always considered myself a midfield player, not a winger. It's true that when I had the ball, on most occasions I would run at the full-back, but my starting position, certainly from the time Joe Mercer gave me a more withdrawn role at Coventry, was tucked inside in the middle of the pitch. Apart from my last season at Coventry when I had swapped to accommodate Steve Hunt, this was on the left-hand side of the team. At City, we had Paul Power rampaging down the left so I was used mostly on the right.

The plan for the Ipswich game was to hit them on the break. When they had the ball, Gerry and myself would be like glue on our two Dutchmen. When we got the ball, we would break away into space. Bond's thoughts, which proved to be correct, was that they would not be as inclined to chase us as we were them. The game at Villa Park was very tight, with few chances at either end. I remember heading a Kevin Beattie header off the line but that was about it. In extra time, Dave Bennett was brought down on the edge of the box and Paul Power, producing a shot to match his name, saw the ball fly into the top corner of the Ipswich net. We held out for the final few minutes.

The feelings of elation I had as the referee blew the final whistle were as great as those I had experienced in a Scotland shirt after the Czechoslovakia game all those years before. We were to play in the great showpiece match of the English game and our opponents were to be Tottenham.

The cup final – two games, as it turned out – will live with me forever. We were only ten minutes away from a glorious victory when fate or bad luck, call it what you will, stepped in to snatch everything away.

My move to Coventry meant regular First Division football and a chance to show the Scottish selectors what I could do.

Had we known how bad our World Cup song would be, perhaps we wouldn't have been so overjoyed to beat the Czechs! Willie Ormond is chaired around Hampden.

My best game for Scotland came in this 1-0 defeat to Northern Ireland, 1974.

It was a bitter disappointment that I didn't have more time on the pitch in the 1974 World Cup finals. I feel that I could have had a real positive impact as I did in this game against Yugoslavia.

A perk of winning the Coventry Telegraph's player of the season award was that you won a car. This one was presented to me on the pitch at Highfield Road before a game.

Lynn, John and myself outside of our house in Allesley, Coventry. The car was a Chrysler Sunbeam, the first of two cars I won.

Myself dressed as a sheik. I'm not sure what my Coventry friend John, the infamous Coundon snooker referee, is dressed as!

The infamous chocolate brown Coventry kit may have been voted the worst ever, but it won me a few quid from my mates.

I think that you can tell by the look on my face that my stay in Seattle was certainly not a holiday as far as I was concerned.

A very sweaty me is interviewed by a television guy after my debut for Seattle Sounders.

When we moved to Manchester, Cindy the poodle (Joyce's puppy, secretly called Rover) came too.

Two of the goalscorers in the 1981 Cup Final games. Unfortunately, one of us scored for both teams and it wasn't Ricky Villa.

Chapter 29

Ten Minutes from Glory

FROM THE moment you reach a cup final, it is as though you are in a very special bubble. Inside that bubble, it is a warm, expectant and exciting place and this bubble seemed to cover the whole of Manchester. Back in the north-west, everyone of a blue persuasion seemed to be in a similar, euphoric state. This sense of elation was intense. There was a real buzz about the place everywhere we went and in everything that we did. City fans and even some non-blues wanted to know you, wanted to befriend you and wondered if, just on the off-chance, you had any spare tickets.

Most of the people who stopped me for a chat were genuine, lovely people, who wanted to wish me well and wanted me to know how much reaching the cup final meant to them. Like everyone else connected with the club, the fans were just beside themselves with delight. This final was to be even more special as 1981 marked the 100th anniversary of the FA Cup. We would be playing in the Centenary Final.

We were measured for club suits and did the round of media interviews, both local and national. When I was spoken to by the press or by TV, the main focus of the chat was on my age. I would be the oldest player on the pitch at nearly 34 years of age. I was asked if I felt that I could contribute in this final like George Eastham a few years before when, at the age of 36, he had scored the winner for Stoke in the League Cup Final against Chelsea. My age was never an issue and I was only ever governed by how my body felt. I felt that I was as fit as I had ever been.

After the final league game of the season, John Bond arranged for us to escape the madness around in Manchester by spending the week leading up to the cup final at a hotel in South London. There we could train in peace, prepare for the game, relax a little and even play a bit of golf. We trained at a local facility and on one occasion some of the press were allowed access. As usual with John Bond, the focus of our session was on attack and we were practising crossing and shooting. Myself and Ray Ranson on the right, Paul Power and Bobby McDonald on the left would take it in turns, running down the line and supplying crosses, some near-post, some far, to our strikers in the middle.

Dennis Tueart was one of the players we were picking out with our crosses. Dennis was a good player and a good pro but he had lost his place earlier in the season and hadn't played in the later rounds of the cup. There was a sizable press group who were lobbying for Dennis to be included in the 12 players for the day. On one occasion, I ran down the line and crossed it into the middle where Dennis met the ball on the volley and sent a screamer past Joe Corrigan into the net. The watching press boys were in raptures and let everyone present know their thoughts on Dennis and his goal. As I jogged back down the line, past the watching John Bond to collect another ball, he said to me, 'That lot can shout and say what they want, but I can tell you, Dennis won't be playing on Saturday!' Fair play to Dennis. He must have been devastated to miss out on the game but he never let his head go down, never sulked and always did his best in training.

On the day of the game, we travelled up to Wembley with the usual TV cameras on the bus. There was a helicopter overhead with another camera filming the progress of our bus. In those days, coverage of the final began about nine or ten o'clock in the morning for a three o'clock kick-off. It was a massive event and millions would watch on the TV at home and around the world. It is such a shame that the advent of the Premier League with all its money has led to clubs playing weakened teams in early rounds which has devalued the competition with the resultant knock-on effect of poorer attendances at some games.

The journey to the stadium seemed to take a long time. Lots of the boys were interviewed on the way by TV guys with the usual jokes, jibes and mickey-takes going on in the background and the occasional paper plane floating past. I either wasn't asked anything or I have forgotten, which is entirely possible. The journey up Wembley Way was memorable. We passed many fans, some waving good luck and shouting encouragement, some waving two fingers and giving us dog's abuse!

While the cup final itself was a new experience, I had already played at Wembley for Scotland. I've told people who have asked, that the only difference between the two occasions, cup final and Scotland international, is that at the end of the cup final the goalposts were still there! I've never particularly suffered with nerves before games and I was quite settled as we made our way into the dressing room and out onto the pitch for a look around.

I had the ability to blank out the occasion and the crowd. I could have been playing for the Bluebell at Moorside or Man City at Wembley and my game would have been the same. The only difference was that at the Moorside you could always hear what people were saying. I did have a word with some of the younger boys reminding them that because of the sheer size of the pitch that they would have to put a little bit extra on long passes to make them carry. We were a bit surprised with the state of the pitch. I think they must have had some event like the Horse of the Year Show on it as several bare patches had been covered with green sand.

For John Bond, the occasion was made even greater because we were playing a London team. As always, he especially wanted to come out on top whenever we played a team from the capital. For the players, we wanted to win it for ourselves and our families, for our club and for our fans, but also for John and the management and backroom team who were all respected and liked. Irene and my children were there, as were many family and friends from Scotland, although my mum was back in Fife watching on TV.

The preliminaries for the match seemed to take a long time and we were itching to get started. It was a relief when we got the word to line up in the tunnel alongside our opponents and begin the march from the shadows into the light and the noise of the stadium bowl. We still had the national anthem and shaking hands with dignitaries to get through but eventually we were able to break and warm up at the end where the City fans were congregated.

Tottenham had a very good team with some world-class players. The pick of them were the midfield pairing, Osvaldo Ardiles and Glenn Hoddle. Gerry Gow had been detailed to sit on Ardiles and we were supremely confident that, come 4.50pm, the cup would have blue ribbons on its handles. Both teams started the game well and made chances but we gradually got on top and started to dominate. It was only deserved when we took the lead in the 30th minute. The goal may have been expected; the scorer and the manner in which he scored were not!

The ball was worked out to the right and, when Kevin Reeves laid it back into the path of Ray Ranson, I knew a first-time cross was coming in. It's ironic that in all those crossing and shooting sessions we had on the training pitch, I was one of the ones doing the crossing. Now, as Ranson shaped to cross the ball, I found myself on the edge of the box. As all good strikers are taught, I ran across my marker. Looking back, I saw the ball arcing its way to me.

As it arrived, I dived and flicked it with my head intending to send it on to one of our forwards behind me at the far post. Instead, I caught it wrong. As I hit the floor, to my delight, I saw the ball rocket past Milija Aleksic's outstretched hand and into the top corner of the net. If you watch the replay of the goal, it looks like the ball went where I intended, but I am confessing now that this was not the case! Nevertheless, I was honoured to have scored in such a prestigious game. I found out later that it was the 150th goal to have been scored in a cup final.

I took a lot of good-natured stick in the dressing room at half-time with most of my team-mates wondering how a player like me had scored a goal like that. It is an understatement to say that I was not known for my aerial prowess. However, as the second half progressed, it seemed more and more likely that my head had done the trick and that silverware would be travelling north up the M1 and M6. Then tragedy! Gerry Gow had done a great job in stopping Ardiles but with ten minutes to go he brought him down on the edge of the box, giving Spurs a free kick in a very dangerous position.

Glenn Hoddle was a free-kick specialist and we had worked on what to do if they got a kick in this sort of area. We had toyed with the idea of putting a man on the post but had abandoned the idea as it would have brought the Spurs players right in front of our goal. We knew that Hoddle would aim for our near post. To ensure he did this, Joe Corrigan lined up our wall a man short on the near-post end, giving Hoddle a bigger target to aim at.

My starting position was on the far-post end of the wall, even though we were certain Hoddle wouldn't hit the ball that way. As soon as the whistle went and Spurs shaped to take the free kick, I was to leave my place, run around the back of the wall and fill the space deliberately left there. It all worked swimmingly except that I overdid my movement by half a metre. Instead of hitting me in the chest as it should have, the ball clipped my right shoulder and spun past the helpless Corrigan into the far corner.

I had scored for both teams in the Centenary Cup Final! I sunk to the floor, head in hands. Football can be a cruel game. It had taken me from the heights of scoring a goal that seemed likely to win us the FA Cup to the lows of putting one in past my own keeper to bring the other team level. I was walking on air one moment and walking the plank the next. Corrigan picked me up and I did my best to put what had just happened to one side.

We played out the last few minutes and extra time with no further goals, so it was that we would be going back to Wembley for a replay on the following Thursday. I had asked John Bond to bring me off in extra time as I was feeling the pelvic injury I carried and I was replaced by Tony Henry. Despite this, I was confident I would be fit for the replay. Both teams mounted the steps to the royal box and we all got to shake hands with the Queen Mother. Having met the Duke of Edinburgh previously, I now only have the Queen to meet to complete the set!

I got annoyed after the match when I passed Glenn Hoddle doing an interview and heard him saying how pleased he was to get the equaliser, his third consecutive goal at Wembley apparently. Well, I wasn't in the best of moods after what had happened and I told him in no uncertain terms that he hadn't scored. It wasn't that I wanted the goal to be given to me. I just felt that it was purely down to bad luck that we had conceded, not down to anything special he had done.

We were all feeling down in the dressing room. We felt we had done enough to win and had been much the better team. I'm sure Spurs were delighted and felt that they had got out of jail. My team-mates were fine with me and no one was pointing the finger saying I had cost us the game. Later on, when the hurt of the own goal had subsided a bit, I was able to pull the leg of the other players, telling them I had earned them a nice little bonus since we were paid extra for each FA Cup appearance, including the cup final replay!

It was only the second drawn final in FA Cup history. The previous one between Leeds and Chelsea had been replayed at Old Trafford. We felt having our game back at Wembley gave Spurs an unfair advantage. Our team would be in a hotel for another few days and the fans would have to travel again.

Our mood wasn't helped when we heard that the FA had released 20,000 tickets for open sale, but only in London. Most of these would be snapped up by Spurs fans. Indeed, on the evening of the replay, it was estimated that the London club had over 50,000 followers in the ground, a much bigger proportion of the crowd, with all the advantages this gave them.

We spent the time recovering from our exertions in the first match planning how we would win the second one. We did have a break when we were able to travel to Wembley again in the week. This time we were spectators as we watched England lose to a Zico goal for Brazil.

As we took the field for the replay, we were still very confident that we could beat Spurs. We had seen nothing in the first game that suggested we could not win. We were surprised when we saw that Ricky Villa, Ardiles's Argentine team-mate, was selected again. He had been brought off in the first match as he had been ineffective and we had expected him to be left out. For us, Dennis Tueart was sub in place of Tony Henry. Once again both teams started well and created chances. But we were shocked when after only eight minutes Villa scored from close range after an unlucky deflection from a great save by Corrigan.

We were still flying, however, and scored a wonderful equaliser from teenager Steve MacKenzie. I nodded a Spurs clearance into his path on the edge of the box and, with fantastic technique, he exploded a shot into the top corner. In any other game Steve's goal would have been praised from the rooftops. Because of what happened later, it has been unfairly overshadowed. In the second half, Dave Bennett was brought down in the box and Kevin Reeves put us ahead once again.

With 20 minutes left, Crooks equalised for Spurs, thereby setting up the scenario for one of the best-remembered FA Cup winners. In the 76th minute, Villa picked up the ball. He drove into our box, went past Tommy Caton, then Ranson, before beating Caton again and slotting past Corrigan. A great goal no doubt, but one we should have stopped. Ranson could have done better but was afraid of bringing Villa down. We had one or two half-chances but it wasn't to be. Our chance had gone and the cup was destined to stay in North London.

This was perhaps my last chance of a major trophy. I remember sitting in the Villa Park dressing room after our semi-final win and saying to Gerry Gow what a long old road I had been on to get to a final. I sensed that, for me, that road had come to an end. We were a dejected group of players. We were too raw to appreciate that we had been major contributors to two fabulous games of football. On the bus home the following day, as we headed north through London, I caught a glimpse of Wembley Stadium. I turned to Corrigan. 'Joe, I hope I never see that place again!' My wish was partly fulfilled. I had played my last game there.

We had a great spirit among the team and it was this that helped us get so close to glory. I think the closeness of the group was best summed up by Dragoslav Stepanovic, our Yugoslav defender. He had been out of the team and didn't get near to playing in either game. As our weary group of players slowly walked up the steps to our hotel for our post-match reception, Stepanovic stood at the top, spread out his hands and shouted, 'Boys, you are my heroes!' A lovely gesture that eased our hurt just a little! I have no regrets about anything and I don't think I could have done anything different. It was great to experience both the cup run and the two finals, the memories of which will stay with me always.

We were off on our travels at the end of the season. We played a tournament in Spain with Real Betis and Belgian team Beveren. The match against our Spanish hosts was anything but friendly. I was the victim of a shocking tackle by a Betis player that resulted in the hyperextension of my knee, leaving me with torn ligaments. As I lay on the ground in agony, all hell broke loose. Dennis Tueart was sent off for kicking a Spanish player and I think the only two City players not cautioned were me and our goalkeeper, Alex Williams.

Corrigan was incredulous that Williams hadn't joined the melee. 'Where were you?' he said to Alex after the match. 'I can't believe it. There's a riot going on and you never joined in to help your team-mates?' Alex was only a young boy so thought it best to stay where he was, in goal, but there's no doubt where Corrigan would have been had he been on the pitch!

One of our directors stood up to give the vote of thanks to our hosts at the dinner after the game. He obviously wasn't too pleased with the day's events or our host's overall arrangements for the tour. He stood up and was brief and to the point with his address, 'Thank you for the three-hour coach journey we had here from the airport and thank you for the reddies.' With that, he sat down! From Spain we flew to Canada for a game against Vancouver. The club kindly hired a car for me so I could pop over the border to see my friends in Seattle with Bobby McDonald keeping me company on the trip.

At nearly 34, I still felt I had a lot to offer. I had loved my first season at City and I loved working with John Bond. I had no thoughts of retirement. Indeed, the move had rekindled my ambition to carry on for as long as I could in English football. Although I had felt my chances of major trophies may have gone after our cup final defeat, our form in the first few months of season 1981/82 made me think again. It had me dreaming that perhaps I was on my way to a league title. With Bond in charge, I felt anything was possible!

Chapter 30

Top-Flight Farewell

THE PROMINENCE of the FA Cup back in 1981 is illustrated by the number of friendly games we were invited to play in pre-season and also throughout the league campaign. Even the losing FA Cup finalists were big box office. I was told that the club was charging at least £30,000 for each friendly that we appeared in. There were a huge 18 friendlies either before or during the 1981/82 campaign, almost half a season of friendly matches. In pre-season alone we played seven games in six different countries. We started in Devon, playing a match in Bideford to officially open the local club's new ground. We then made a ten-hour coach trip to Glasgow to play Rangers.

This was my one and only appearance at Ibrox, the home of the club I followed as a boy. It was a real thrill! My old mate Willie Johnston played for the Gers that day. It was less of a thrill for Dave Bennett, however, as he understandably became upset at the racial abuse he received from some of Rangers' less-enlightened supporters. This included being pelted with bananas when he went to take a corner. Racism may still be with us but thankfully such blatant behaviour is much rarer, in this country at least, and would now result in sanctions of some sort being applied. In those days nothing happened and players like Dave were just expected to get on with it.

Two days later we were in Germany and fortunately I didn't play, considering John Bond's reaction to the result. We were beaten 8-0. Tommy Booth and I were sat on the bench and would glance at the gaffer as the game went on, noting his near-apoplectic mood! We agreed that the team talk following the game wasn't going to be good! Seventy-two hours later, another country, Holland, another friendly, PSV. This time we managed a creditable draw in Eindhoven. Next up were two games in Iceland. The first of these was on a cinder pitch which, if you went to ground, cut your legs to ribbons. The next day we played an Icelandic national team. Six games in 13 days had certainly got the blood pumping.

Then we had a break of a week or so before our final pre-season game in Milan against AC. The night before our flight to Italy, David went over the handlebars of his bike, concussed himself, and was left with a few road chippings embedded in his forehead. I had to say goodbye to him while he was kept in the hospital overnight for observation, which was hard. We lost 1-0 in the Italian friendly and I chatted to my old Scotland colleague Joe Jordan after the game. Joe had just signed for AC Milan after moving from Man United. John Bond joined us and listened while Joe explained he was baffled as to why Milan had signed him. He played his usual game, made his usual runs, but the Italians didn't play the ball into him, they didn't put high crosses into the box. 'A'hm just runnin' doggies back and forth across the pitch waiting for the ball.'

Bond was really interested. 'Just stick it out for this year, Joe, and next summer I'll be in for you and I'll bring you to City.' As it happened, Joe stayed in Milan for two years and had another year afterwards playing for Verona. Either he got used to the Italian game or they discovered his footballing strengths. Whichever was true, he never made it back to Manchester. Over the coming season we played exhibition games in Norway, Ireland, France, Wales, Sweden and Kuwait, as well as several in England. An end-of-season tour took the club to Trinidad and two more games. By that stage, however, I was elsewhere having my own adventures in a foreign country.

We made several top-notch signings that summer which indicated that the club was going to have a real go this season. Trevor Francis, presumably fully recovered from his pummelling at the hands (or should I say the feet) of George Curtis, was a great signing. If I was picking a team of the best players that I played with, Francis would be in it. He was a wonderful player. Another good signing for us was Martin O'Neill who arrived from Norwich.

Martin didn't have the best of starts at City, perhaps down to the fact that none of his new team-mates had told him about one of Joe Corrigan's pet dislikes. Joe was a huge guy, six feet four inches, and had a massive frame. He could also have a massive temper. One thing sure to get him going was if he was chipped in training. He hated it. One pre-season day, we were practising shooting. We would lay the ball up to John Bond on the edge of the box and he would pass it short, left or right, for us to have a shot. O'Neill took his pass from Bond, saw Corrigan leave his line to narrow the angle and with the deftest of chips lifted the ball over Joe's head and into the net.

Martin made three mistakes. The first was the actual chip, the second was chuckling about his cheeky piece of skill in front of Joe, the third was walking past the keeper to retrieve his ball from the net. Still smiling as he passed Joe, he never saw the almighty elbow that the keeper landed on his torso. I'm sure Joe never meant any real harm but he ended Martin's training session, leaving him in great pain with what was later confirmed as two cracked ribs. Joe was no respecter of hierarchy and treated all who beat him with a chip in the same way. John Bond himself should have warned Martin not to do it as he himself had suffered the same treatment for the same crime against the keeper.

The only exception that Joe made to the no chipping rule was me. I explained to him that due to the delicate nature of my groin muscles, I couldn't hit the ball hard for fear of injury. He grudgingly accepted this but, even so, any ball that ended up in his net from a chip by me was unceremoniously booted to the other end of the training ground by a disgruntled Corrigan. A few minutes fetching my wayward ball was still a better deal than a dig in the ribs!

Joe was one of a number of big characters in the City dressing room. Tommy Booth was a funny boy with a dry sense of humour. Then there were pranksters such as Phil Boyer. Corrigan used to arrive at Maine Road for training each day on his bike. He would give it to Little Jimmy, the kit man, to lock away in his storeroom. Boyer watched this ritual every day and decided to have some fun. He got hold of Jimmy's key, let himself into the storeroom, let down the tyres on Corrigan's bike and took his pump. The next day before training, Corrigan stormed into the dressing room and wanted to know who tampered with his bike. He did not see the funny side of having had to cadge a lift home the previous day.

If the scene had been remade in cartoon form, Corrigan would have had steam coming out of his ears! Most of us didn't know who the culprit was and Boyer would have got away with it had he not piped up and tried to pass the blame off on someone else. Joe saw through his ruse, picked him up and dumped him fully clothed in the bath! I think the moral of the story was: if you play a trick on Big Joe, don't get caught!

Some people might have thought that with so many good players coming in – Asa Hartford and Kevin Bond (reunited with his dad) joined with Francis and O'Neill – that my place in the team might have been under threat. I was confident that this wasn't the case and that I would still be in the starting line-up. I did have a brief falling-out with John Bond; however, it was quickly sorted out. I got back from training one day and Irene showed me the back page of the *Evening News* which had an article stating that Bond was looking to get rid of the older squad players and have a younger team. Irene was obviously a bit concerned by this, as was I.

It shows how precarious the life of a footballer can be. You can go from being ten minutes away from being a cup-final hero to being surplus to requirements a few months later. I saw Bond the next day after training and told him that if I was to be shipped out, he could have told me before he told the press. I also told him of the worry the article had caused Irene. He apologised for what had been written, said that his words had been misconstrued and that they hadn't been about me at all. I was still in his plans and was going nowhere as far as he was concerned. I think he showed his class too. In the time it took me to get home, he had sent Irene a big bouquet to say sorry. Even better was the fact that he gave me a pay rise!

I was certainly in the team as we opened the new season with a win at home to West Brom. I scored a very satisfying goal that day, a training-ground routine that came good on matchday. There was a diagrammatic plan of the goal complete with arrows and cartoon players that appeared in the next edition of *Shoot!* magazine. It was my last league goal for City and my last ever in the First Division. Even though I say it myself, it was a good goal to go out on!

Trevor Francis came into the team for the first time, away at Stoke, and introduced himself nicely to our fans with two goals in a 3-1 win. Trevor was a pedigree player and it was a real treat for me to play with him. You'd see him lining himself up to shoot in a game and you'd be screaming at him inside your head, 'don't shoot from there', before watching him score a wonderful goal from an impossible position. He was a real flying machine. Whereas Kevin Reeves and I could be timed with an alarm clock on our sprints, Trevor was a real thoroughbred. He was quick of thought and quick with his feet too. The only downside to Trevor was that he was so injury-prone.

Things were going really well. We were looking like worthy candidates to challenge for the First Division title, confirmed by our Boxing Day win at Anfield. Liverpool were having a poor season by their standards but our record there was terrible. Apparently, City teams had regularly turned up with the expectation that, however well they played, a losing outcome was almost guaranteed. This game was different. True, we were helped by some questionable goalkeeping from Bruce Grobbelaar, but the fact was we thoroughly deserved our 3-1 win.

This result kept up our challenge at the top of the table and left Liverpool in mid-table. If you had told those present that one of those teams would be league champions, most people would have said the winning team would be Manchester City. As so often was to happen with the Liverpool team of that era, they confounded their critics and went on a storming run to end up champions. When they collected their title in May, I was no longer a City player.

We were still very much in the title race when we played Coventry at home in the fourth round of the FA Cup. If we had dreams of repeating the previous season's glorious run to the final, we were given a cruel awakening by the Sky Blues who deservedly beat us 3-1. The decisive goal, a Peter Bodak chip, would have left Joe Corrigan raging. We followed our cup exit with defeat, away at Southampton. Perhaps these two games showed the writing was on the wall for us as title contenders. I think they also show that even before I left, our fortunes had started to wane. The Southampton game was my last for City and would be my last in the First Division. Sad to end on a defeat, but there it is. The Coventry game had huge significance for me for other reasons.

There had been changes afoot at Highfield Road since I had left. Gordon Milne had been moved to general manager while Dave Sexton had been brought in to look after team affairs. Ron Wylie spoke to me on the day of the cup game and told me that he was leaving Coventry. He told me he had accepted a post to coach Bulova, a team in the thriving Hong Kong football league. He wanted me to come and play. He had cleared it with John Bond to speak to me, so everything was above board.

I had heard tales of players going to Hong Kong, not being paid properly and living in poor conditions. Ron assured me this wouldn't be the case. I trusted him. He had secured my successful move to the US and if Ron said things would be okay, I believed him. I spoke to John Bond and he said it was up to me. He told me that I had always done my best for him and that, knowing the salary figures that I could earn, he wouldn't stand in my way.

And so it was that in February of 1982 I found myself on a plane to Hong Kong sitting next to my friend and mentor Ron Wylie, setting out on what seemed to be a real adventure for me. There were certainly risks involved, and a degree of heartache too. I would be leaving Irene and the children behind for three months while I saw how the land lay for us as a family in Hong Kong. I was also signing on permanently with Bulova. Unlike my stint in the US, there was no English parent club to come back to this time. However, with everything that Ron had told me about our likely lifestyle in Hong Kong and with the wages quoted – which for the first time would give us as a family some financial security once my playing days were over – both Irene and I felt that it was a risk worth taking.

So it was with both excitement and a little bit of apprehension that I walked down the steps of the plane and into the heat. I was about to find out that life as a footballer in Hong Kong would never be dull!

Chapter 31

Mr Gentleman

THE PLAN was that I would spend three months out in Hong Kong on my own and then Irene and the children would join me for what would have been the final month of my contract. The Hong Kong season was already underway when I arrived so I would only be playing part of the season, still lucrative considering what I was being paid. I would then return to Seattle and play again for the Sounders, who had offered me a contract. I would be living in the Hong Kong Holiday Inn and the family would join me there. This wasn't a problem as it was a lovely place. As usual, things didn't always work out as we had planned.

We flew out to Hong Kong in February of 1982: me, Ron Wylie and Phil Boyer. Ron had been interested in signing Boyer, a Man City player, who like me was well into his 30s, and he had asked me what sort of character he was. Phil was a good, honest pro so Ron was happy to take him. Phil had also asked me about Ron and I had told him what to expect in terms of what you could get away with and what you couldn't get away with. One of the don'ts was making sure you didn't abuse your body with too much alcohol.

I was surprised then when Ron bought us a few drinks at the airport before our flight out. I was even more surprised when he did the same at the stopover in Dubai. I turned to Phil when Ron was at the bar and said to him that this wasn't the Ron Wylie I had known at Coventry. It was as though he had lived a life of strict discipline up to this point but was now loosening the shackles a bit. Once we were up and running at Bulova, however, Ron was completely professional again in everything he did.

We arrived in Hong Kong after our nine-hour flight and were surprised when Ron told us that we were going straight to training. I am normally up for training and would never usually object, but with jet lag and tight hamstrings from sitting down for nine hours, I had anticipated a few hours of rest at the Holiday Inn. Ron was adamant though. He told me in no uncertain terms not to mention my tight hamstrings to CP Wong, the club owner, who we would meet at Happy Valley, the training ground we were to use. CP wanted to see us train. He wanted to see what he had bought.

He had been stung before, spending big money in bringing former England international Charlie George to the club. It hadn't worked out well. George was mostly injured, sometimes with hamstring trouble, and had only made seven appearances. Ron was anxious that we got off to a good start with no mention of any ailments. We had the session and I experienced for the first time the humidity of Hong Kong. Within seconds of putting on our training kit, we were drenched in sweat. The session itself was fair enough. A bit of passing and shooting practice, then a five-a-side game to finish and get to know everyone there. As far as I could tell, CP Wong seemed satisfied with what he had purchased.

The training facilities weren't very good. Most of the teams had to hire places to train. We had to share the same stadium with the other clubs in the league, so there was no training there. Happy Valley training field was in the middle of the racetrack of the same name. We would train when we could, starting sessions at 8am to avoid the worst of the heat. If it wasn't available then we would use Kowloon Park. Here, there were a series of 30-odd concrete five-a-side pitches on a public space.

It wasn't uncommon to have to halt training as local people wandered through. I remember one time seeing an elderly lady carrying a bird in a cage, the bird sheltered from the sun by the umbrella that she carried in her other hand. She tiptoed across our space nodding and smiling to us as we waited for her to pass. Often our access to some of the pitches was restricted due to groups of people practising tai chi. It goes without saying that training on concrete wasn't great whatever space we had.

The other facilities we got to use, but only occasionally, were the pitches at Stanley Fort, a British military installation which Ron managed to get us into sometimes due to contacts he had. This was the only place we trained that had changing rooms and showers. We usually came to training in our kit and showered back at the hotel. The facilities may not have been great but the sessions that Ron put on were always enjoyable and worthwhile.

Our squad was a mixture of European players and local lads. Other teams in the league varied. One club went for only Brazilian players, another only Dutch. South China FC would only play local boys. Hong Kong Rangers had a recruitment policy closer to my heart. The only foreign players they would recruit were Scots, never any English, because they felt us Celts showed more courage and appetite for work than our Anglo-Saxon cousins!

Because Ron Wylie had recently worked at Coventry, he recruited players from there who he knew and trusted. As well as myself, my close mate Barry Powell arrived, as did a young youth player from Coventry, Clive Haywood. Ron was keen to add some bite to the team, so when he received a call from Alan Dugdale, an ex-Coventry centre-half who had been playing in the US, he was interested. Recent photos showed that Duggy had put on a bit of weight so Wiley asked him, 'Will I be getting the Duggy I used to know or the present bigger version?' Dugdale assured him he would be slim and trim by the time he played, so he came on board too. Peter Foley from Oxford was another English signing.

I had a new room-mate at the Holiday Inn after a while. This was Don Masson, a fellow Scottish international, although his caps came after mine. We shared the dubious honour of both having missed a penalty for our country. His was arguably more catastrophic than mine as it came against Peru in the 1978 World Cup. He got off to a bad start with Ron. We met up with him for the first time in the hotel bar for a chat. He told Ron that at Notts County and Minnesota, his last two clubs, he had taken the training as well as playing. He hoped he would be able to do the same at Bulova. Ron was someone who prided himself on his coaching and on the standard he set at his clubs.

There was no way he was going to relinquish any of his duties, but he said to Don, 'Nae bother, son. Ah'll be able to have a wee rest then with you around.' Don obviously was immune to the sarcasm in Ron's reply and he outlined his plans for training. When he disappeared to the toilet, Ron says to me, 'Tommy, when you get back tae your room tonight, put this guy right and how things work oot here, okay? Cos if you don't, Ah'll be giving him a ticket home.' He didn't like it when I told him that night, but I put him right and Ron continued doing the coaching!

On the pitch, Masson found things tough in Hong Kong. He had a reputation for being a midfield lynchpin in his teams, someone who could spray the ball around the pitch with pinpoint accuracy. On the face of it, he was an ideal addition to our team, as in the heat it wasn't possible to run with the ball all of the time, it was a passing player's game. He should have been more suited to the conditions than a player like me. However, out of possession, Don was a liability. He either wouldn't or couldn't do the work necessary to close down the opposition. We were almost playing a man short in these situations.

We had two local lads who would help out behind the scenes with the kit and any other tasks needed. Neither of them were particularly athletic and one of them was quite overweight. They would help the team warm up, however, taking part in the circular, quick-passing piggy-in-the-middle exercises. It was embarrassing for Masson that even with these two lads in the circle, when he was 'piggy' he could never get the ball.

He didn't seem to read people very well in social situations either. Not only had he missed Ron's sarcasm but he didn't see the genuine annoyance he was causing Alan Dugdale when we were having a drink together in the hotel bar. He would do silly things like flick an ear then look away pretending it wasn't him. After an evening of tricks like this and after a few drinks, Duggy had had enough. He was from Kirkby in Liverpool and, like a lot of lads from that city, he had a tough upbringing. You only had to look at Dugdale to know that he was a guy that it was probably best not to mess with. He had a craggy, hard face in the Tommy Smith mould that should have warned anyone not to mess with him.

Masson was obviously oblivious to this. Dugdale said to him, 'Which window do you prefer?' Don looked at him quizzically. 'What do you mean?' 'I'm asking you which window you want me to put you through if you don't stop annoying me,' replied Alan. That was my cue to leave. I said my goodbyes, leaving the two of them to it, and went off up to my bed. During the night, I got up to use the toilet and picked up the towel after washing my hands. I had dried myself when I noticed the towel was covered in blood. I thought I had unknowingly cut my hands somehow, but I wasn't bleeding at all. I washed my hands again and, after thinking of the previous evening, had a good idea as to what might have happened. When Don emerged from his bed in the morning, my suspicions were confirmed. His nose was a mess, bloodied and spread across his face. Don had obviously not heeded the warnings he was given!

One of the quirks of playing in Hong Kong was that we were paid in cash. We would collect our wages from the secretary and deposit it in the safe when we were back at the hotel. Phil Boyer became a bit concerned, developing a bit of paranoia. 'Hutch,' he said after a few weeks out there, 'you can't be sure who's watching us when we collect our money.' Due to his worries, we started to vary our times and our routes on payday. He was probably right to be careful, but I have to say that Hong Kong was perhaps the safest place that I ever lived. I never had any concerns about Irene and the kids being out and about. Hong Kong was a very law-abiding and kindly society.

The stadium situation was a bit odd in that there was only one main place to play, the national stadium. The pitch wasn't great and the playing surface seemed to be made up of green weeds rather than grass. Every team played their matches there, so the surface suffered. One stadium also meant that games were much more infrequent in Hong Kong. We might play a game and then have a two-week break before the next match.

The only team in Hong Kong that had a fan base was South China, the all-ethnic Chinese club. They would have about 10,000 partisan followers at each of their games. Every other team were watched by generally unattached fans who just wanted to watch a good game. Because of this, attendances varied widely.

A match between two of the lower teams might only attract a few hundred people while a game between ourselves and Seiko, our main rivals at the top of the league, could see attendances of 25,000-plus. The stadium was cut into the side of the mountain and was quite a spectacular place to play. I remember my first game there, a night match against South China, looking up in the darkness at the sheer side of the mountain, seeing what appeared to be the red light on the underbelly of a plane very close to the face of the mountain. It was only after staring for a few moments that I realised it was a bus on a road cut high up on the mountainside.

Once you saw the stadium in daylight, it wasn't an impressive sight. All the stands were wooden affairs and the whole place looked worn, tired and old. Catering within the stands could be a little unusual by UK standards too.

I went to watch a game with Irene on one occasion and we sat behind the goal. There were vendors with baskets moving up and down the aisles selling small bags of food. We assumed they were a variety of nut, perhaps peanuts. Loads of people were buying these little bags and getting stuck in so we assumed it must be good grub. The people in the row behind bought a bag and soon all we could hear was a biting sound followed by a spit and the sound of chewing. We carefully turned our heads trying to see what was going on without making it too obvious. Well, Irene's face was a picture when we saw what the delicacy was. The bags contained cooked chicken feet. To eat them you had to bite out and spit away the claw, which left you with the skin and tendon to eat. Funnily enough, I couldn't persuade Irene to try a bag!

There was a smaller stadium at Mong Kok which was used infrequently, only if the main stadium had been booked out to another event. I only ever played in this stadium once. Once was enough. Facilities there were very poor. The changing rooms were tiny, not big enough to fit the whole team in. I had noticed that the local boys would always give way to the European players. Even in the national stadium, they would change in a group on their own away from the Europeans.

I had never experienced this before and didn't like it. As far as I was concerned we were a team with no superstars and no whipping boys. Getting changed for the game at Mong Kok, I noticed the Chinese lads had started to strip off in the toilets, hanging their clothes on handles or on cubical doors, presumably to leave the limited space in the main room to the foreign players. I decided to join them in the toilets and hung my clothes in the same fashion.

This began a trend. When we were back in the main stadium, the other European boys made sure they got changed in among the Chinese lads too. The rationale was simple: if we were to be a team on the pitch, we had to behave like one off it. Each week, the club arranged for a night when all the team and backroom staff would come together for a meal. One week it might be at the Holiday Inn, the following week it would be at an authentic Chinese restaurant. It worked wonders for morale.

It did take me a while to get an understanding of the psyche of my Hong Kong team-mates. They certainly seemed to have an inferiority complex when it came to playing and training alongside their foreign colleagues. This I could not understand. I could see that they were good players, many of whom could have played professionally in the European leagues. If they were taken out of their comfort zone and asked to try something new and they didn't immediately succeed, they would down tools and be unwilling to try again. After witnessing this a few times, I lost patience and had a go at a few of them. My tirade was met with stony silence and even stonier looks.

After training that day, Tony Tse, the general manager, took me aside for a chat. He told me that in Chinese society, not losing face with your peers was a huge thing. Getting something wrong and making a mistake in public was humiliating and would result in others laughing at you. He used the example of few local players wanting to be strikers because misplacing a shot too often – something accepted in our culture – would result in the losing of face. He felt it was natural for his countrymen to feel less valued than their overseas team-mates when the former had arrived to pick up big salaries, far greater than they were getting. He told me that if I wanted to change things I should go easy with them and use the carrot, not the stick.

In future I bit my tongue when it came to criticism and praised my team-mates whenever I could. By the end of my stay with Bulova, our team ethic was excellent and there was no sign of the us-and-them attitude I saw when I arrived. I think trust developed within the team, helping our local players overcome their fear of failure.

Tony Tse was the Mr Fix-It at our club. If there was anything that you needed, anything that had to be sorted, he was the man to go to. He was a former journalist who CP Wong entrusted with the day-to-day running of the club. He was the man who had been tasked with finding the right coach for the team and it was he who did the research and eventually found Ron Wylie. Ron was a disciplinarian and Tony loved the way that he worked. He demanded the absolute best of everyone that he worked with, a trait that Tony very much appreciated.

Tony told me that they had got me in to show a professional attitude, not only to the local players, but also to the foreign signings. Too many times a high-profile foreign player had arrived with a big reputation only to disappoint as they treated their stay as a holiday and didn't put in the effort required. Ron Wiley knew me well from our Coventry days and had convinced the club owner and Tony Tse that I would always give of my best, in training and in games, and that I would set the tone for the club.

Our family had help settling in and finding our way around Hong Kong from a chap called Walter Gerrard. Walter was a Glaswegian who had played lower-league football in Scotland before finding his way to Asia. He was among the first foreign players to play in the leagues over there and had played for Hong Kong Rangers, Seiko and Caroline Hill. The famous Brazilian team, Santos, played a friendly against Caroline

Hill and Walter found himself in opposition to the great Pelé. Late in the second half, just by coincidence, both teams made a substitution with Pelé and Walter being taken off. As they were walking to the dugouts, Walter put his arm around the Brazilian and said, 'Pelé, these coaches son, they don't know a good footballer when they see one!'

Walter was certainly no Pelé but he must have made a good impression on the Chinese fans as he was given a nickname. Due to his size and barnstorming play, he was christened 'Water Buffalo'. When he finished with football, he stayed in Hong Kong for the rest of his life, marrying a local girl and becoming a very successful businessman, mainly in the wines and spirits industry, but with fingers in other pies too.

He also had an interest in the Nike sportswear company. He asked me if I could help him by promoting the Nike brand. He provided me and all the family with Nike sportswear and asked us to wear it when we were out and about. As a foreign footballer I had quite a high profile and was always being photographed. If I was wearing Nike gear, so much the better for Walter. I was the subject of a documentary for Chinese TV and they filmed me and the family going about our business, at training, playing football with my kids in the park, in a restaurant where the children tried Chinese food for the first time. In every scene, we were living adverts for Nike. Walter's bosses were delighted and we had an endless supply of sports clothes.

Ron had got to know Walter well after moving to Hong Kong. He was a valuable person to have as a friend as he seemed to have contacts with everyone and solutions to any problems. If Tony Tse wasn't able to resolve any particular situation, Walter was the next port of call. We were a bit concerned about lack of play facilities for our kids so Walter arranged for us to become members of the prestigious Kowloon Cricket Club. This was a posh institution with membership costing up to £20,000 each year. Our membership, courtesy of Walter, was free. At the club, you could play tennis, go for a swim or have a meal. Membership extended to all the family so Irene and the children were able to use the facilities.

Walter also arranged an annual friendly football match between expat Scots and another group of nationals, say the Dutch or the Germans. This took place at the Hong Kong football club, an institution with a clubhouse and a stadium but no team. Various friendlies would take place there. For Walter's game, the Bulova Scottish contingent went along and were treated well. We received a huge bottle of whisky and a commemorative plaque. The only Scot from our group who didn't take part was Don Masson, who said that he didn't take part in 'silly games'. It was a shame as money raised went to charity. Walter is well remembered for his charitable work, particularly on behalf of the Hong Kong Society for the Protection of Children.

The language barrier could potentially have been a difficulty when moving to a country overseas. For me to try and learn Cantonese would have been impossible. I find it difficult enough making myself understood when speaking English! Fortunately, most of the players, even those native to Hong Kong, spoke very good English. Still, Ron Wiley was taking no chances of misunderstandings on tactics and team plan and he asked Cheung Chi Doy to act as interpreter. Cheung was the first Hong Kong player to play in a top European league when he joined Blackpool in the First Division, so his English was spot on.

Ron would say the first sentence of his team talk, perhaps 'Right boys, let's keep things tight for the first few minutes.' He'd then turn to Cheung for him to repeat in Cantonese. Switching English football terms to Cantonese must have been a very involved process because Cheung would go on and on, eventually finishing and looking at Ron for the next instruction. 'It's very warm today boys, so let's make the ball do the work, lots o' crisp passing, make this lot run their legs off.' Ron would then turn to Cheung who went off again in Cantonese. Much to Ron's obvious frustration and to the amusement of the European players, Cheung's explanation would take on epic proportions, and leave Wiley asking him, 'Are you sure Ah said all that?'

At all the clubs I had been at, before playing for Bulova, the players were expected to turn up on matchdays wearing a suit. It had become a part of my working life. Not surprisingly, in Hong Kong all the players arrived at the ground on matchdays in T-shirts and shorts, by far the most sensible form of dress for the heat and humidity of the country. For my first few games out there, I went along and dressed the same as everyone else. However, something was missing. It just didn't feel right going in to do my job dressed in that way. It was like being a painter and decorator but not wearing my regulation pair of white dungarees.

I said to Irene that it didn't feel right, so, I started to wear a shirt and tie to games (even I thought wearing a suit jacket would be too much in that heat). I took a spare shirt with me to wear after the game as the one I arrived in would be soaking in sweat as I changed out of it. I now felt much better prepared for the game ahead. The local players took note of my sartorial change and I found out a little later that they had started to call me 'Mr Gentleman' in honour of my matchday dress. It wasn't the only nickname that I received in Hong Kong. I was also called 'Zhang tui Zhameng' which translates as 'Long Legged Grasshopper'! In Chinese culture, apparently, it is an honour and a measure of acceptance to be given a nickname. I viewed the two that I had been given as a compliment.

I got to know the owner of Bulova, CP Wong, quite well. He was always at games and would often have a chat with the players. He was extremely wealthy. When I was in Hong Kong it was rumoured that he was trying to buy Pan Am Airways. On one occasion, Doug Ellis, the chairman and owner of Aston Villa, was staying at the Holiday Inn. Villa had been one of Ron Wylie's clubs and the two were good friends. Ellis had been to watch us train and play. Ron introduced him to CP Wong and after chatting for a while CP said he would like to buy Villa from Ellis. Doug insisted that Villa wasn't for sale. CP handed over his cheque book to him and told him that whatever figure he wrote on the cheque, CP would meet it in order to buy the club. No sale went through and the passing over of the cheque book may seem like an act of bravado, but it was typical of our owner's attitude to money. He certainly had a lot of it to spend.

Originally CP had been the owner of Bulova's great rivals, Seiko FC. He become bored with football for a while and had given that club to his brother. After a while his appetite for the game returned and he took charge of Bulova. It was CP's money that had enabled Tony Tse and Ron Wiley to bring in European players such as myself. He had a very hands-on approach to the running of the club and I am sure there were times when Ron Wiley had to bite his tongue when it came to being advised on football matters. At the start of every game, CP would stroll onto the pitch and gather the team around him in a huddle.

All the European players joined in but as he spoke in Cantonese, we hadn't a clue what he was saying. The local boys seemed to hang on his every word, however, and would cheer and clap after he had finished. They would run over to the section of the crowd where their families were sat and shout something up to them, resulting in more cheering and clapping from the crowd. After being part of the pantomime a couple of times, I asked one of our Chinese players what was going on. He told me that when CP formed the huddle, he was telling the Chinese players what their win bonus would be for this particular match. They would rush over to their wives and families and give them the good news! I would often ask my team-mates, 'So what are you on today boys?' just to make them smile.

As a family, we enjoyed living in a completely different culture, a different way of life. We loved exploring the markets. In Stanley Market you would often find very cheap sportswear. When I first arrived in Hong Kong, my laundry was taken away and I would be reimbursed by the club. Looking at the prices of shirts and other gear in the market, I realised it was cheaper to buy new stuff than to pay for my dirty clothes to be washed!

The stuff sold was copies of major brands but the quality of the items was top notch; you would be hard-pressed to tell the difference between the real stuff and the counterfeit. On a couple of occasions, I was looking at items for sale when I was quickly ushered away from the stall, covers were thrown over the goods and the venders quickly disappeared. Policemen had been spotted wandering through the market and business was suspended!

In Mong Kok there was an exotic market selling all sorts of things. It was within a long goal kick of the airport and it felt as though you could almost reach above your head and touch the Pan Ams as they came in to land. All sorts of unusual (to European eyes at least) livestock was bought and sold. One day we were there with the children walking through the hustle and bustle when John suddenly yelped and started rubbing at a small cut on his arm. I looked around and saw a Chinese lady disappearing into the crowd. She had a pushchair to which was tied a plastic bag. A live chicken had pecked a hole in the bag and its head was protruding. As she strolled along, the angry chicken was taking its revenge on the human race, pecking anyone within range!

At least for the chicken, its fate was delayed. Other creatures there were dispatched on the spot. If you fancied a bit of frog or snake for tea, you could select your victim from a tank. They were hauled out, killed, skinned, chopped, weighed and bagged within seconds. I don't think you could have had fresher meat. While the meat on sale there did not appeal to us, the fruit and vegetables certainly did. The produce was fresh and of excellent quality. We would go down there once or twice a week to stock up on provisions.

At another shop, Irene and I were taken by the beauty of some of the furniture we saw, so much so that one day we decided to take the plunge and buy several pieces. We went into the store and the salesman showed off a handmade rosewood dining table and chairs that we had asked about. To demonstrate its inflammability, he took out a lighter and held it to one of the spars on a chair. 'See,' he said proudly, 'impossible to burn this furniture.'

We had the furniture we had bought shipped back to the UK when we left Hong Kong. Despite the hefty cost, we still felt we had a bargain. We kept it all until I finally retired from my football development job and Irene and I returned to live in Fife. The house we have now was too small for our Hong Kong fittings so we passed it on to our son David. Forty years on from Hong Kong, our tables, chairs and cabinet are still going strong. David has added other Chinese furnishings to go with our original stuff. Furniture made to last!

One of the few things we had to pay for in Hong Kong was for our children to go to school since education over there was through private providers. Our kids were happy and we thought that the standard of education in the schools was excellent. In the summer months they had to arrive at school for an 8am start. They would finish in the early afternoon before the real heat of the day. They would come back home, where I had joined Irene after training, to sit with us by the pool. We would maybe have a barbecue for lunch and spend the afternoon together. As a family, it was an idyllic time.

We may have had to pay for schooling, but healthcare was provided by the club. However, I still found it a bit surprising that there was no in-house medical team at Bulova. That said, any injuries we picked up would be treated at local clinics or hospitals. Simple niggles such as the odd muscle strain we would try to treat ourselves through time spent in saunas. One technique that I was told about that helped to loosen my often-tight hamstrings was to take a block of ice into the sauna and sit on it until it had completely melted. The contrast between the extremes of hot and cold seemed to help.

On the football front, things could not have gone any better. The season was six months old when I arrived and we were unbeaten in all of our remaining games. We came second to Seiko in the league, missing out by a point, but we won the Hong Kong FA Cup and the Viceroy Cup, both prestigious trophies. Getting to the final of the Viceroy Cup caused another dilemma for me with regards to Seattle Sounders. Days after we had played and won our semi-final, I was due to leave Hong Kong and fly to the US where I would sign for the Sounders on a permanent basis. When CP Wong found out I was going to miss the final, he was adamant that I was to stay with Bulova, not only for the final but for the following season too. The financial offer he made changed our minds. I signed on for another year in Hong Kong and played in the final as we beat Eastern 2-1 after extra time.

After I signed on for the extra year, we moved into an apartment block in Mong Kok. The apartments themselves, four on each level, were lovely and cost about £2m each. The whole block was owned by CP Wong. As we lived on the 14th floor with a good few levels above us to the top, you can see what a wealthy man CP was. However, although lovely, the apartment wasn't suitable for a family with young children as there was nowhere for them to play.

I had a word with Tony Tse and he arranged for us to be moved to another apartment block, New World Buildings, on Kowloon Bay overlooking the harbour. The apartment block was again very expensive, with each apartment costing £4,000 a month to rent in 1980s prices. Luckily for us, the club paid our rent! It was built above one of the biggest shopping centres in the world, a huge indoor mall where you could buy anything you could think of and, being Hong Kong, lots of things you would never think of. It's an indication of how safe we felt there that we had no worries about the children going down to the shops in the lift and mooching about in the centre or buying themselves a bag of sweets.

My second Bulova season almost exactly mirrored the first in terms of league and cups. Again we lost to Seiko in the league, this time on goal difference, but again we won the two cup competitions. My salary was heavily based on incentives. If we won, I received a substantial bonus. Our good form helped the family from a financial point of view. That second season saw us lose the only competitive game that I can remember getting beaten in during my Hong Kong stay, to Seiko in the second game. The loss caused CP to panic and he insisted we get away for some intensive training. We would also play a friendly match which would bring us back to winning ways.

We flew off to South Korea to play Hallelujah FC in Seoul, a club we were told was formed based on Christian principles with all the players being committed Christians. Before the game, all the Korean players went into a huddle and prayed together. Unfortunately for us, their Christian ideals went on the backburner once the whistle blew and they proceeded to kick lumps out of us, running out winners too. CP's master plan seemed to have backfired, but he need not have worried, as the rest of the season went swimmingly.

I got on well with CP but I was a bit concerned about his involvement with the team when I first arrived. We were in the changing room before a match when he came in and told me what he wanted me to do during the game. I was tempted to tell him where to go, but I glanced at Ron and he gave a little shake of his head, so I said nothing. When CP had gone, Ron told me to just let him play the president, listen and nod if he gave me advice and carry on with our game plan and ignore him. The second time he came into the dressing room and spoke to me, I wasn't given advice, I was given an order, but on that occasion, I was more than happy to comply.

We were at the national stadium playing against Eastern in a cup semi-final. The sun was beating down on the field with the temperatures in the high 30s. During the first half I had played in the shade of the stand, which at least kept me out of the sun. I knew I would feel its full force in the second half. CP came to talk to us and to urge us on to give every effort in the second half. As he was leaving, he turned to me and said, 'Hutchie, this half, you play on the right, you stay in the shade.' He then turned to our right-sided midfielder, Clive Haywood, pointed at him and said, 'You, Haywood, you're young. You play on the left and stay in the sun.' I said to Clive as we went out for the second half, 'You can't argue with the boss. He knows his stuff!' So, I happily stayed in the shade leaving Clive to fry!

The heat was a factor out there. On a day-to-day basis I didn't mind it, in fact I quite enjoyed it. In games you could only ever play in bursts. There was no way that you could run for 90 minutes. The objective was to keep possession, keep the ball moving and make your opponents chase. I felt John Bond's advice, to get my head up more to pass rather than always running with the ball, stood me in good stead in Hong Kong. In fact, Ron would sometimes say to me 'Passing game today, Hutch, limit your running.'

Even at 35 or 36, my body was holding up well and I never felt at a disadvantage to my younger opponents or team-mates. All the feedback I got about my performances was very positive. I played well out there.

I suppose confirmation came in the invitations that I had to play in representative games and to guest for other clubs in friendlies. I played three games for the Hong Kong FA so you could say I am a Hong Kong international!

Guesting for other clubs was very lucrative. Each team in the league was allowed to play one high-profile friendly each season in order to raise funds. I played in several, including one for Hong Kong Rangers against Celtic. CP had to give permission for me to play in these games and he insisted they paid me. Playing against Celtic, I earned £1,000. You can see why my 18 months in Hong Kong were the best paid of my career.

Ron Wylie had returned to the UK at the end of my first season with Bulova, a bit of a blow as I really enjoyed working with him despite him being a hard taskmaster. With Ron, there was virtually no carrot, only a big stick. He simply expected everybody to have the same professional pride as he did and to work for their rewards. This approach was fine with me. I think Ron must have had a big say in his replacement as our new coach at Bulova was an old playing colleague of his from Birmingham City. Geoff Vowden was also very professional in his outlook and expectations, although I think the carrot-to-stick ratio was more balanced with Geoff. I got along fine with him. His softer approach wasn't any less demanding and things carried on much as they had before.

At the end of our time in Hong Kong, Irene and the children had to travel back to the UK without me because Ron Atkinson, the Manchester United manager, asked me to play some exhibition matches for them on their tour of Australia with Frank Worthington and Peter Barnes. They were short of some of their players due to the last-ever Home Internationals taking place. I played against Forest, Juventus and the Australia national team. Mark Hughes, who I would later work with in Wales, was breaking into the team and it was obvious what a good player he would become.

My final game for Bulova was our second Viceroy Cup victory, a lovely way to finish my time with the club. At the end of my contract, I had decided that I would return to the UK and back to the football league. I had two firm offers on the table, both from historically successful, well-established clubs. One was in the First Division, one in the Third, but both were managed by men I had worked with before and who I liked and respected. Who should I choose?

Chapter 32

It's Raining Again

WHEN I returned to the UK in the summer of 1983, I was approaching my 36th birthday. During my time playing in the English football league, I had played only two seasons outside the top flight and had never played below Division Two, the second tier. Even now, in my advanced footballing years, I had the chance to continue to play in the top division. Ron Wylie, my friend, mentor and manager at Bulova, had taken over as boss of West Bromwich Albion and offered me a contract. It seemed a perfect move. The owner of Bulova, CP Wong, had warned me that if I did not sign for Ron at WBA, he would hold on to my signature meaning that I couldn't play anywhere. He was only half joking.

The problem I had was that there was another offer on the table, from John Bond. He had left Manchester City during my time in Hong Kong and was now the manager of Burnley. Although never one of the glamour clubs, Burnley had a fine historic reputation and had been league champions as recently as the 1960s. Now they had fallen on hard times and had just been relegated to the Third Division.

On the face of it, First Division versus Third Division, it should have been no contest. The difficulty was my loyalty to Bond. I had enjoyed working for him more than any other manager. He had let me go to Hong Kong when I was still under contract at Man City and still in the team every week because he knew the financial rewards the move would bring for my family. He had also said that when I returned, he would have a place for me at whichever club he was at. And so it was that I turned down Ron Wylie's offer, one that would have given me a considerably higher wage, and signed for Burnley.

The appointment of Bond was a departure from the norm for Burnley. In the past they had employed managers who had a historic link to the club as a player or coach. To take someone as high profile as John, someone who was regularly in the national media, was something new. Bond was enthusiastic and full of confidence when I arrived. He felt that this was a club with bags of potential and he could restore it to its former glories. Certainly, I was impressed by the infrastructure.

Turf Moor was a good, traditional stadium and the training ground was a huge and well-cared-for complex on a par with Coventry and much better than what had been available at Maine Road. It looked as if the estate that the training ground was built on had once been something akin to Downton Abbey. There was a huge mansion-like building that stood next to the training pitches.

Halfway through the first season, before a game against Oxford in the cup, I was interviewed on the TV by Ian St John, the former Liverpool player turned TV presenter, a lovely, funny chap. I stood with my back to the mansion as he talked to me. As the interview ended, he wished me all the best for the game. I thanked him, nodded over my shoulder at the big house and said, 'Right-o. I suppose I'd better go and see if the wife's back from the shop yet. They've done really well with the club houses here.' He had a laugh at that and they got me to do it again so they could tag it on the end of the interview.

Bond's recruitment was based on bringing in tried-and-trusted faces. Arriving were Gerry Gow, Kevin Reeves, Willie Donachie, later Denis Tueart and Steve Daley, all with Bond at Man City, and goalkeeper Roger Hansbury who he had at Norwich. John Benson would again be Bond's assistant.

Steve Daley had been at Man City when I arrived there. He had been signed by Malcolm Allison for a colossal fee and given a nine-year contract. He was being paid a huge weekly wage for the time. John Bond spoke to me about Steve, saying that he needed to get him off the Man City books. As a player, he hadn't justified either the fee or his wages and his salary was drowning the club. By coincidence, Seattle had shown interest in signing Steve. Bond wanted me to convince him it would be a good move.

That wasn't a problem. I could speak with honesty and conviction as I loved my time there. I must have done a good job as Steve signed for the Sounders for £300,000, a fraction of what he had cost Man City.

However, Bond had nothing against Steve as a player (although I don't think he saw in him what Allison had), hence he was happy to have him at Burnley.

I am sure many Burnley fans wondered what Bond was up to when he signed me. Many were probably suspicious of a soon-to-be 36-year-old signing for their club. Some would have thought that I had come for a last payday. They didn't know that was not the way I operated. I think by the end of my stay they knew that I cared about the way I played and my contribution to the team.

I didn't get off to the best of starts at the club when Bond handed me my contract. It showed the trust I had in him that I initially signed a blank contract, leaving him to fill in the details. I was dismayed to find that I had been given only two years, not the three that John had promised. When I saw him about it, he apologised and said that the chairman, because of my age, would not be moved on the two years. He did point out, however, that I now had a signing-on fee, something not in our verbal agreement. I was happy enough with that.

Burnley fans, waiting to see what the new, big-name manager would do for their club, were not impressed to say the least when I was handed the captaincy of the club in place of fan-favourite and club-legend Martin Dobson. Martin was a Lancashire boy who had played over 400 times for Burnley in two spells. He was an ex-England international, a cultured midfielder and someone who attracted a record transfer fee when he ended his first spell at Turf Moor to move to Everton.

There were rumblings and grumblings aired by and in the local paper, but Bond's decision was fine by me. I had been captain at Coventry and I was always a vocal player, so it wouldn't affect the way that I played. I never knew why Bond made that decision. He may have felt that things had been too cosy and he wanted to shake things up and put his stamp on the place. I know that he wasn't impressed by a newspaper article that Dobson had written where he said that winning trophies was not his goal. He was happy to go training, do his best on a Saturday and go back to his family. For Bond, this was the wrong attitude. He wanted his players to want to be winners. All of this made no difference to the Burnley public.

The first time that they could publicly show their disapproval, they did. The supporters weren't in the best of moods when, in what was hoped to be a promotion season, we started with a 4-1 defeat at Hull. The dressing rooms and tunnel at Turf Moor were in the stand

The moment I thought that I may have scored the winner in the FA Cup Final for Manchester City. Celebrating with my two Scottish mates Bobby MacDonald and Gerry Gow.

It looks like I am about to stamp on Garth Crooks. Perhaps that's what the ref Keith Hackett thought too. In fact, I was just letting Garth know that I felt he had dived and I wasn't too pleased about it!

John Bond and I at an awards ceremony in Manchester. I was voted the North-West Sports Personality of the Year for 1981.

Winning the Viceroy Cup, the most prestigious trophy in Hong Kong football, with Bulova. Tony Tse is back row third from the right.

It was at Burnley, well into my thirties, that I felt physically, I was at my strongest.

Even playing for Swansea I couldn't get away from sky blue kits. We were in our change strip for this game at Northampton when I was 40.

Welcome to the Vauxhall Conference. The tackles were still hard to take playing for Merthyr.

At the PFA Awards where I was presented with my Order of Merit award by Sir Alex Ferguson.

Myself and David at John's Passing Out Parade for the RAF. David is strategically placed on the kerb to make himself bigger.

I have enjoyed going back to Coventry for Legends' Days organised by the former players' association.

TOMMY HUTCHIS

Myself and daughter Lynn at the Legends' Wall.

You can't beat fish and chips at a family get-together. David, daughter-in-law Julie, Thomas and Olivia tuck in with Irene and me.

Irene and I at Lynn's wedding. Our kids are really fond of this one.

behind the goal. As managers, staff and subs emerged into the light, they had to walk half the pitch to get to the dugouts below the Main Stand. Considering this was Bond's competitive debut as manager of the club at home, I would have expected that a little leeway would have been given, but it seemed the fans had made up their minds based on the treatment of Dobson, not helped by our opening-day thrashing, and Bond was roundly booed as he made his way from tunnel to dugout.

It set the tone for this season and for my two-year stay at Burnley. I loved the Lancashire people during my time at Blackpool and Manchester City. The Burnley public came from the same strong, working-class type of background as my former clubs. The difference here was the feeling of anger and disappointment that seemed to hang over the town. To be fair to the Burnley fans, they did have a lot to be angry and disappointed about. Sadly, things were to get much worse. Thinking back on those days, it always seemed to rain in Burnley. Certainly there weren't many sunny days on the pitch.

As always, John Bond's emphasis was on attack. He wanted to win but he wanted to win in the right way. Although we weren't pulling up any trees in terms of a consistent run of winning results, we were playing good football and goals were arriving in good numbers. That first home game for example, despite the catcalls that greeted Bond, we struck five goals past Bournemouth. In November we hit seven against Port Vale. We also had big wins against Lincoln, Exeter, Scunthorpe and Wimbledon. Kevin Reeves and I had an excellent understanding of each other's games built on our time in Manchester and it continued at Burnley. I knew where and when his movement would take place, he knew that when he made his run, I would find him. We combined well for a lot of our goals.

Considering the players we had, it is not surprising that during the first part of that season we were challenging, if not for automatic promotion, then for a place in the play-offs. As well as the contingent from Manchester, we had Irish international Billy Hamilton up front and a good defensive combination of Mike Phelan (who would go on to play for Norwich and Man United) and Vince Overson at the back, and another Burnley legend, Brian Flynn, in midfield. Despite losing the captaincy, Martin Dobson was obviously rated as a player by Bond as he too played regularly.

The move to Burnley worked out well from a domestic point of view. We had kept the house that we had in Wilmslow when we went to Hong Kong. Gerry Gow still couldn't drive so me and Kevin Reeves, who also lived nearby, shouldered the chauffeuring responsibilities to training each day. Gerry had been a popular player with the fans at Bristol City and in Manchester. By the time he arrived at Turf Moor he was having trouble with his knees and it was starting to show on the pitch. Gerry's wife and family used to go to games with Irene and our kids. She found it hard listening to the criticism from the stands for her husband, some of it very unfair and more to do with his association with Bond than his performances on the pitch.

Gow had been a smoker for most of his adult life and I would often make the old joke about the election of a new Pope if I went into the dressing-room toilets and saw his smoke rising from a cubicle. On one occasion he resolved to stop and give up the filthy habit. He managed to stay off the tobacco for a few weeks but felt that his form dipped considerably so he took it as a sign that he needed to go back on the cigarettes to start playing well again. Unfortunately for Gerry, things didn't work out for him at Burnley and by October he was out of the team, never to play league football again.

John Bond was never afraid to try new things if he felt it would give the team an advantage. In those days, almost every team played a rigid 4-4-2 system. Bond decided to give me a radical new position in a 3-5-2 line-up. I was to be the sweeper playing behind our two centre-halves, Phelan and Overson. The full-backs would become wing-backs with responsibility for both attacking and defending.

I was never going to be a traditional centre-half and my two mates at the back were told that I wasn't going to be sending towering headers back up the pitch from our box. My role was to tidy up behind those two, pick up any bits and pieces that came my way and, with my positioning, give them the licence to attack the ball. I would also be able to use the ball creatively to set us on the attack. The change worked reasonably well. I found it an easy position to play, spending most of the game looking forward and having the time to read the game and to use the ball, although I wouldn't have wanted to play there long term.

Having had the opportunity to travel quite a bit during my career, it was quite an eye-opener to mix with some of the younger Burnley lads who hadn't had the chance to do the same. Mike Phelan was a lovely lad and a very good player. I couldn't understand why it took so long for a higher club to come in and snaffle him up. He was a local, born down the road in Nelson. Soon after I arrived, I asked him where in Burnley I could get a good meal. He gave me the name of a café and I asked what the food was like. 'Oh.' he said, 'Don't worry Tom, you'll get plenty of grub there.' I said to him, 'But what's the food like?' I had to laugh. For Mike, quantity seemed to mean quality.

Later that season we were playing in London and were having a meal at our hotel. Mike was looking at the menu and he asked, 'So, what's the difference between sirloin steak and fillet steak?' Quick as a flash someone said, 'About three quid,' but it was the simpleness of Mike's life up to that point that made me smile as much as the joke. Something as simple and commonplace as steak was out of his orbit.

John Bond was not finding it easy. The fans never really took to him and their hopes of an immediate return to the Second Division, something that Bond's appointment seemed to promise, added to their feelings of discontent.

He probably didn't help himself by letting two promising young locals leave. Bond told it how it was (at least in his eyes). He expected those he managed to listen to his advice and instructions and to act on them. If they didn't, they were likely to feel his anger. Maybe Brian Laws and Lee Dixon, the two lads concerned, didn't like this approach. Both of them went on to have excellent top-flight careers. Dixon had a stellar time with Arsenal, playing over 400 games while picking up 22 England caps. In fairness to Bond, both of them took a while to reach the top of the football tree, but their value to Burnley had they stayed could have been immense, both on the pitch and for the bigger transfer fees they might have earned the club.

Our chances of making the play-offs faltered then disappeared late in the season when we managed to win only one of our last 12 games. Why the wheels game off so drastically it is hard to tell. The dip in form only deepened the mood of gloom and anger that seemed to hang like low cloud over Turf Moor. I was still convinced that the following season we would be on our way out of the third tier of English football and that John Bond would be the man to achieve this. I was right on only one of these counts, and not in the way that I hoped.

Chapter 33

The Only Way Is Down

JOHN BOND went about his business of trying to improve the Burnley squad that summer with enthusiasm. He seemed to have lost none of the confidence in himself, that he was the man to improve upon the previous season's disappointing 12th-place finish. In came Kevin Hird from Leeds and my old Coventry and Bulova team-mate, Barry Powell. We also signed Alan Taylor from Hull City. Taylor had made a name for himself by scoring goals in the West Ham team that won the FA Cup in 1975.

Apart from myself, all the previous season's ex-Man City big hitters had moved on. Kevin Reeves had been forced into retirement by a hip injury. He told me that he did not blame all the twisting and turning that he did, nor the heavy tackles that he endured. No, he told me, it was having to constantly turn and chase the overhit crosses that I had floated into the box for him!

Having spent the summer making plans and bringing players in, it was a major surprise that Bond left shortly before the new season started. His reasons for leaving weren't shared with me and I was as in the dark as everyone else as to why he had gone. As far as I was concerned, John Bond was a good coach and a good manager. That first season at Burnley hadn't been good, but I felt that if he had given himself time, he could have turned things around. Perhaps he was fed up working under the clouds that hung over the club. Some fans would say he was responsible for the rainy weather, and there may be some truth to this. However, I also think that working in an atmosphere of negativity, of constant criticism from fans and the local press, may have taken its toll. Maybe his wife Jan had a quiet word reminding him that he didn't need to do the job.

Perhaps surprisingly given he was John Bond's man and the boardroom regime may have wanted to distance themselves from the Bond era, John Benson was given the manager's post. I liked John, got on well with him and felt he was an excellent assistant manager, but I was surprised he hadn't gone with Bond and I wasn't sure he was the right candidate to be in the hot seat. I was unfortunately proved correct.

The season was a disaster from start to finish. For a club of Burnley's stature to be in the Third Division was bad enough. By the end of the season, things had gone from bad to worse and we were relegated to the bottom tier for the first time in the club's history. In the 46-game season we managed to win on only 11 occasions. As a team, we were truly terrible and finished fourth from bottom of the league, the club's worst-ever finishing position. That we won two of our last three games disguised how grim we were – with one less point we would have been second from bottom.

Incredibly, we had two huge wins that season, one of them record-breaking at the time. In February, Rotherham came to Turf Moor and we somehow managed to beat them 7-0. They finished in mid-table, so goodness knows the frame of mind they were in when they crossed the Pennines that Saturday morning. The other big win came in the FA Cup when we were drawn away at Penrith Town. It was the second time I had played there as Man City had taken the cup final team to Penrith to play a friendly. Fortunately, Burnley weren't in a friendly mood that day and we comprehensively avoided a shock by winning 9-0 with hat-tricks from Hird and Taylor.

Taylor wasn't always in John Benson's good books. He felt that he did not work hard enough in games, but he did score a few goals for us. Hird was a good player. He was about seven stone wet-through but he had dynamite in his boots and he could strike a ball hard. There were times, watching him play, that I would wonder, 'What are you doing playing for us?' He was such an easy-going boy, always dressed in old jeans and a T-shirt, quite happy to come in, do his training and go home. He had no ambition to play anywhere higher. He was as happy playing his guitar as he was playing football.

Before one game, he had arranged for the team bus to pick him up from his house. When we pulled up on his street, John Benson couldn't believe where he lived. The street was like something from the pit raws back in Dundonald. The accommodation didn't seem to bother Kevin.

Had he been single, you could just about have understood his lack of concern for where he lived. As he was married, you would have thought he would have lived somewhere nicer. He wasn't on a fortune at Burnley but equally he wasn't poor, so his choice of house was odd.

Looking back on that season and why it went so wrong, the only conclusion that I can draw is a simple one. As a team we just weren't good enough. We had good players, but perhaps not enough of them. As a unit we didn't gel. It would be easy to lay the blame at the feet of John Benson, but I think he was only part of the picture. When a team is struggling as we were, he probably didn't have the experience to pull us out of what was a catastrophic nosedive. Could another manager have saved us? That is hard to judge. It was to be my second relegation but it was a far worse feeling than Blackpool's drop from the First Division. At least on that occasion we had gone up to the top flight, hadn't strengthened and returned to where we started.

A club like Burnley should never have been in that position. I had been a member, indeed captain, of the worst team in Burnley history. It was a horrible feeling. From a personal point of view, I had no regrets. I don't think I could have worked any harder or played any better. Over my two seasons at Turf Moor I had played every league and cup game, so I felt I had given the club good service. Others must have agreed as I was voted both supporters' and the sponsors' player of the season.

By the end of the season John Benson had gone and the club was looking for its third manager in three years, one that would lead them out of the basement division. I was asked to apply for the job and advised by John Bond to go for it. I had the interview and was led to believe that the job was mine. I had no intention of giving up as a player. It was at Burnley that I felt physically at my strongest. Why should I give up? When the job was confirmed then I would be player-manager. I knew already whose would be the first name on the team sheet!

It was a shame that a celebration dinner to honour the Burnley heroes who had won the First Division title 25 years previous came on the back of the club's most disastrous season ever. Nevertheless, the dinner was held and I represented the club as manager-elect. There I was given my player of the season awards. So it was to my surprise, and I think to a few others as well, when a couple of days later I heard that my old Scotland team-mate Martin Buchan was to be the new manager. I was never given any explanation. As usual, with all that goes on in football, I accepted my deselection as Burnley manager and put it down to experience.

Martin Buchan asked to see me and we had a walk out on the Turf Moor pitch. For once in Burnley the rain had stopped. Like John Bond before him he spoke about the tremendous potential of the club. He said to me, 'If we get it right here, I think we'll stroll to promotion.' He offered me the assistant manager's job, but I had to tell him that I wasn't interested. I didn't feel it would have been a good move for me to have gone for the number one position and settle for number two.

It was a fortunate decision on my part. Things didn't go well for Martin or Burnley and with only two months of the new season gone, they were looking for boss number four. Hard to believe that over the coming seasons, things were to get even worse for the long-suffering Burnley fans when the club came within a game of being relegated from the football league. When that happened I was still an English football league player, despite playing in a different country!

Chapter 34

Into the Hot Seat

JOHN BOND was back in football within a few months of leaving Burnley. This time, Swansea City chairman Doug Sharpe decided he was the man to revive the Swans' fading fortunes. Under John Toshack, they had risen through the leagues and reached the upper levels of the First Division, finishing in sixth place in their first season there. It was a great achievement by all concerned with the club, but what happened over the next few years indicated that perhaps the spectacular rise was funded by money that they didn't have. They were now back in the Third Division, having suffered two successive relegations. Bond's immediate task was to stop it from becoming three.

I played for Burnley against Swansea with only three games of the previous season left. We were on the way down and it was distinctly possible that they would be joining us, particularly when a goal, made by me and scored by Alan Taylor, sent them to a 1-0 defeat. After that game, John Bond said, 'See, Hutch, that's why I have been telling the chairman that we need to get you here.' We agreed that if I did not get the manager's job at Turf Moor then I would sign on with him again, this time in South Wales. And that's how things worked out.

Ever since leaving Alloa, Irene and our growing family had followed me around the globe, wherever football had taken me. This time it was going to be different. The family were settled in Wilmslow and my initial contract with Swansea was only for a year. At nearly 38, my football future was the most precarious it had been, with no guarantee of any more contracts. We decided that for one year at least I would live alone in Swansea. I would travel home after my Saturday game for what was left of the weekend before travelling back to Wales on a Sunday night

232

or very early on a Monday morning. I took up residence at the Mermaid Hotel on the Mumbles.

My introduction to my new team-mates came during a pre-season tournament in Malaysia with Kuala Lumpur as our base. How the club were able to afford such an exotic location for a pre-season visit was something that I pondered when the financial chickens came home to roost later in the season. At the time, it was just another exciting place that playing football had enabled me to visit.

After one of the games, John Bond gave Colin Pascoe such a roasting that he was in tears. Some of the Welsh boys felt that they were singled out for criticism more than the English boys. I told Pascoe this wasn't the case and that Bond just wanted players to act on advice and improve. I told him, 'Pasc, the time tae start worrying is when he doesnae speak tae you as that means he's givin' up on you.' Bond would become genuinely frustrated by players who couldn't or wouldn't act on his advice.

The boss hadn't pleased the Swansea fans at the end of the previous season when he released local boy Dean Saunders, who had scored a few goals for the Swans, for the very reason that he would not act on the things he was being asked to do (mainly to delay his runs in behind defenders as he was frequently and unnecessarily caught offside). Saunders, like Dixon from Burnley, went on to have a fantastic top-flight career.

It wasn't looking too good for John when the chairman sided with the fans and criticised the decision to let Saunders go. Bond also didn't inspire much confidence as to what his players could achieve when he declared that it was the worst squad of players that he had ever seen! He didn't tell me that when I was signing on!

Once the season started, the mood of the fans did not improve. We lost the first four league games. By early November we had won only four times, but by then there were bigger fish to fry than league position. We were facing a battle for the very survival of the club. The first hint that I had of the looming situation was in October when HMRC called for a winding-up order against the club due to unpaid taxes. We muddled along until Christmas when the real hammer blow fell. A High Court judge ruled Swansea City insolvent and effectively wound the club up.

The players met in the Vetch Field dressing room to hear the news and were devastated. As far as we knew, we were now out of a job. John Bond was removed as manager and the stadium was closed and padlocked. Our game against Walsall the following day was postponed.

It seemed as if Swansea City was dead. However, it was not quite the case. There was still the flicker of a pulse in the almost-moribund body of the club, giving a small glimmer of hope.

The fans immediately rallied around with fundraising schemes. Two groups of local businessmen, one led by current chairman Sharpe, set about putting rescue packages together. On Christmas Eve 1985, the club was granted a three-week stay of execution to see if it could be saved. Jeffrey Paine was installed as general manager of the club operating under the supervision of the official receiver.

I was asked to look after the playing side. I would be assisted by my fellow senior pro, goalkeeper Jimmy Rimmer, and Ron Walton, who had coached and scouted for John Bond. I was finally to become a manager, albeit a temporary one in the most unusual and difficult of circumstances, six months after missing out on the Burnley job.

One thing that I made clear to Jeffrey Paine was that I would be continuing as a player, something he had no problem with. Any issues to do with the playing side of the club was completely down to me. He would have enough to do in trying to keep the club afloat. My remit was to find a way of fielding 11 players to make sure we fulfilled our fixtures and simply do our best. Winning or drawing would be a bonus. Two days after being appointed, I took charge of my first game, a 1-0 defeat in the South Wales derby with Cardiff. Four games in, I had my first win in the rearranged game with Walsall. Of the first five games we played with me and Rimmer in charge, we won two, lost two and drew one; a reasonable start.

However, it was pounds, not points, that made prizes. With that in mind, I called upon contacts and friendships to try to ease our situation. I had known and had been friendly with Manchester United manager Ron Atkinson since our early playing days at Blackpool and Oxford respectively. I had guested for United in Australia at the end of my stint in Hong Kong. Now I asked him a favour. Would he bring his United team to Vetch Field to play a fundraising friendly to help our cause? He was only too pleased to help and, at amazingly short notice, brought a nearly full-strength team on 13 January.

They showed real class in taking no payment, no expenses, even for the cost of travel. A full-house crowd raised over £45,000 and this, along with the fundraising efforts of the fans, meant our stay of execution was extended to the end of the season. The patient that was Swansea City was still in a chronic and life-threatening state but at least it was now sitting up in bed.

The sad thing about such a terrible financial situation is that it affected many people who had worked at the club for years, often giving loyal service for low wages. Many now found themselves unemployed. For Jimmy Rimmer, Ron Walton and myself, we had to become 'Jacks' of all trades (appropriate when you think of the nickname for natives of Swansea). Any task that needed to be done to keep the club functioning, we would do it. Among the people to lose their job was the lady who used to wash the kit.

Responsibility for clean shirts now passed to me. I organised a rota of the apprentices for them to take a turn. A pair of lads came to find me one day to tell me we had run out of washing powder. We had reached the stage where, not surprisingly, no one would extend us credit or deliver to the club without cash being handed over. I sent them to find the secretary to ask for some cash so they could nip over to the local shops for some detergent. They came back in a few minutes saying that the secretary wanted to see me.

When I went into his office, he said to me, 'Tommy, you're putting too much powder in that machine. You need to use less of the stuff.' I told him, 'See when tomorrow's washing needs tae be done? Well, I'll be sending all of the dirty kit tae you and then you can use as much or as little powder as you like.' The amount of powder we used wasn't disputed again! On another occasion we had two games in the north, at Rotherham and Preston, in the space of three days. It was economically better for us to stay in a cheap hotel for a couple of nights than to incur the cost of travelling back and forth to Swansea.

As we now had no kit man, another one of my duties was to organise the gear along with the apprentices. We needed two sets of kit for the games plus training gear. The first match went off without a hitch in terms of kit, although a 4-1 defeat didn't help our league position. When we got to Preston and opened the kit baskets for the second game, they were empty! The lads in Swansea had put the wrong ones on the coach. We were in the embarrassing position of having to use Preston's away kit to compete in the game. In our position, each completed fixture, however we managed to do it, was a mini-victory.

I could see the secretary's point. The situation with money was desperate. When we travelled to away games, we couldn't afford proper pre-match meals so we would stop at a restaurant or a hotel for tea and a couple of slices of toast, not the best preparation for 90 minutes of intense athletic activity. I remember we did this at a hotel in Stone in Staffordshire (the place where I signed for Coventry all those years ago) before a game.

As we were about to leave for the match, I went up to the receptionist and asked her to send the bill to the club. She told me that she was sorry but that we had to settle in cash. I glanced out of the entrance of the hotel and could see the team milling around beside the bus, unable to get on as the hotel manager was standing in front of the bus door. I paid the bill with my own credit card so we could go. The manager apologised but said that they had been stung several times by clubs not paying their bill. He knew our financial situation and he wasn't taking any chances.

Jeffrey Paine wasn't a football man but he was sympathetic to the situation we were in. I enjoyed working with him. When he heard what we were doing for pre-match food he was shocked. He insisted that athletes had to be properly fuelled. After that conversation we were much better prepared for games. He would drip-feed money to me for anything I deemed essential. I much preferred working for him than I did for Doug Sharpe. Everything with Jeff was honest, open and transparent; three words that I wouldn't associate with Doug.

As a manager I intended to be strict but fair. There would be no favourites and I was prepared for the inevitable falling-out with players, particularly those who weren't being picked. I used the experiences I had of working with so many different coaches and managers when making decisions. During my six-month spell as caretaker, I was reminded a few times of John Bond's saying, 'Good players are easy to coach, it's the not-so-good ones that make a manager's life difficult.' The likes of Trevor Francis, Dennis Mortimer and Kenny Dalglish were top players because of their natural talent but also because of the way they trained and the way they looked after themselves. They also worked on their weaknesses.

I wanted the Swansea team under my control to play with simple tactics. The ball would be played up to the front men and laid back to our centre-midfielders. They were told not to dwell on the ball but to return it to our strikers running the channel or to play it out to our wide players. We had practised and drilled these movements time and time again until the players had them off pat, each knowing their movements and their passing options. I can remember my frustration with Ray McHale who got the ball in central midfield, had the ideal opportunity to play it forward, but dwelt on the ball too long. He was caught, dispossessed and we conceded.

As a manager, it's hard to take when you see something like that happening. A move that has been practised and drilled so much but was then ignored with dire consequences. No wonder managers go grey! I was not a shouter so Ray didn't get the hairdryer treatment from me when they came in at half-time. A lot of the players in the Third and Fourth Division just didn't build on their natural talent, their mindset was different to the players at the top. They tried to do things that more skilled players in the First Division wouldn't have attempted because they had the football intelligence to know that such a move wasn't on. For someone like me, who had played with Francis, Mortimer and Dalglish, it was hard to take and harder to explain. Players at that level often didn't listen, or listened but still did their own thing.

Organisation of the team was made more difficult because several of the players who had signed for Swansea were based elsewhere. We were now in a situation where we couldn't afford to pay for them to stay in local hotels or flats or even their expenses to travel into training, so they were having to train on their own at home and travel to Swansea or the away ground we were playing at on the day of the game. I was now paying my own hotel bill in order to stay in Swansea.

There would have been no way to incorporate those non-local players to work on shape or on tactics that had gone on that week. They were paid their travel expenses on the day of our home games from that day's gate receipts. They had to accept whatever form of money we could give them: 50-pence pieces, 20-pence pieces or whatever the secretary could find.

We were operating on a skeleton staff both on and off the pitch. I had an article published in *Shoot!* magazine where I launched an idea called 'Vetch Me a Star'. It was a scheme where any would-be footballers could write to the club and we would allocate them a place in a series of trial matches that we were to hold over a two-month period. Ron Walton did all the arrangements. Each candidate was given the time, date and venue details but had to make their way there at their own expense, bringing their own kit. We did have the embarrassing situation at one of the trials when council officials refused to let us go ahead as the club had not paid the £25 rent.

On the whole, however, the scheme ran smoothly. Some of the lads who turned up were a bit like those hopeless singers seeking five minutes of fame on *Britain's Got Talent*, having no skill at football at all. Some were grossly overweight, some turned up without boots, but most of the boys could at least play a bit. It was a good PR exercise and it did give some of the locals who turned up a closer contact with their club. We hoped we might unearth one or two hidden gems but in the end we only took on one lad who, although a reasonable player, never made the first team.

One of the most difficult tasks I had when I took over as caretaker manager was to tell the apprentices, in the company of their parents, that they were going to be released. We didn't have the money to keep them on. Not surprisingly, it was a hammer blow to their dreams. Some had been told by John Bond that they would be offered a professional contract. There were tears from parents and boys alike. I did my best to help two of the more promising youngsters. I phoned Mick Brown, the assistant manager at Manchester United, and told him that we had two very good young lads about to be released by the names of Nigel French and Andy Melville. He told me to send them up to Manchester and they could have a month's trial.

I had noticed in my short time in Swansea that many of the Welsh players, particularly the younger ones, were very much homebirds and were reluctant to travel. I wasn't thinking of this when I asked the two young lads into my office. As far as I was concerned, I was doing them a massive favour – not only saving them from a likely spell on the dole but giving them the chance to join one of the biggest and best clubs in the world.

I asked them what they would do if, as was likely, we were to close. They both looked blank and obviously had no idea what they would do. I thought they would be delighted with the proposed offer from Man United. I was wrong. When I told them, one of them asked, 'Would we have to stay up there?' When I told them yes, the other one said, 'What, we won't be able to come home?' I was disgusted and told them to leave before I blew my top. As it happens, they were both able to stay when the club was saved. I do think that Andy Melville would have progressed quicker and become an even better player had he been able to benefit from the coaching he would have received in Manchester.

I had heard from other player-managers the difficulties they had in combining the two different roles. I did find it hard during games to operate as manager too. With Jimmy Rimmer still playing as well, our 'eyes on the side' belonged to Ron Walton. Some of the decision-making during matches was allocated to him. I didn't have the self-confidence of Terry Yorath to criticise another player's performance when playing poorly myself. I needed to be our star man before I felt that I could point out the shortcomings of those alongside me on the pitch. This was an area that Ron helped out in. Likely substitutions we would discuss at half-time, but he had authority to change it as he saw fit, tweaking things here or there, even bringing me off if he felt it was needed.

As the season progressed, the club's financial problems began to ease. A combination of the infrastructure being cut to the bone, fan fundraising efforts and the money we received from the Man United game meant that we began to trade in profit. Doug Sharpe put in £72,000 to pay off some debts and it was his consortium that regained control of the club. On 20 July 1986 the winding-up order was lifted. Thanks to the combined efforts of all who loved it, the future of the club was secure once more. However, we would be plying our trade in the Fourth Division. For the second successive season, the club I was with was relegated to the basement division.

We were in the relegation zone when I took over and there we stayed. We finished bottom, six points from safety. The Swansea fans had been great with me and the team. They knew our predicament. The fact that we had managed to save their club was a cause to celebrate.

My own future was insecure. My playing contract was up and I had been only the interim manager. I was delighted when I met with Doug Sharpe that summer and he asked me to be the permanent manager. I was happy to accept as long as he agreed that I would continue as a player. He said he would sort out the paperwork. Football is certainly a unique industry. I know of no other where you can find yourself the manager of an institution one day, then three days later find that someone has taken your place!

Chapter 35

Sharpe by Name

ASTON VILLA chairman Doug Ellis had the nickname 'Deadly Doug' due to his quick trigger finger shooting down managers he no longer saw as doing their job. We had our own cheaper, pound-shop version in South Wales. While I was informing family and friends of my soon-to-be-signed contract as player-manager of Swansea City, the South Walian Doug had taken himself off to Leeds for the day. He was at that very moment drinking lager in the back garden of my friend and former playing colleague, Terry Yorath, trying to persuade him to become the next manager of Swansea.

While Terry didn't know that I had already been offered the job, Doug, with his less than comprehensive knowledge of football, didn't know that Terry and I had been together at Coventry and were friends. Yorath was assistant manager of Bradford City but keen to try his hand at being a number one. Though not that impressed with Doug, Terry agreed in principle to take the job with the details of his contract to be finalised at a later meeting in Swansea.

Before the announcement was made, Doug called me in and told me that he had had a change of heart and that he was now going to appoint a young tracksuit manager. In my disappointment, I could have told him what I thought of him and what he could do with his job. Fortunately, on hearing who the young tracksuited manager was to be, I decided to hold fire and see how the land lay.

When Terry arrived in Wales for his meeting with Doug Sharpe, the chairman was less than happy to find out he would be discussing terms with Terry's wife Christine, who was a businesswoman in her own right. She drove a much harder bargain than Doug was expecting and he was not at all pleased to have been outdone by a woman. The upshot was that Yorath was appointed and he wanted me to be his assistant. Had it been anyone else, I would have walked after the way Sharpe had treated me. But Terry was enthusiastic and felt that together, despite 'Deadly Doug Mk2' we could achieve something there.

I told him that I wouldn't sign unless it was for two years at least. The travelling was killing me and the only time I talked to my children was to tell them off! We weren't going to move unless we got that bit more security. Financially too, things weren't great as they were. I was paying all my travelling expenses and hotel bills. This left us with about £90 a week which, considering all the hassle we had, wasn't worth it. Initially Sharpe was reluctant to give me that contract. He thought that I was finished as a player. However, Terry insisted and, in the end, he got his way and I got my two years. As it turned out, I quickly regretted my decision to sign.

The ink was barely dry on the contract when I received an offer to return to Coventry. I went to speak to John Sillett and he asked me to take on the role of player-coach. The job would have involved working with and bringing on the youth team. It would also have meant that I would have the chance to play again in the First Division, even at the age of 39, a prospect I would have relished and one which Sillett saw as realistic. Terry was disappointed that I might go. 'Stay,' he told me, 'we'll do alright here.'

The matter was settled by Doug Sharpe, who saw a few pound signs in front of his eyes and told Coventry that he wanted £10,000 for me. I told him that he was having a laugh, that it was unfair, that he had got me for nothing. He had told Terry when negotiating the two-year deal that I wasn't worth it, that he thought my legs had gone after Christmas of the season just closed. Now I was worth paying for. It was all to no avail. Coventry wouldn't pay and the matter was closed.

Sharpe's heart was in the club but he should never have been in charge. It was just so badly run and seemed to have been for years. This was brought home to me several times in my five Swansea years. During my first caretaker stint, I had looked at the files from some of the previous big-name signings. The wages that had been paid to those players were unbelievable, clearly unsustainable for a club with Swansea's income.

Sharpe could not be held responsible as he only became chairman at the tail end of the period, but the craziness, a lot of it non-financial, did not stop when he took over. He seemed to have little common sense and few social skills. He would arrive at the club some days wearing an oddment of clothes, none of which matched. John Bond, when he was in charge, would say to him, 'And so who dressed you today, chairman?'

Initially, Terry and I shared an apartment in Swansea and his family stayed in Leeds. He would do the same as I had and commute back up north at the weekends. I didn't envy him. After house-hunting together with Irene, we found a lovely place on Caswell Bay and for the first time in over a year we were back together as a family. It was a beautiful place to live and all of us loved it, my daughter Lynn so much so that she stayed when the rest of the family moved on and she still lives there with her husband.

The season started well enough. I enjoyed working with Terry and I think we made a good team. On the pitch we were doing okay and challenging for promotion, until our influential striker Ian Love suffered a broken leg and we seemed to fall away.

As we started to flounder, I tried to talk Yorath into making a comeback. He was still registered as a player and was a few years younger than me. He joined in with our training but not always with the high-intensity stuff so he probably wasn't match-fit. There is no doubt in my mind that he could have got himself to the required level if he had stuck at it. In the end my nagging paid off and he included himself for a match against Wolves. Not surprisingly, he was off the pace and didn't play his best. For him that was it, the end of his playing career, and he put his boots away. If he had continued, increased training and played himself into form, he could have come back, but this time Terry was adamant. As far as he was concerned, he was now an ex-player.

Even though the team's form had tailed off, I was pleased with the way my 39-year-old legs were holding up. My personal view that I was doing well was confirmed one day by Terry when he called me into the office. He told me he had just spoken to Terry Dolan, an old colleague of his from Bradford City, who was now the manager.

Bradford were in the division above us and Dolan had been sounding Yorath out about any good players he had come across in our division. In particular he was looking for a left-sided midfielder and wide player. Yorath told him that he knew the best player of that type in the division, but that Dolan wouldn't be able to get him. 'Why's that?' asked Dolan.

'Because I already have him here,' Yorath told him. Even at 39, it was still nice to hear compliments like that!

I was very proud to be recognised by my fellow players, those from the teams we played against, when I had been voted into the PFA Fourth Division Team of the Year for season 1986/87. It was a thrill to receive the award and nice that I could travel to the ceremony in London with my Swansea team-mates Colin Pascoe and Terry Phelan, who were also selected for the team of the year. It was further confirmation that I was still a good player, still pulling my weight and making a difference for the team.

We finished 12th that season, not great for a club like Swansea, but there were encouraging signs that we could do better. Some of the new players we had brought in had shown that they could play and with another close season under their belts, things were looking good. One of these players was Gary Emmanuel, a Swansea boy who we brought back from Bristol to play for the club that both his dad and his uncle had played for.

Gary was a good player and one of the better ones in our squad. He was a real trier, desperate to do well for us and always gave 100 per cent. He was, however, hugely self-critical. If he had a bad first half, I would have to go over to him in the dressing room and try and talk him out of his black mood before we went out for the second half. He was one of those players who could never appreciate the good things that he did. His focus was always on his mistakes.

By this stage, my kids had transferred their football allegiance from Coventry to Man City to Burnley and now to Swansea. My son David had become a keen student of our team. Every Saturday morning he would go up to the loft and get out two sets of his many Subbuteo teams; one would be Swansea, the other would be in the colours of the team we were playing that day. Having seen us play many times now, David picked the team he thought Terry Yorath should be playing. He would come downstairs before he started his game to tell me his Swansea line-up, and then again when his game was over to tell me by how many Swansea had won. (I don't think, with David as manager of his plastic men, Swansea had ever lost!)

I would tell all the players how we had fared on the Subbuteo table that morning. Gary Emmanuel was going through a poor run of form and his chin was on the ground. I said to him after a game, 'Come on, Gaz, we'll go doon the pub now n' have a beer.' 'Okay, Tom,' he said to me, 'after that performance I could do with a drink.' As we left the dressing room, I turned to him and said, 'I dae have some bad news for you though, Gaz.' 'Oh aye, what's that then?' he asked a bit anxiously. With a solemn voice and a straight face, I told him, 'Just looking at your form lately, David's had tae drop you from his Subbuteo team.' Thankfully he took it in the right way and started laughing and said, 'Just shows how bad I'm doing when I can't even make the Subbuteo team!'

Managing a football club is a hard task. It's made even harder when the manager and the chairman don't see eye to eye. Doug's insistence on interfering with football matters meant that often our team-building plans were scuppered. Terry had agreed a deal that would have brought Geoff Thomas from Crewe to Swansea. Thomas went on to have a great career and became an England international. We saw great potential in him. He would have improved our team greatly as a player and would have earned the club a lot of money when he would inevitably have been sold on.

Doug had initially said yes to the deal, but then he heard that the package we had arranged did not include the player's signing-on fee or his wages. He wasn't happy. He told Terry to go back to Crewe and renegotiate. (Football negotiations were beyond Doug and even he realised he was better staying out of them.) Terry knew that the deal agreed was already in our favour and wasn't going to be improved upon and so the transfer never happened. Sharpe just didn't have the confidence in us to trust our football knowledge and instinct in matters like this.

Sharpe had his own building business which had been successful and had given him his personal wealth. In his own line of work, he was used to having his own way and calling all the shots. He found it difficult at the club because Terry and I would stand up to him on football matters and his bully-boy techniques did not work. We were the people he had hired to make the football decisions and our reputations would sink or swim depending on the results we achieved. We weren't going to let someone like Doug, with no football experience, tell us who to sign, who to pick or the tactics we would play.

Relations between us and the board – essentially Doug – were always tense. An example was when, on a couple of occasions before matches, Sharpe and another director asked Yorath what the team would be for those particular games. On the first occasion, Yorath reeled off the names of the starting 11. Well, Sharpe disagreed with the selection of one or two of those players and argued with the manager, trying to get him to change the team. Yorath was having none of it and told the two of them to stay out of team affairs. A week later, Sharpe was there again, asking for the team before the game. This time Yorath was ready for him and simply told him to look at who ran out from the tunnel at 3pm.

Despite Sharpe and his continued attempts to meddle in team affairs, we arrived at the end of the season just scraping into the final play-off position. The play-offs had only been going for a couple of years at that stage and their format was different from those of today. Scunthorpe and Torquay had finished the season in fourth and fifth positions and they would play in one of the semi-finals. We had finished in sixth place and we would play Rotherham, who had finished fourth bottom of the Third Division. In effect, the play-offs gave one team the chance to avoid relegation as well as giving three clubs a chance for promotion. Over the two-legged semis, Torquay and ourselves came out on top. We would now meet home and away in the two-legged finals – no Wembley in those early play-off days.

We took a 2-1 lead to Plainmoor for the match that would decide the immediate future of the club, and probably its management team too. On an absolute bog of a pitch, we raced into a 2-0 lead and appeared to be sailing serenely back to the Third Division. But Torquay roared back with two quick goals to draw level. Alan Davies restored our lead just on half-time. Torquay weren't finished and a second equaliser brought the score on the day back to 3-3. We were desperately hanging on but somehow managed to see out the game. We were up!

What should have been the best managerial experience seemed strangely flat. The players, quite rightly, were ecstatic, as were the fans. As we sat on the coach back to Swansea, Yorath turned to me and asked what I was feeling. 'Nothing,' I said, and he said he felt exactly the same. The black cloud hanging over us and over the club was Sharpe. His thriftiness we could perhaps understand considering the excesses that had nearly killed the club but his criticism of us and the players and his attempts to meddle in team affairs were steps too far. As well as managing the team, we were having to manage Doug, and both of us felt the stresses and strains of the latter were greater than that of the former.

Nevertheless, we enjoyed our open-top bus ride around Swansea and I got a cheer on the steps of the town hall before our civic reception when I said that I would be playing again next year. A new season too, this time back in the Third Division, was an exciting and promising prospect. I had played over 40 games in our promotion-winning team and was confident that at 41 years of age I would be able to cope with the rigours of a Third Division season. But for how much longer could Terry and I put up with Sharpe?

Chapter 36

Back in the Hot Seat

THAT COMING season, 1988/89, would see me still playing league football at the age of 41. When I was the captain at Coventry, I would write a column in the matchday programme. In one I wrote that I could see myself playing until I was 40 and that I would have no problem in dropping down the leagues if it meant that I could keep on going.

That column was written in my early 30s so it turned out to be an accurate prediction of what I did (except, ironically, this season I was actually on the way back up the divisions again after promotion). I also said, perhaps a little tongue in cheek, that I was only halfway through my career. I had played around 450 games by that stage but went on to play a thousand. As a prophet, I was doing a pretty good job!

When I started at Blackpool, I would have been happy to have had ten years as a player. As my career progressed, I knew that, barring injury, I would play for a lot longer than that. Some players were almost persuaded into retirement by their age and not by how their body felt. One of the fittest players I ever played with was Jimmy Armfield. He retired in his mid-30s and at the time I felt he could have carried on. I firmly believed that if you looked after yourself, kept yourself fit, then there was no reason to finish just because you had hit the magic age of 33 or 34. I did feel that if you stopped playing and changed your mind, it would be a difficult thing to get muscle tone back on an older body.

I once heard Bill Shankly say that the older a player got then the more sleep they needed. I found it to be the opposite in my case; I needed less rest than in my younger days. I had also always been lucky that I could play from a cold start, never had to warm up before a game. There must be something in my physical make-up that allowed me to do it. I maintained a good level of fitness throughout my career.

I continued to look after the youth team, something I had done since my early days at Swansea. On one occasion, when we were short of players, I played with the youth team at Haverford West on a Wednesday afternoon and for the reserves at the Vetch that night: 180 minutes of competitive football in an eight-hour period. Even at that age and after so many years as a professional, I just loved to play; there was nothing to beat the feeling of being out on a pitch and competing. Don't get me wrong, the ageing process and the effect that it has on your body will win out in the end and overcome even the most enthusiastic athlete. But through lucky genes and hard work and dedication, I managed to carry on a lot longer than most.

On the pitch, we made a reasonable start to the season. Coming up to Christmas we weren't too far off the play-offs. Despite this, relationships with Sharpe hadn't improved. He was unhappy that Terry had accepted an offer from the Welsh FA to manage the international side. Instead of seeing it as a feather in the cap of the club, he thought that Terry wasn't going to give his all to his role as Swansea manager. He couldn't see that Yorath pitting his wits against some of the top managers of the day would improve him as a coach, or that a manager with a higher profile would attract better players to the club. Up and coming Welsh players would want to play for Swansea with the international coach working with them every day.

On a week that Terry was with the Welsh team, we would talk after Swansea's Saturday game and decide on the outline of the training programme for the week ahead. I would put together the actual drills but I knew that by 9.30 on Monday morning I would receive a call from Sharpe. He would ask if Yorath had given me a training plan. I would confirm that he had. He would then want to know the details of what we were doing and I would give him the headlines.

Inevitably, he would tell me not to bother with any of that. What the players needed was to be run. 'They're not fit enough, Tommy,' he would tell me, 'run them.' I would listen, not comment and get rid of him as quick as I could by simply agreeing, 'Aye, okay chairman.' Of course, I had no intention of doing any of what he had said. He had a friend who would drive to the top of the training ground at Morfa, park up, watch what we were doing and no doubt feed back to him. Because neither Terry nor me were bothered by his bluster, he never came back to us on what we did or on how we failed to follow his directives.

It was a busy but enjoyable time, apart from having to deal with Sharpe. As a player I was still training full time in the mornings and playing Saturdays and sometimes midweek too. In the afternoons I would take the youth team training and I would manage them for their game on a Sunday. On a Thursday evening I would also take scholars training, the school-age boys. I would help out with anything else that needed doing; sorting the kit or even marking out the pitch.

On a Thursday, Terry would be down to watch the scholars or even join in with them. After the session we would return to the Vetch with Ron Walton and another coach, Tony Abel, to have a chat about how things were going. On one occasion, Terry said it would be nice to have a beer while we chatted, so he went off to the boardroom in search of a few bottles. He came back and said, 'No good, they've locked us out.' I went to have a look and I noticed high up on the wall above the door, there was a switch. I got a broom and with the handle flipped the switch. Hey presto! The door clicked open and we helped ourselves to a few bottles. It became a regular event at our Thursday chat, but we always remembered to flip the switch back. We thought of it as a small victory against Sharpe's petty mindedness.

After a game on a Saturday, I would always go up to the boardroom and take back a few drinks for the opposing team's manager and staff, and maybe for the referee and linesmen too. It was all official and above board, having been grudgingly approved by Sharpe, as even he recognised some hospitality was needed. On one occasion, I went in there after a game as usual. Old Les, who acted as barman, handed over the drinks but said to me, 'The chairman thinks that too much unexplained beer is going out of here. He has a chippy coming in during the week to change the lock.' It was with a heavy heart that I had to tell my fellow conspirators that our Thursday beer-drinking sessions looked to be numbered.

Terry and I were in his office the following week discussing a forthcoming match and we could hear the chippy across the corridor fitting the new lock to the boardroom. When he finished, a knock came on the door. The chippy said, 'I've finished the job now, can you pass these keys on to Mr Sharpe?' Terry took the keys and said, 'No problem, I'll make sure he gets them.' As soon as the chippy had gone, Terry called in an apprentice, gave him a key and told him to pop down to Timpson to get another one cut. The Thursday night beer club was back on and now we didn't even need the broom!

Yorath's frustration at how things were run at Swansea was increasing. A bonus that he should have been paid upon promotion was withheld by Doug Sharpe as the agreement had only been a verbal one with nothing written down. As I had found out to my cost, Doug's word was certainly not his bond. The team's impetus gained with promotion seemed to have stalled. Terry had also spent the best part of three years living away from his family in Leeds. When Bradford City came in for him to be their new manager following the sacking of Terry Dolan, he had no hesitation in saying yes to a move that meant he could live at home again.

Sharpe wasn't pleased and lots of litigation followed Terry to Bradford. One thing was clear, that Swansea needed a new manager. I was asked to take over again until a permanent appointment was made. I was in charge for a month during which the most significant occurrence was beating non-league Barry Town over two legs to reach the Welsh Cup Final. Because our opponents in the final were Kidderminster, an English team, we were now guaranteed to be in the following season's European Cup Winners' Cup competition as the representatives of Wales.

A new manager came in for the final run of games. Ian Evans, a former Welsh international who had been assistant to Steve Coppell at Crystal Palace, was appointed by Sharpe. He may have played for Wales but you have never heard anyone speak with a more authentic Cockney accent than Ian. He got off to a less-than-auspicious start with us. Out of the 12 league games for which he was in charge, we won only two. We did beat Kidderminster 5-0 at Vetch Field in the Welsh Cup Final and so he did have an early trophy on his managerial CV. It was clear to see, however, that Ian wasn't going to be a match for Sharpe. Where Terry would have stood up to Doug, particularly on football matters, Evans was too easy-going. I'm sure that Doug was delighted that he now had a manager who would do his bidding.

Sharpe showed his contradictory nature again when he came to me after the appointment of Evans. He offered me the continuing role as player-assistant manager, recognising that Evans's inexperience could be a problem. While I was grateful for the offer of the contract, I couldn't help but remind him of what he had said about me in the past. 'Wait a minute, two years ago, you said that ma legs had gone, now you're saying that Ah can still play?' 'Ahh,' he said, 'this is different, this is management.'

I didn't understand how being 'management' gave life to my legs. I also didn't know what he thought I had been doing for the previous two and a half years. Had he forgotten that I had been the interim manager after John Bond and then Yorath's assistant? Who knew with Doug? I signed what was to be my last football league contract. However, I wasn't finished yet. The next 18 months would see me break new records.

Chapter 37

Deadly Doug Strikes Again

AFTER THE poor end to the previous league season, Ian Evans really needed the team to get off to a good start. He was to be disappointed. Out of the opening nine games, we won only one, went out of the League Cup to Exeter from the division below and went out of the Cup Winners' Cup at the first hurdle. Evans was under pressure straight away, emphasised by an article in the local press where Sharpe aired his disappointment at our early exit from money-spinning European competition.

I got on okay with Ian Evans on a personal basis but professionally we didn't always see eye to eye. His management of the players wasn't to my liking. I liked to see things done fairly, all players treated in the same way whether they were team superstars or a young squad player. Ian had his favourites and other members of the team could see that some of their colleagues received preferential treatment. When you are losing most weeks, team spirit will generally be poor. I think Ian's man-management style made things worse.

In some ways Ian was ahead of his time in the way he looked at the game. Every time we played a match there would be apprentices sitting in the stand. Each player would have an apprentice watching him all game recording his data: passes made, passes completed, tackles made, etc. Ian looked at the information given to him and used this as part of his rationale for team selection. Every league team nowadays uses a similar, much more complex computerised system to analyse player performance. I had no problem with having this information to hand, but I felt Ian put too much emphasis on it and not on what his eyes were telling him.

We disagreed sometimes on team selection too. We had a lad playing for us, a striker, who I would rather not name as he was a good lad and

I have nothing against him. I felt he was not having enough impact on our games and was not scoring the goals that he should have. I raised the issue of his place in the team with Ian, stating my concerns and saying I felt he should be left out. Ian totally disagreed and after rummaging through a file handed me the striker's data sheet. Ian pointed out that he had completed more passes than anyone else in the team. 'Yes, but how many of those are of the five-yard variety or sideways or backwards?' I asked him. Ian stuck to his guns and the striker remained in the team. I told Evans that if he persevered with him, he would find himself out of a job. Prophetic words.

Personally, I felt I was still playing well and my data must have been good too as Ian generally kept picking me! The first of the records I broke came in the away leg of the Cup Winners' Cup. When I played against Panathinaikos in Athens, I became, at 42, the oldest debutant in European competition. I am sure that when the Greek left-back heard he was up against a 42-year-old European debutant then he would have had a smile on his face. As always, I was confident that I would give a good account of myself. As a team, we certainly didn't do ourselves justice. Due to two keeper errors, we went in at half-time 2-0 down. Both the game and crowd were feisty and our subs were unable to warm up on the sidelines as every time they appeared they were showered with coins.

When we conceded a third goal just after half-time, the tie looked done and dusted. However, we hit back with two goals from my corners to reduce the arrears and even struck the bar in the last few minutes. In the return at the Vetch, we played well and led on the night, first 2-0, then later 3-1. I had another assist from another corner. It looked like we were going through. However, we ended the night broken-hearted as two late goals, this time from Panathinaikos, saw us knocked out of the competition.

We were out on the night, but we very nearly didn't start that evening. Ian Evans had decided to take us to Aberystwyth for a few days to prepare. We travelled back to Swansea on the day of the game. There were no major roads between the two towns in those days and we had an arduous journey on twisty country roads that left us travel-sick. Worse was to come as the coach we were in broke down. As the clock ticked on, we waited for a replacement. We eventually got to the Vetch with time to spare but it had been a bit hair-raising. Imagine the Greek team ready to go out only to be told that the local team still hadn't turned up yet!

Results did pick up a little in the autumn, around Christmas and we had a little run in the FA Cup. We were drawn against Liverpool at the Vetch in the third round. At that time, under Dalglish, Liverpool were the top team. With players like John Barnes in their side, they were capable of ripping First Division teams to shreds, never mind Third Division Swansea. I decided to even things up a bit. One of my duties before games was to pump up the match balls before giving them to the ref. As our physio looked on, I said, 'Barnesy will no' be bending these balls intae the net tonight!' He laughed when he saw me putting a good few extra puffs of air into each ball making them hard. 'Let's hope the ref doesnae notice,' I said as I went to hand them over.

Whether the unusually hard balls made a difference, I don't know, but we managed to keep Barnes and Co at bay and hung on for a creditable draw and a replay at Anfield. At the end of the game, Dalglish came to find me and say hello. The physio was a big fan of Kenny's and was delighted when I introduced him to the great man. Kenny is a funny boy and he had the physio and me in stiches with his stories. As he was in full flow, a knock came and one of his Liverpool staff was there to tell him that the TV people were ready for his after-match interview. Kenny said okay, that he'd be there in a minute. As he said goodbye, it was as though a veil had come down over his face and his persona changed completely. The physio noticed and commented on it. 'Aye,' I said, 'that's the face he has for they boys out there,' meaning the TV people. Kenny was always wary of the way that his words could be manipulated in the media.

I don't know whether Ian Evans had shares in a west Wales hotel or not, but it was back to Aberystwyth before the Anfield replay. Me and Robbie James had been injured and Evans pencilled us in to play for the reserves before the cup tie in order to get some fitness. No problem with that, until I heard that the reserves were playing in Yeovil and that we were in Ian's favourite hotel in Aberystwyth. (In reality, it turned out the hotel was owned by a friend of Sharpe.) After hours sitting in a car on the way there, playing for 45 minutes (we didn't play 90 with the cup tie coming up) followed by hours sitting in the car on the way back, neither Robbie or I were best pleased.

We were even less happy after another tortuous journey from West Wales to Merseyside to find out that neither of us had been included in the team. I felt it was a huge mistake by Ian. Although Robbie and I didn't have the legs that we once had, we had know-how and experience and both of us had played at Anfield several times. Our boys took a real beating that night and were ran ragged by Liverpool, ending up on the wrong end of an 8-0 scoreline. Sharpe was not happy and made his views known in the press, calling our performance and the result embarrassing.

We continued to bumble along in the league, just about keeping our heads above the relegation waters. In March we travelled to the Isle of Man to play a friendly. Ian Evans didn't come with us, wanting to stay behind to sign a new player, Alan Knill. When Sharpe saw me before the game, I knew the writing was on the wall for Ian. Sharpe told me to ignore whatever team Evans had picked to play and to pick the team myself. As it happens, Ian had left me in charge and told me to pick the team anyway, but Doug wasn't to know that. It was no surprise when Sharpe told me soon after the Manx trip that Ian had gone.

It may have been no surprise that Evans was out, but Sharpe's choice of his replacement was a bolt out of the blue. Terry Yorath was coming back to South Wales. While I was delighted to be working with my old pal again, I couldn't help wondering if he was doing the right thing in jumping from the frying pan, being unemployed at home in Leeds (Terry had already lost his job at Bradford), back into the Swansea fire. He told me later that even when he signed the contract, he was unsure if he was right to come back. If he knew what was to follow, he would never have returned. There was certainly no miracle improvement in his first round of games back in charge. We won three but lost seven of Yorath's 13 games at the end of the season. We limped over the safety line from relegation.

Then came a boost. That summer, Doug found some money! Whether he discovered the £65,000 pounds we used to buy Terry Connor and Jimmy Gilligan down the back of his settee or under his mattress, Terry and I didn't care. The fact was we were able to get two decent, proven strikers. However, the fact that we had spent that amount of money now put us under even more pressure. We had to deliver, we had to improve on last season and be pushing upwards towards the top of the league. We started the new season consistently. Unfortunately for us, we were consistently poor and consistently losing. Of the first 11 games, we won only two. Yorath's record since returning was played 24, won five. That was poor by any standards. He and I were going to find things difficult unless we improved.

A few games into the season I stormed into Terry's office to see him. I wasn't happy. He had left me out of the first team the previous

Saturday. Although I never took kindly to being dropped, that wasn't the issue. I had just seen the reserve team for their upcoming midweek game pinned to the noticeboard. I hadn't been included in that either, and I wanted to know why. 'I was thinking of you. I honestly thought you would enjoy the rest,' Terry told me. 'Ah'll have enough rest when Ah'm six feet under, thanks,' I growled at him. 'If you think Ah'm finished as a player, think again. A'hm not ready to hang up ma boots an' Ah'm far from finished.' He made me even angrier when he started to laugh at me. 'You've just given me a great story,' he said. 'Wait until I tell people that I once had a 43-year-old player bang on my door wanting to know why he wasn't in the reserves.' He did tell that story, with relish, when I was in his presence. I had to laugh.

The fact was that football still gave me so much joy. I got the same thrill out of playing now as I did as a young lad running around with my mates, chasing a ball around The Square in Dundonald. When I put my boots on and crossed the white line onto the pitch, I was on a high, troubles and cares vanished. All that mattered was the game. I didn't want that feeling to end. I wasn't ready to give it all up. I enjoyed managing and coaching, but nothing gave me that buzz like playing did. To be fair to Terry, all he needed to say when I came roaring in was, 'You want to know why I've left you out? Look at your birth certificate!' but he was too kind to do that.

Amazingly, out of nowhere, we went on a good run, the team gelled and results picked up. Had that form continued, we would have been challenging for a play-off place. However, following a heavy defeat in an FA Cup third-round replay at Rotherham, the wheels came off the season. We went on a run of ten straight defeats. During this run, I played my final game in the football league, a poor 4-1 defeat at the Vetch by Southend. It confirmed my second age-related record in two seasons. I was already Swansea's oldest-ever player but the record would stand at 43 years and six months.

After such a run, Terry and I knew what was coming. Sharpe had already said that the performance against Mansfield that season was the worst by a Swansea team he had ever seen. We knew that the axe was in Doug's hands, poised, ready to strike. The only thing we didn't know was when it would fall. We were together at the Vetch watching a reserve game when the hatchet fell. A steward tapped Terry on the shoulder and said that Doug wanted to see him in the boardroom. He rolled his eyes at me and off he went. He told me later that Sharpe had told him that he wanted him to resign. There would be no compensation to pay if he did that. Terry wasn't going to finish that way and he told Sharpe that the only way he was leaving was if he was sacked. He came back into the stand and told me that he was out. Deadly Doug now wanted to see me.

What Doug said to me tells you a lot about his mentality. He stated, 'I don't care if the crowd give the players stick. They pay their money to get in; as far as I'm concerned, they can call them what they want. And see you two, I pay you a good wage. If the crowd start giving you stick, well that's okay too. But see when they start giving me stick? Then, something has got to change.' I told him, 'Fair enough. It's your club.' After the run we'd had, I could hardly complain. He was going to pay up the rest of my contracts, as a player and as assistant manager, although not a big sum as I only had a few months left on each. Doug said to me, 'Well, you've taken it better than Yorath. I'll tell you what, why don't we tell the press that you resigned and you won't have a sacking on your CV?' I wasn't having any of that, 'No way. Ah'll no resign, you sacked Terry and that's what you're doing to me.'

And so that was it. My career as a football league player was over. It was the first and only time in my life that I had been sacked. I found my dismissal hard to take, but harder still was the thought that my football career might be finished. I also needed to work and provide for my family. Who would employ someone who was possibly now an ex-footballer?

Chapter 38

Going the Full Circle

I HAD known the lads at Swansea since they were young. I knew them well and I liked them. I felt sorry that now they would be working with this guy. I could understand why Sharpe had appointed him. He thought that shouting at and abusing players was the way forward. 'Get them going, get them wound up and get them running.' That was his mantra. It was no way to get the best out of young lads, to get them to learn and to improve, but Sharpe couldn't see that.

Jimmy Rimmer had known Smith since their days at Manchester United. He didn't like him either. If we met at youth or reserve matches, Smith would often try to reminisce with Rimmer about their glory days as 'Busby Babes' at United. After one of these occasions, I said to Rimmer, 'I can't remember him, I don't think I've ever heard of him as a player.' Jimmy told me that he never got near the first team at United, he only ever played for the youth team. If that was the case, then I had actually played more games for United than he had – I played four friendlies as a guest on their Australian tour!

I woke on the day after my conversation with Sharpe and I was lost. For the first time in my life, I had nowhere to go. I had spent most of my working life making sure I was fit and sharp enough to play a game at the weekend. Now there was no game to aim for and no training to go to. After a couple of days, I decided to bite the bullet and see Frank Burrows to ask if I could train with the youth team. He said that would be no problem.

For a week or so I went in every day in order to keep myself fit. I still intended to play and I wanted to make sure I was ready when a club came in for me. The plan failed when the physio came to me one day and said he was sorry but he had been asked to tell me not to come in anymore. The reason he gave was that, according to Smith, the youth-team boys were listening to me more than to him.

At the end of that season, I had some good news that dispelled some of my unemployment gloom. I had been given another award by the PFA. I was presented with the PFA Merit Award for making an outstanding contribution to professional football by my fellow Scot, Alex Ferguson, an honour for me in itself. I remember being asked by a journalist what was the secret to having a long career in football. I was obviously still feeling quite bitter about Sharpe. I told him, 'Hard work and never trusting chairmen.'

During the summer, I signed on for the coming season with Merthyr Tydfil in the Vauxhall Conference. I had now gone full circle, finishing my career as I had started it, playing for smashing people at a non-league club in a mining town. There were a lot of similarities between Merthyr and the Bluebell, not least in the boisterous and funny 600-odd who turned up every other Saturday to meet their mates and watch their team in a ramshackle stadium. (Actually, there were parts of the stadium that were far from ramshackle as I will mention later.) The manager at the time was Winford Hopkin and, even though I was signed by the chairman over his head, we got on fine.

I was now training twice a week, in the evenings, as Merthyr was a part-time club. It was at this stage that I was approached to take on the role of football development officer for Taff Ely Council. This would certainly take me out of my comfort zone, not least because I had never worked in schools. I now had to adjust to a more normal working day. Football provided our family with jam but our bread and butter came from the community scheme. One advantage of this job was that I would work out of a small office at Penydarren Park, Merthyr's stadium.

The Conference was a national league and I played in some far-flung places, at least far-flung as far as Merthyr was concerned. There would be mammoth trips to Colchester and Barrow. With Merthyr's limited finances, there were no overnight stops and games would sometimes be played at the end of five-hour coach trips. The travelling never bothered me. I enjoyed the odd sing-song, the fun and the conversation on away trips. A pillow became an essential part of my kit for longer away days as it made a nap on the way home slightly more comfortable.

There was also no such thing as a pre-match meal on away days with Merthyr. We would stop somewhere and players would get their own food, often eating stuff that wasn't great for fuelling 90 minutes of endeavour. I started to bring a couple of bags of sandwiches and rolls so that the players had a healthier alternative to some of the motorway junk they were eating.

As well as bringing my limited culinary skills to my new club, I also brought some new playing talent too. Over the course of a couple of months, I was contacted by several of my old youth-team charges at Swansea who were disillusioned at how they were treated there and wondered if they would get a chance at Merthyr. We were happy to have them and three of the boys were able to use their stay as a way back into the league and full-time football. David D'Auria was typical. When I heard that he had been released by Swansea, I got him down to Merthyr. He matured with us and went on to have a good career in league football.

I also brought along Des Trick, Simon Davey, Phil Evans and Chris Thomas, who all did really well for Merthyr. I always felt that clubs released a lot of their youth players too early. At 18, they were still growing into their bodies. The player they were or could have been at 19 or 20 was often more suited to the rigours of a career in football, being that much bigger and stronger. D'Auria and some of the other boys were a case in point.

Soon after joining Merthyr, I started to have a few fitness issues. The hamstring on my right leg was causing me problems. I was helping out our manager Winford Hopkin and I would often take training on a Tuesday or Thursday night. I would sometimes be on my knees in agony after these sessions. I was still managing to play, albeit in great pain, but during half-time I would have to walk around the dressing room as I was too uncomfortable to sit. The condition was diagnosed as a problem with my sciatic nerve, but it didn't matter what treatment I received, nothing seemed to help.

My daughter Lynn had been on to me to go and see a lady she knew who was a faith healer. 'Dad, she will sort you out if you give her a chance,' she told me. I was a complete sceptic and had no intention of seeing this lady. One day, Lynn told me that she had just seen the healer. 'Dad, she told me that you were in bed suffering with back problems. I haven't mentioned you to her, how does she know?' I didn't have an answer, but I still had no intention of meeting her. However, as time went on and I remained in pain with no relief from conventional medicine, she wore me down and I agreed to go.

I arrived at the lady's house, at the appointed time. As I walked up the path to her front door, the high wall on my left was decorated with a selection of old fireplaces removed from houses and hung up there. That was strange, but there was more to come. I was let into the rather dingy house by a Scottish lady with long white hair. She led me along a corridor that had a ceiling from which hung lots of drinking mugs. One side of the corridor housed a selection of slot machines, the other was festooned with a variety of Elvis memorabilia. My qualms about coming hadn't been helped by what I had seen. I wasn't greatly impressed that her treatment room was full of stuffed and ornamental elephants of all shapes and sizes.

I took a seat as invited and I mentioned that Lynn had been coming to her for readings. She told me, 'I do give readings, but my main gift is as a healer.' Well, I was there against my better judgement and, having seen her house, I was even more sceptical now. I would try and catch her out if I could. I knew Lynn hadn't told her anything about me apart from confirming that I had a problem with my back. I was surprised then when she said, 'I can see you're in pain with your back. You've also had problems with your neck too.' I confirmed that as true but I was still giving short answers, determined not to give her any information that she could recycle.

The treatment began when she put her hand at the back of my shoulder, then at the top of my leg. She told me that I should feel a warmth. The sceptic in me still wonders if, in planting a seed in my mind, she caused me to go along with what she said would happen. I did indeed feel a warmth from the touch of her hand, more than you would normally feel when someone touches you. She said that I was going to be fine.

By this stage, any movement was causing me problems and I asked her how soon it would be before I would be able to run again. She told me I would be running within ten days and that my problems would gradually clear. If they started to return, I was to associate this visit to her with a number that was significant to me. I thought about it and said that the number five was the one I would choose. One of my uncles had given me my first football shirt when I was a young boy. I loved that shirt. It was a white Airdrieonians top with a big red 'V' on the front and a big red number five on the back. She said that if the problem reoccurred, I was to visualise the number five in my mind. Think of it in different colours, think about tracing it in the snow, actually trace it in the air or in the soil with my finger. I could also phone her up and she said that talking to her on the phone would sort me out again.

When we finished, I asked her what I owed her. She told me that she wasn't allowed to profit from her gift so there would be no charge. However, as I was leaving, I left a £5 note on the table to help with the cost of all the feather dusters she must go through to keep all of her nick-nacks clean! Despite my scepticism, I was jogging again in ten days and the problem gradually cleared.

Merthyr was a friendly, homely club but, in my three years there, we didn't really pull up any trees in terms of success on the pitch. Indeed, my second and third years would see my team-mates and me battling to ensure that we stayed in the Conference. Early on in my time there, I received a call from the club chairman, John Reddy, asking to meet me at a café at the Head of the Valleys road. He told me that he thought there needed to be a change at the club. When I put the phone down, I got straight on to the manager, Winford Hopkin, and told him that the chairman wanted to see me. Did he know why? The only thing that Winford knew was that the chairman had told him he thought I was finished as a player due to my fitness issues. This surprised me as I had thought from his tone that the chairman was talking about the manager, not me, when we had spoken.

Meeting up with him, I at first assured him that I was fit and ready to play and was in the team for that day's game. He told me he was pleased but that the team as far as he could see needed more than just me returning. He felt we needed a new manager. Would I be interested in the job? My suspicions were confirmed. I asked him if he had told Winford. He said no. I said maybe we should have the meeting with Winford present. Again, he said no. In the end, I told him that I wasn't interested in taking over.

Working full time as well as the playing and training commitments were enough for me. I also told him that I thought he already had a good manager in Winford. I told Winford about the conversation and he wasn't particularly surprised. He laughed and told me that at a meeting he had with the chairman, John Reddy had asked him to get rid of me because I wasn't playing. It looked like at least one of us was on the way out! As for Winford, he said he would carry on until he heard otherwise. Within weeks, he was relieved of his duties and my old Swansea friend and colleague Robbie James took over as player-manager.

You might think that from the way John Reddy dealt with Winford Hopkin, he was the Doug Sharpe of Merthyr. This was not true. I actually got on very well with him. He had a great deal of pride in the club. The boardroom at Merthyr was a very impressive place, much better than the one at Swansea. There was also a nice players' room at the stadium too, again much better than anything Swansea had to offer. John was a member of St Mary's Catholic Church, just around the corner from the stadium. I think we must have been unique in world football because the barmen in the Merthyr bar were two Catholic priests. They worked at the club as a way of generating funds for their parish.

St Mary's Church needed a new roof and John Reddy was determined to help. He asked me if I could get Celtic to send a team down from Glasgow to play us in a fundraising friendly. I knew Tommy Craig well and he was coaching at Celtic at the time, so I thought it was a possibility. Reddy said that I would earn £400 for my trouble if I could get them to come. I got in contact with Tommy and a friendly was arranged.

Celtic were great and sent down a competitive team. The Celtic fans showed fantastic support and the stadium was packed with as many Scots as Welsh that night. Considering the crowd that turned up, we should have raised a fair amount for the church. The problem was that John Reddy absolutely loved events like this and he went to town on commemorating the occasion. The Celtic party were booked in to play golf at the exclusive Castle course and their accommodation was top drawer. Each Celtic and Merthyr player was presented with an engraved tankard, the management from both sides were presented with engraved decanters.

I was worried we'd actually make a loss. If you factored in that each policeman on duty that night would cost the club £85 and there were dozens of them on duty, that in itself was a huge cost. It was only when I saw that the crowd were being entertained at half-time by the police band that I realised that John had got a BOGOF deal with regard to the local constabulary! I never did find out what was raised for the church roof. I suspect it may only have been £400 as I certainly never received my arrangement fee!

I had spent my working life with players who were committed to the lifestyle of being a footballer and would look after themselves. There were some who drank too much, ate the wrong food and who weren't committed in training. They didn't tend to last long and were in the minority. I found the mindset of a lot of the Merthyr players very different. For a start, they played for the fun of the game. The few extra quid they got from playing was simply a bonus.

We had players who, without doubt, could have played league football had they wanted too. Dai Webley, a goalscorer on a Saturday and a foundry worker in the week, was one such player. I told Frank Burrows at Swansea about him and we arranged that he would have a few days' trial when the foundry closed for the Easter holidays so he wouldn't lose any wages. In the end, Webley decided not to go. He was happy enough in the valleys and didn't want the hassle of travelling to Swansea every day.

I remember one occasion when he came to a game unable to play due to burns on his foot. He had an accident at the foundry where molten metal dripped onto his shoe and burned its way through it. Despite events like this and his hard-working life in the foundry, he preferred it to full-time football. He was the best non-league player I had seen.

Another good player we had was a boy called Ceri Williams. He worked in the week tarring roads. He would often put in a shift on a Saturday morning before playing for Merthyr in the afternoon. His lifestyle certainly wasn't one of an athlete as he smoked like the proverbial chimney.

To make sure he got to games on time, I would often pick him up from the site where he was working as I came through from Swansea. The first time, he went to get in my car wearing his tar-spattered overalls. I made him take them off and put them in the boot before he got in. He was only wearing his underpants and T-shirt underneath but that didn't bother him. Every time I picked him up, he was the same. When we arrived at Penydarren Park, he would simply wander from the car park into the changing room in just his pants and shirt! I did find a successful way of winding him up too.

He was the most tattooed person that I had ever come across. I would say to him, 'George,' (yes, his name was Ceri, but for reasons I never knew or I have forgotten, everyone called him George) 'tha programme hasn't been delivered yet, Ah' need something to read, come over here so Ah' can read your back.' He would groan and roll his eyes at me, but it gave me a smile!

I think the Five By Five Club, a group I neither wanted to or indeed could have joined, summed up the attitude of some of the players. Games would end roughly about 4.40 on a Saturday afternoon. To join the Five By Five Club, a player would have to leave the pitch, go straight to the clubhouse and down five pints of beer before five o'clock. For some, playing football at that level wasn't about fitness or dedication, it was a social event, a time to have fun with your mates.

My return to non-league football meant a return to more interaction with the crowd. Just as at Dundonald, you could hear everything spectators shouted at you. Playing in front of bigger crowds, I rarely heard individual comments or any abuse, even when playing on the wing. I was playing in front of mainly working-class crowds and on most occasions, you worked hard and always gave your best, then you would do for them.

I did feel for players that were on the receiving end of some unpleasant chants or catcalls. There was a lack of understanding from people doing this. If you go to work in a tractor factory in Coventry, say, you are able to get on with your job without anyone trying to stop you. In my line of work, I had someone who was equally as skilled, as fit and as determined as me trying to prevent me from doing it, sometimes with people shouting at me telling me I'm rubbish too.

I have to say that nobody on the sidelines ever made me a bad player. If I was being cheered and encouraged then that inspired me, but so did receiving abuse. That made me determined to prove to those people what a good player I was. At Merthyr, I had no Uncle Brickie telling people what he would do to them if they didn't stop shouting insults at me. Fortunately, I quite enjoyed that sort of thing. When I would go and take a corner, someone would inevitably shout, 'Here comes the pensioner. Where's your zimmer frame then?' They thought they were an almighty wit and I hadn't heard anything like that before. I would turn and look at them then, which inevitably unnerved them, and I would say, 'You've forgotten tae mention tha pension book and tha walking stick.' Their mates would then start laughing at them and you would have them on your side.

I returned to Swansea with Merthyr for a Welsh Cup game and the crowd there started to chant 'Swansea reject, Swansea reject' as I went to take a throw-in. Now, I had given six years of good service to that club, helped to save them from liquidation and had been forced to leave against my will, so I wasn't having that. I turned round to face the crowd and spread my arms towards them with a gesture of 'why?' Fair play, the chants stopped, and they gave me a round of applause.

The joy I felt when playing was very much still there at Merthyr and could sometimes get the better of me. I scored an absolute belter of a goal in a game against Farnborough. The sense of euphoria when you score can sometimes make you do daft things. As the ball hit the net, I wheeled away and did a somersault near the touchline, landing on my back. This brought wild applause from the crowd but left me bent double as my back still wasn't in the best of condition. Irene had stopped coming to games by that stage but my antics got back to her as Robbie James lived across the road from us in Swansea. I had no secrets. Robbie and I were quite similar in appearance and even his little lad called me 'Dad' by mistake a couple of times. The postman would also hand me letters for Robbie if he met me outside. When Irene heard the story, she wasn't as impressed by my goal and my backflip as the Merthyr crowd!

When it came time for me to leave Merthyr, chairman John Reddy was very good to me. He marked the occasion of my leaving by holding an event at the local Hoover factory. Hoover were a major employer in South Wales and they also sponsored the club. John used the large Hoover employees' social club to put on a farewell dinner. He arranged for my friend, mentor and footballing hero Denis Law to come down to Merthyr to say a few nice words about me and to present me with an ornate rose bowl. As I say, John liked putting on celebrations like this and seemed to get a lot of pleasure out of arranging them. I was grateful to him as he didn't have to do anything for me once my contract was up.

It was at the end of my third Merthyr year that I made a decision that I really didn't want to make. I had been dreading it. At the age of 46, I decided to bring the curtain down on my football career. I had been paid as a player on a part-time or full-time basis for over 28 years, in a profession where the average span of employment is only eight years. In the end, what made me call time was the expansion of my role as a Football in the Community officer. I no longer had the time to train and play, with so much of a Saturday spent travelling too. I had no regrets over what I had done or where I had been. I had loved every minute of my time as a professional footballer, but it was time to move on.

Chapter 39

Life after Football

IT WAS through my role as youth-team coach at Swansea that I first came into contact with the PFA officer for South Wales, John Relish. He would come to the club once a week to make sure our young players were being looked after properly. I got to know John quite well during these visits and we would often have a chat. One day he asked me if I had considered what I would do when my playing days were over. Had I thought about working for the PFA on one of their development projects? At the time, I was working long but fulfilling hours at the club and I told him that I hadn't even considered retirement, or what I would do when no longer a footballer.

Within a few weeks of signing for Merthyr, John contacted me. He told me that the PFA and Taff Ely Council were setting up a development programme that would be run out of Merthyr Tydfil FC. Would I be interested in taking on the role as the football development officer? I was at first unsure what I should do. I needed a job, as playing part-time for Merthyr only gave me part-time wages. But could I do this job? Would I be capable of fulfilling the role?

I had a chat with my old Manchester City and Burnley team-mate Kevin Reeves, who had a similar job at Birmingham City to the one I was being offered. He was positive about the work he did, which was reassuring. Both the PFA and the council had been running similar schemes to the one they were proposing. I knew that I would be presented with lots of children to work with and all the equipment I needed. What I didn't understand until after I started was that it was up to me to generate the courses for children to attend and, through these, generate my income. I had no guaranteed wage, which was a bit daunting.

Initially, I worked on my own. I would contact a school and tell them that they had six free football coaching sessions for their children, delivered by me. Some headteachers who were followers of the oval-ball code were reluctant to let me in as they didn't want their children playing the wrong game! Schools that I did manage to get into often gave me their football team or their Year 6 children (to begin with, I only worked in primary schools). I told them I didn't want to work with their football team and ideally not Year 5. I wanted to start with Year 3 and return each subsequent year to work with the same children, therefore ensuring progression.

Most schools in the end worked this way. I was supposed to be accompanied at all times by the class teacher. This was the case to start with, but when they came to see that I could be trusted and that I had control of the class, a lot of them were happy for me to get on with it in the playground while they completed other tasks.

For me, the goal wasn't to produce better footballers, although this could be a by-product of what I did. My objective was to use football as a vehicle to teach the values of working hard, good communication and of teamwork. I hoped that the children would learn to communicate more effectively and that their levels of concentration would improve.

Through teacher Malcolm Brown I got involved with Ty Coch, a school for children with special needs. Malcolm had been a player at Merthyr and he promoted my work brilliantly, so much so that I ended up alongside him taking a Welsh special needs team of young adults to an event at Wembley before the Charity Shield between Blackburn and Everton. For three days prior to the Wembley date, we stayed at Windsor Castle and I worked with the group, some who had Down's syndrome, some who had cerebral palsy, on basic skills. Young adults with similar needs were there representing England, Ireland and Scotland.

My friend from my Blackpool days, Derek Fontane, turned up at the castle while we were there after hearing I was involved. I chatted to him for a few minutes and introduced him to Malcolm Brown. He went off for a bit and turned up a little while later with a bag full of drinks for our team. It was a really hot day and I was a bit concerned that we would be having cold drinks in front of the players from the other three countries who were practising nearby.

I mentioned this to Derek. 'Ah, tae hell with them.' It makes Derek sound harsh and uncaring but nothing could be further from the truth.

It was simply that he was my friend. I was managing the Welsh team and for those few days, Derek, a proud Scot, would be an honorary Welshman. When Derek left, Malcolm was upset that we couldn't give him a security pass so that he could join us inside Wembley. I told him not to worry as Derek would get in. 'Tha' man can get intae places tha' mice would struggle with,' I told him.

At that time, Derek was working as a London cabbie despite never having taken 'the knowledge', the test on routes through London everyone had to pass if they were to drive a London black cab. It was the occupation he had taken up after working as a press photographer. His qualification to be a press photographer? He had bought himself a good camera. He hung around Heathrow or Gatwick and snapped celebrities as they came through arrivals. He managed to somehow get himself pictured alongside famous people, such as Liz Taylor.

On the day of the game, the security gates closed behind our coach at Wembley, we had our paperwork checked and the guards ensured that each one of us had the correct coloured wristbands. Security was tight. As the bus came to a halt, I tapped Malcolm Brown on the shoulder and pointed out of the window. Not only was Derek there ahead of us carrying his camera but he was being followed by a senior security guard who he somehow duped into carrying his photographic equipment. He told me later that he had announced himself at the gates as the official photographer for 'Welsh News'. Through a mixture of bravado and the use of his silver tongue, Derek wormed his way in, as I knew he would.

We took our teams out onto the pitch before the main match. Derek may have been the supposed photographer for Welsh News, but here he was striding all over the holy turf of Wembley taking photos of all four teams. Each corner of the pitch had one of the teams showing off a drill to the crowd. After a few minutes, all the teams moved on to an adjacent corner and a new skill would be demonstrated. Our team, male and female, decked out in Welsh international kit provided by the FA after much cajoling by Malcolm Brown, were having the time of their lives.

Once we had finished our routines, the teams made their way up the famous 39 steps to the royal box to receive their medals. As all four teams stood on the balcony, having received the applause of the crowd, the official photographer on the right-hand steps spoke to the group and carefully composed them, ready for his final portrait. He was just about to take their picture but, before he could say 'cheese', a shout of

'This way everyone' came from the left-hand steps from the Welsh News photographer, who duly clicked away with his camera, leaving his colleague lost for words on the other side of the box!

The event brought me to the attention of Taff Ely schools. With Malcolm as my advocate, this time cajoling headteacher colleagues, my pathway into schools became much easier.

During the school holidays. I ran fun days all over the county on council fields or in sports halls. On these occasions I called in favours from my Merthyr team-mates and asked them to volunteer to coach the children. The Merthyr lads were as good as gold and they came along and helped me out. It gave them a bit of experience of working with children and of coaching, even if it didn't give them any extra cash.

I worked in some pretty deprived areas with children who had very little in material terms. One such area was Gurnos in Merthyr. The council asked me to run an evening session there. I had two groups to work with, nine to 11-year-olds followed by 12 to 13-year-olds. The sessions were held on a floodlit all-weather pitch and the aim was to cut down on anti-social behaviour and petty crime in the area by giving the children something worthwhile to do. There was a nominal charge of something like 20p but I aways allowed in anyone who didn't have the money, asking them to pay next time. In almost all cases, that is what happened.

The pitch was enclosed by a combination of wood and mesh fencing. As the younger children began their first session, some of the older kids gathered outside; first to watch, then to throw stones in. We ignored what was going on as best we could. At the changeover from younger to older children, I recognised many of those now entering the enclosure as the stone throwers. I told them to form a line at the top of the pitch. Our warm up, I said to them, was a series of stretches. I informed them, 'Ah want you to slowly walk forward, and every time you see a stone, Ah want you tae stretch doon and pick it up. We don't start playin' until you've stretched for every stone.' It must have taken us 20 minutes to clear the pitch but the stone throwing never happened again!

When I told my old Swansea mate Ron Walton, who came from Merthyr, that I would be working in Gurnos, he rolled his eyes and told me not to take my car in there as it would soon be wheelless and balancing on bricks. I had a nice red Mercedes at the time but it never bothered me to leave it in the area when I was working. The kids got to know me, to know I was fair and was on their side. I never had any bother and my car was never touched.

One of my tasks in Taff Ely was to organise an annual five-a-side competition sponsored by the PFA between the primary schools. It involved a league system followed by a knockout competition. The winner in Taff Ely would go on to compete in area semi-finals. The winners in my area, two years in a row, were the team from Goetre Primary, the school which served the Gurnos district. Most of the children in that school had travelled very little outside of their community. To get to an area final that would take some of them to London was a huge event.

The area final for the first of these two year groups was held at QPR's ground, Loftus Road. In our first game we played a school from Chelsea. My team froze and lost. I told them that the children may have been from a school in Chelsea but that they had nothing to do with the football club of that name. They were just ordinary kids like we were. This seemed to work and the Goetre kids went out and played with freedom in the rest of the games in the area finals, so much so that we won this part of the competition. We were now through to the national finals to be staged at Wembley.

The whole area was lifted by the success of the school football team and a coach was hired to take families and anyone else who wanted to go see their children perform in the English national stadium. The competition was to take part on the Wembley pitch before an England game. Although we didn't win, the experience that the children had that year will have stayed with them forever. Above all, it showed them that kids who came from Gurnos could succeed, often against children who came from more privileged backgrounds. The belief generated by that first Goetre team was passed on to the year group that followed them. They also reached the area finals and, although they went out at that stage, they too had a tremendous experience. The power of sport to lift the lives of people was clear to see after the exploits of the local school football team.

After three years working out of Merthyr, I was approached by John O'Callaghan of Vale of Glamorgan Council to see if I would be interested in running a similar scheme for him, this time in conjunction with the Welsh FA. John had previously worked for Taff Ely Council and was impressed by what I had done there. My new job would involve working with a much larger number of schools and with a big increase in workload.

I was already doing a lot of travelling up and down the Taff Valley. Working for Glamorgan Council would mean having two additional valleys to navigate, the Rhondda and the Cynon. It was at this point that I decided to call time on my playing career. I was already finding it hard to devote the time I needed to do myself justice on the field. For the first time ever, I wasn't enjoying training or the travel to away games. I was also suffering more and more injuries. It made sense to finish.

I had enjoyed working and playing in Merthyr, but once again it was time to move on. My time working for Taff Ely had shown me that I could both set up a football development scheme and run it successfully. More importantly, I found out that I really enjoyed working with children, particularly those who came from difficult backgrounds. It gave me a real thrill to feel that even in a small way I might be helping to improve their circumstances. I was hoping for more of the same in my new position.

Chapter 40

Football in the Valleys

ONE OF the main attractions to me of the new job was that my wages would be paid directly by the council and by the Welsh FA. Working for the FA was a bit of a problem. As far as I was concerned, I was finished with the professional game. I had come to believe that the only role that I wanted in professional football was as a player. That time of my life had now passed. However, if I wanted this role, I would have to put some of my scruples aside. The Welsh FA wanted me to run their centres of excellence. To do this, over two years, I had to take my A, B and C coaching qualifications. To cut down on travelling we moved house from the Mumbles to Llantrisant in the Vale of Glamorgan.

John O'Callaghan was into his sport and, somehow, he managed to convince the council to fund a fantastic floodlit 3G facility complete with plush changing rooms in Pontypridd. It was a great place to run our courses. My old friend and colleague from Swansea, Tony Abel, worked alongside me. While I was out and about working in schools and running fun days, Tony was responsible for the day-to-day running of the centre. Because of the facility, we were able to put on sessions for a wide range of children. I got to know many of the children and their families very well. One little lad, Chris Harris, regularly attended and was always brought by his granddad. I was taking this boy's group one day when I noticed that his movement seemed a bit strange. He would swing at the ball and miss and seemed to fall over for no reason.

I spoke to Granddad after the session and what he had to tell me was devastatingly sad. He told me that the boy had been diagnosed with a brain tumour. That was bad enough, but he also told me that his older teenage brother had been told he had cancer in his back. Worse still,

Chris's dad, this man's son, died the previous Christmas, also from a tumour in his back. Granddad said that he had been going to tell me this awful news that night and to ask me for some help. The family were hoping to send the older boy, a rugby player, to an overseas rugby tournament. Chris, they wanted to send to Disneyland. I told him to leave things with me and I would see what I could do.

I wasn't keen on organising some sort of bucket collection for this family. I immediately thought of using my football connections to raise money. There was a nice little stadium in Pontypridd used by local teams, set in the middle of a park with a great pitch. My initial thought was that I could get a few of my old footballing mates together to put on some sort of all-stars game. However, someone had a conversation with me about an upcoming Wales international match. It put a grain of an idea in my head. The Welsh squad were together at that very moment only a few miles from Pontypridd. I got on to the Wales manager Bobby Gould, explained the circumstances and asked him: if I found someone for them to play, would he bring a team to Pontypridd in two days' time? Gould was fantastic and agreed straight away. Next, I was on the phone to Cardiff manager Phil Neal. He was as good as Gould, if you pardon the pun! Cardiff would send a team too.

Game on. I contacted John O'Callaghan at the council. When he heard the story, he immediately swung council resources behind what we were doing. It seemed that all other council business stopped for a couple of days. Flyers were produced in record time and distributed all over the county. I organised a good local ref to come in and take control of the game and a quick call to Umbro meant we had top-quality match balls.

It was unbelievable that so many people came together to make sure the event took place at short notice. On the night of the game, we had volunteers on the gates to the park collecting the admission money in buckets. We asked for a minimum £2 donation to get in, but most people gave much more. Cardiff and Wales brought very strong teams to play and both Gould and Neal deserve great credit for taking on an extra game they could have done without. We raised £23,000 that night for the two boys and their family. They were both able to go on the trips planned for them.

I went to see Chris at his house after the fundraising match. I was disappointed to see that the family and their neighbours were living in streets that very much reminded me of the pit raws from Dundonald, the streets I had grown up in. How was it that nearly 40 years after the raws were demolished as unfit to house people, there were still places like them, housing families in Pontypridd? Anyway, I chatted to Chris and his mum. I felt really sorry for her. She had lost her husband and now there was a real possibility that she was going to lose her two sons too. I asked Chris who his favourite player was. He told me it was Eric Cantona. Later that day, I gave Alex Ferguson a call, told him the story, and asked him to send me a photo of Eric with a personal message to the boy. When I took the signed photo around to him, Chris was really made up.

Things were not looking good for Chris. I went to see him when he was admitted to hospital in Cardiff. He was very poorly and sadly he passed away. We organised for a trophy, an engraved cut-glass bowl, to be presented in remembrance of him at his school, Cilfynydd Primary. This was given out annually to the boy or girl who had made the greatest effort to improve in sport and academic work. For the first two years of the award, I went into the school and presented it myself. I am pleased to say that the memory of Chris is still being kept alive in the school today, nearly 30 years after his death, as the trophy is still presented every year. Thankfully for his family, Chris's elder brother was able to beat his illness and was cured.

Working in communities such as Cilfynydd was the thing I liked best about my work. Football was such a powerful tool to make a real difference to the lives of the children that I worked with. The part I was least fond of was running the Welsh FA centres of excellence, something I had to do because the FA were part-funding my wages. It was too close to the professional game, which I no longer wanted to be a part of. At the start of my time in the Vale of Glamorgan I had a meeting with a representative from the Welsh FA. He outlined what was expected of me. I was to take boys with potential from 11 to 15 years of age and coach them in year groups. I asked him how the centres would be funded, who would pay for kit, resources, venues, coaches. He told me that I would collect subs from the boys, 50p a session. Now that sort of money, even in the mid-90s, wasn't going to go far. It also bothered me that a boy's presence at the courses would depend, not only on his footballing ability, but on his family's ability to pay. I knew families where finding a spare 50p would be difficult.

I knew that the Welsh FA had no money. It was something that Terry Yorath had often mentioned. In the end, I told the chap from the FA that I wouldn't be charging the boys to come to the courses. I would find other ways of funding them. He went off happy, knowing the centre of excellence courses would be up and running with no cost to the Welsh FA. I was happier knowing that I was footing the bill – it gave me a much greater autonomy. The first thing I did was to change the age range I was taking. I would have seven to 13-year-olds. I would start with younger boys. Only when lads we had worked with ourselves got to the age of 14 and 15 would we run those age groups. I wanted the boys to have developed the right attitude and habits.

Funding would come from fun days that I ran. I knew the coaches would be happy to give their services for free. The venues we would use would be council-owned, such as our lovely 3G facility in Pontypridd. My council connections would mean these were available free of charge, including floodlighting and changing facilities. The only thing I would have to fund was the equipment we would use.

A career in football is a great way of building connections. Due to the Hoover's sponsorship of Merthyr, I knew many of the managers in the factory. I contacted one of the guys and asked if he would provide a bit of sponsorship for the Welsh FA's elite boys groups by providing a washing machine and tumble dryer for our centre in Pontypridd. 'No bother, Tommy.' The equipment duly arrived with the washing machine plumbed in by local firefighters who used our centre as a base to keep fit.

I went around a number of local stores and asked them to donate towels for the boys to use. These were generously given to us. Each boy who came to the centre was expected to shower afterwards. They would each have their own towel with their name on, which would be washed after each session. It was another way of removing barriers to attendance due to the embarrassment of having either no towel or only having one that had seen better days. Showering after matches and training was one of those good habits that I wanted to instil in my boys. It also gave them a chance to have a proper wash, something not always available at home.

I picked the boys who came to our programmes. Their selection was based on what I had seen going around the schools. The purpose of the centre of excellence programme was to improve the boys as players and showcase them to the Welsh FA and to professional clubs who, when the boys were older, would take the better ones on as apprentices.

During my time working in the Vale of Glamorgan, I was contacted by Mark Hughes, who had been given the Wales manager job. He asked me if I would coach and look after the under-16 team. I said to him that I was interested, but the only problem was I was Scottish! He laughed and said my nationality wasn't a problem, he just wanted someone who could do the job, which was a nice compliment. I was happy to take on the role as long as I could make my own decisions.

I remember we had a trial game for likely candidates for the team. The young goalkeeper in one of the trial sides was doing okay but made a howler of a mistake when he came for a cross and got nowhere near the ball, costing his team a goal. A few minutes later, he came again for a cross and again missed the ball. At the end of the game, when I told the players and their parents who I was taking through to form the squad, I could sense the surprise when I picked that lad as part of my squad. I decided to explain my decision.

He had shown courage and confidence in putting his first mistake behind him to come for the ball the second time. This mental resilience, added to his generally good performance, warranted his selection. The good keepers I had played with – Glazier, Blyth and Sealey at Coventry and Corrigan at Man City – all had the mental ability to not let a mistake ruin their overall performance. I had seen these qualities in this lad. I was happy to back my judgement and not always go with the easy or, at least on the surface, more obvious answer. Mark Hughes was content to leave these decisions to me so I enjoyed working for him for a while.

I finished this part of my association with the Welsh FA in the end because I didn't like the interference from the selectors of the Welsh Schools FA. While Mark was happy for me to make the decisions I felt were best for the young lads in my care, this was not always true of the selectors, who I felt had too much power. I took a squad of potential under-16 players on a training camp for a week with Ian Docherty, who worked with me in the Vale of Glamorgan. Our brief was to work with the boys on closing down opponents and restricting their space with the ball. We put together some quite detailed reports on the players we worked with and had drawn up a provisional list of names who we thought should be in the final squad.

At the end of the week, a group of school selectors came to meet us. We passed on our reports detailing the strengths and weaknesses of the boys in the group and handed over our provisional squad. It was already disappointing that we didn't have the final say as to which boys would go through. We had worked intensively with them and had a far better knowledge of the players than these guys who had just turned up. We were even more annoyed when we joined the group of teachers as they were coming to their final decisions as to who was in and who was out.

They had disregarded virtually everything we had said and were basing selection to a large extent on geographical location. There is some animosity between North and South Walians and they wanted to ensure that there was a balance of boys from both regions. Similarly, those from the South were selected so that there was a balance from the different areas, particularly Swansea and Cardiff. It was an amateurish way to put together a squad and totally unfair on the boys.

The final straw was when one of them questioned my loyalty. We played in a four-team tournament against Scotland, Ireland and England. We got through to the final and were going to play the Scots. A Welsh selector came up to me as the boys were warming up and, in all seriousness, asked me who I wanted to win. I asked him which team's tracksuit I was wearing. He huffed and walked away.

I told Mark after that game that I was going to finish. Ironically, I had a disagreement with the Scotland coach, a boy from Celtic, that day too. I saw that my purpose as a coach was to improve the lads I worked with as players. Winning was nice but was not the primary concern with boys of this age group. I used to coach from the touchline, alongside our defensive line. The Scottish boy objected to this, saying I was telling the boys what to do, and not liking the fact I wasn't stood on the centre line. We had to agree to disagree. As far as I was concerned, improving the boys' performance was part of my role as a coach.

In August 1998 I received news that I had been dreading. I took a phone call from my sister Lizabeth to say that Mum had been taken into hospital with an embolism. They had been debating whether or not to operate but, before they could decide, she had died anyway. We went back up to Fife for her funeral. Although she was 85, her sudden death was still a shock as she had remained fit, active and healthy throughout the 20-odd years she had lived on without my dad. I was lucky that, despite living so far away from home, I always knew she was well looked after, firstly because my two sisters were nearby, secondly because she always had company in the house as she continued to live with my uncles.

At the time of her death, one of my uncles was still around. At her passing, he moved into sheltered accommodation, but he only lasted a few months on his own without my mum. Liz Robertson was a strong woman who had lived a hard life, particularly in her early years. She remained the fiery but kind character she had always been, always willing to give away her last penny to someone she thought would need it more. I always felt she had high expectations of me, something not always easy to live up to. It was as though I had to be a hero to her. Because of my job, I had the satisfaction of being able to help Mum and Dad and then, after Dad died, Mum on her own, with any financial needs. I think that both Mum and Dad were proud of what I had achieved.

Life goes on and Irene and I returned to South Wales, but not for long. To be a football development officer in the Vale of Glamorgan was a very fulfilling role. It did, however, require a lot of energy and hard work to do the job properly. The amount of travelling each and every day to schools and centres up and down the valleys was wearing, and that was before the high-octane task of working with the children. By the end of my time in the Vale, I covered three valleys, as Taff Ely, my old area when at Merthyr, had joined and become my responsibility too. Despite the hectic nature, I had no intention of leaving until John Relish, my old PFA mate, met up with me one day with a new proposal.

Chapter 41

The Last Post

UNLIKE MY two previous posts as a football development officer, my new role didn't require me to set up a programme from scratch. Bristol City – for it was in their community department that John Relish wanted me to work – already had something in place, it just wasn't working very well. As I understood things, my predecessor in this job had been keen to work with the football club. He wanted involvement with the professional side of Bristol City and had perhaps neglected his main objective in the role, that of working in the community.

On the day I came for the interview, one of the directors showed me a leaflet showing the programme of events run by the community arm of the club in the previous year. It was an extremely busy set of activities including something like 20 fun days all over the city. I pointed these out to the director and said, 'This all looks great, running over 20 fun days, what dae you want me fur?' He said, 'Yes, looks great, Tommy, but only six of those fun days took place, and that's typical of what had been going on.'

I wanted to be the opposite of the guy I was taking over from. I told him I would take the post but only on condition that I had nothing to do with the professional side of the club. I wasn't interested in academies, youth teams, any of it. I had said the same in my previous post and still flirted with the professional game due to my links with the Welsh FA. Well, this time I was adamant. My role would be purely community-based. A small part of my wages was to be paid by the PFA. The rest I was going to have to generate from the programmes I ran. Bristol City gave me the use of the Ashton Gate office, stationery and mailshots but nothing else.

The key to the success we enjoyed in Bristol was that we worked as a team, and our team had a clear ethos. We were there to serve the children we worked with, and through our activities try to improve their lives. I worked with Mandy Gardener. She ran academic courses that complemented the work that I did. There was a study centre at Ashton Gate, complete with a suite of computers. It was a really innovative facility in those days and one installed with the purpose of engaging children who would often be totally turned off by academic studies. Mandy and I worked closely, taking the same groups of children. I would put on football-related activities and she would put together academic work, often IT-related with a football slant.

Over the course of two years, we put in two bids for funding from the Football Foundation. These needed to be very detailed to succeed. Mandy was invaluable in completing the forms we had to send in. I was happy to leave all this to her. She obviously did an excellent job as the two bids brought in close to half a million pounds. This enabled myself and coaches such as Geoff Stevens to work intensively in deprived areas such as Withywood, Hartcliffe and Henbury. We had to account for every penny that we spent and we had to ensure that we were spending the money on the areas we had specified in the bid. This is where Mandy's husband Richard came in. He was meticulous in producing our accounts.

The attraction of working in Bristol was that my energies would be directed at running courses and working with children rather than having miles and miles of driving to do as I had in the valleys. We moved house for the final time of my working life and settled into the border town of Chepstow. I would work out of an office based at Ashton Gate.

Working for a community scheme based at a professional club did give me the opportunity of giving out incentives to those taking part in our programmes. Bristol City would give me up to 1,000 tickets to give to children for each home game. We would have a section of the ground given over for kids on our courses and their parents, who could attend a match for a cut-price £5 admission charge. I was surprised at the reaction of some of the children I worked with in places such as Withywood or Hartcliffe. These districts were only ten or 15 minutes outside of the city centre, but many of our kids had never been into Bristol and certainly nowhere near a football stadium. Some of them were amazed by what they saw.

Reaction of the parents varied. I had one dad come up to me and say, 'Thanks for this mate, it's great. I used to have a season ticket up here, but since the kids came along, I can't afford it now. The bonus is, cos' I've had the kids all day, I can go out for a pint tonight too!' On another occasion, I went over to talk to a dad who was more concerned about gesturing and shouting obscenities at the away fans than he was about his embarrassed son or the game.

I went over to him and said, 'Sit doon, sit doon. Where dae you think you are? You're in the kids' section!' At the end of the game, he told me that he didn't like the way that I had spoken to him. 'Who do you think you are telling me to sit down?' He was going to see the club chairman to complain. I told him to come along with me there and then. I'd take him into the boardroom so he could make his complaint to the chairman straight away. He slunk off, declining my generous (and genuine, as I would have taken him to the chairman) offer.

I also had a good relationship with the boy who ran the club shop. He would pass on any pieces of the previous season's kit that he wasn't able to sell. I would give these out as prizes for competitions that I would run. At one point I had around 500 club scarves in my house. Every girl or boy who worked with us would get a red and white City scarf.

Not long after moving to work in Bristol, Irene and I received some worrying news. Our youngest son David had discovered that he had a lump on his testicles. He told us over the phone that he was going to have a biopsy done. It was not the first time that we had been worried about David's health. When I was at Merthyr, we heard the tragic news about Terry Yorath's son Daniel. Terry had been playing football in his garden with his 15-year-old son when Daniel collapsed and died. It was found that he had an undiagnosed heart condition.

Our hearts went out to Terry and his family. The pain of losing a child was unimaginable. You can realise our horror when, just a few months after Terry and Christine lost Daniel, David got up from the kitchen table, took a few steps and then collapsed to the floor. Thankfully he came around pretty quickly and, after various tests and checks, the doctors thought they knew what the problem was. David was still growing into his teenage body but was well over six feet tall. Because of his size, it took a while for his heart to pump blood to his brain if he stood up and moved too quickly. So as long as he got up slowly, he would be okay and the problem would gradually disappear.

We hoped that the medical experts would again relieve us of our worries and tell us that David was fine. I went into the consultant's room with David to find out the results of the biopsy. This time we received the news that we had been dreading. The lump was malignant, David did indeed have testicular cancer. The consultant was very optimistic about his prospects. All things being equal, he thought David would make a full recovery. He operated successfully on David and diagnosed a course of radiotherapy.

David was pretty calm about things. It was typical of him that he wanted to find out all he could about the disease so that he would know what to expect. Needless to say, me and his mum were far more anxious. In the end, the news was good, the treatment was a success and David was soon fit and well. He has since gone on to marry and have two lovely children.

While David's treatment was going on, it was hard to concentrate on anything else. However, in lots of ways my work helped me to take my mind off the worries. Early on in my time in the city, I met up with the chap who was running similar schemes to me at Bristol Rovers. He had been in post for some time and knew the various districts of the town. We were deciding which schools and localities would be Rovers and which would be City. Because of his greater local knowledge, I was happy to defer to him but it quickly became apparent to me that a greater number of the poorer, more deprived areas were going to be red, while most of the well-to-do areas would be blue. Maybe he just wanted to replicate the political map of the city!

What he didn't realise was that I was more than happy with what he was doing. I saw the schemes as a way to improve the lives of the children who signed up. It was far easier to do this when the children I worked with had little to begin with. The kids who came from those areas were also those that I related to best as I came from similar circumstances. For some of the children, I was the only male figure that they came into contact with. There were a lot of single-parent families. Since working with young children, I had learned to tread carefully and build up a relationship with them. It wasn't uncommon for a child to flinch if I made to move towards them. I could only imagine what some of their home lives were like.

I had almost the whole school age range on my courses in Bristol, with children from Year 3 to the final years of secondary school. I did leadership courses with the older children where they had to learn management skills through coaching sessions they took with primary-age children. This was a real eye-opener for some of the kids who hadn't been the best behaved through their school years, having to manage the behaviour of younger versions of themselves. From the leadership courses, I was able to offer some work experience sessions to those who had shown an aptitude for working with younger children. This might also lead to some of them having a pathway into employment through apprenticeship schemes. Some of the lads who went through this process actually came to work for me.

I took on one lad, Ryan, from a special school. I had been impressed with him and arranged with the headteacher of the school to meet up with Ryan and his mum to offer him the apprenticeship. When I told him that I liked what I had seen from him and that I wanted him to join me, both he and his mum burst into tears, even the headteacher was a bit misty-eyed. He told me that it was a rare event for children from his school to be offered a job. I did tell Ryan, a Man United fan, that he would be getting all of the dirty jobs. Due to my Manchester City connections, I was obliged to make life difficult for anyone who was a Red! Thankfully he got the joke and accepted.

Ryan knew his football but was a little slow on the uptake sometimes. However, he really showed his mettle when thrown in at the deep end. We were running a day's course in Taunton and turned up at the sports centre in our van packed with the kit needed. When I was unloading our gear, I found we had left our bags of footballs behind. We had 40 eager kids joining us for a day of fun and football who were drifting into the changing rooms even as I discovered our mistake.

I called Ryan to one side and told him I would dash into town to buy as many balls as I could. I wanted him to start off the session doing a few activities that didn't require a ball and buy me the time I needed. I went into Taunton and bought around 12 balls, an amount that would get us through the day, and hotfooted it back to the sports centre. Well, I needn't have hurried. Ryan had everything under control. All of the children were bibbed up and were having a great time doing a range of activities that Ryan had organised. I was delighted to know that I hadn't been missed.

Ryan's life had been far from easy. He was very down one day. When I asked him why, he told me he had been thinking about his dad. I knew he wasn't on the scene at home but didn't know the circumstances. Ryan told me that his father had treated him badly as a child. Ryan was a big chap and I believed him when he told me that if he ever met up with his father again, he would batter him. I told him the best way he could show his strength and his power over his dad was by carrying on the way he was going and make a success of his life. An easy thing for me to say, but I didn't want to see the justified bitterness that he felt derail his life.

Ryan had been working for me for over a year when he came in one day in tears and told me that he would have to leave. His mum had had her benefits recalculated and now, as a result of Ryan bringing in a wage to the household, they were going to be £80 a month worse off. It was my turn to feel bitter at a system that penalised young people trying to make their way in the world. I did meet up again with Ryan a few years later. He was working in a Bristol sports shop and I had gone in for a new pair of trainers. We had a good chat and I was pleased to see him doing well. I also advised him that the only way he would flog those awful Man United shirts was to offer them at half price!

If you have managed to read through to this point, you will know that nothing else in my life gave me the thrill of being out on a pitch with a ball at my feet. It was sheer bliss! However, there were occasions in my life as a football development officer when I knew that I had a positive impact on a child's life. That ran close to the joy I felt as a footballer.

But what a tool I had at my disposal! What a tool for good football was! It could be used to bring warring factions, groups or individuals together and make them friends. I genuinely believe that if it is used in the right way, football can achieve the almost impossible. Football gave me the opportunity to build relationships with the children I worked with. It was football that allowed me to teach the skills that would be invaluable to improving the lives of the children on my courses, particularly if they came from a disadvantaged background

I took Sean for football at Gay Elms school. He was so keen he would slide tackle on the playground. This would either be courageous or foolhardy, depending on your point of view, for an able-bodied child. Sean, however, suffered from cerebral palsy. When we started working with his class one September, we quickly had to dissuade him from throwing himself about so much. There was no doubt here was a lad with spirit. I was saddened to learn from his teacher that, due to the worsening condition of the muscles in his legs, it was expected that he would be in a wheelchair by Christmas.

I thought about ways we could help Sean and prevent the loss of so much of his independence if he lost his mobility. I devised a plan. Every time we took his group, we had sessions that still involved the use of a football but were built around movement as well. We used the school field to set up a circuit which required the group to run, stretch, change direction, jump and bend. The objective was to improve the children's core and muscle strength. Because these activities all involved the use of a ball and were football related, all the children enjoyed them, including Sean.

When the rest of the group went off to play five-a-side after three circuits, I kept Sean behind to do one or two more before he went off to join his mates. My personal objective was to ensure that when we left the school at Christmas, Sean was still mobile and out of a wheelchair. It was achieved. Sean was still active, on his feet and playing football at the end of our time there.

Two boys I remember very well were Billy and Sam. They were twin brothers that I came to know from my time working in their secondary school. They were well known to everyone in the school and in the area and not for the right reasons. They were coming to the end of their school days and the way they behaved wasn't improving. I had them on one of my football programmes and they weren't the easiest of lads to work with.

I had a visit one day from the local FA officer, James, and we were talking about which of the older kids I would take on for work experience. He asked me if I would take on these two boys. He felt that, despite their troubled history, they had a bit about them. It was something that I hadn't even considered. These two lads were, to use an old-fashioned description, tearaways. They already seemed to be on a troubled path. It was hard to see that they were going to become the sort of adults who would contribute positively to society. I had enough difficulty dealing with them in my sessions; did I now want to work with them all day every day for the next few weeks?

Against my better judgement, I agreed to give them a start. I met up with the two lads. 'So, boys, I hear you want tae come and work with me?' They nodded. 'Well,' I said, 'any nonsense from either wan of you an' you'll be back oot tha' door. You understand?' Again, they nodded.

My initial thought was that we would have more of a chance of making things work if we split them up. It proved to be a good idea.

Sam came out with me. Early on he proved his worth. We went into a local primary school just as the lunch break was ending. We were met by the caretaker who told us that one of the lads we were due to take that day had climbed a tree on the playing field and was refusing to come down. 'He's been performing all lunchtime, I've had enough of him.' And with that he stomped off! He didn't have to tell us about the boy in the tree as we had heard him shouting at the lad as soon as we got into the car park. Sam said he knew the boy and he would get him down.

I left him to it and within ten minutes I saw the two of them, Sam and the boy, out on the field putting out the equipment for the session. When I went over, I asked the lad why he had climbed the tree. 'Tommy, I was playing football at break time and no one would pass the ball to me. I wasn't getting a kick.' The obvious solution from his point of view was to climb a tree! By the end of the session, he was joining in with us and he even went over to apologise to the caretaker. Sam had succeeded because he knew and understood the boy.

When you saw the area that Sam and Billy grew up in, it was not hard to understand why they were the way they were. I had come across them at their school, Withywood Comprehensive, unkindly nicknamed and stigmatised by people from other areas as 'Diviwood' due to the assumption that it was 'divis' who went there. I had also encountered them on a council-sponsored programme I put on at a small sports hall at Broadplain, near to where they lived.

What a place that was! The sports hall was just across the road from the police station, luckily! We used the field at the back of the sports hall and we had to clear a variety of drug paraphernalia before we could start the sessions. Unfortunately, we couldn't clear the drug and alcohol users who were still dotted about the field when we tried to set up. I remember a young mother there, a couple of kids playing around her, another in the pram, swigging from a can of lager as she sat on the grass, surrounded by her discarded empties. This was Sam and Billy's community.

I have to say that they proved me wrong on work experience, so much so that I offered them both a paid apprenticeship. I got them kitted out with new trainers and tracksuit. I expected anyone who worked with me to look the part, to have smart, clean kit on and to take a pride in their appearance. I knew that there was still potential for them to go off the rails and I warned them, 'See tha' tracksuit? Well, tha' has ma name on it. You don't wear it outside, only when you're working with me. When you have tha' on your representing me and Ah haven't worked hard all ma life tae have two muppets like yous ruin ma reputation, you understand now?' I was deliberately hard on them and would give out to them any time that they failed to live up to my expectations. However, they knew I was looking out for them and wanted them to do well, so there was mutual respect.

I talked to them all the time about the choices that they could make. Did they want to spend their days doing drugs and dossing, giving up on life like some in their community had done, or did they want something better, a life where they could be proud of what they had done? We had to fill in forms from the council that showed we had no criminal records and we were the sort of people that were safe to work with children. They were curious about this. I explained to them that whatever they did in the past, it could affect them in their future lives.

I turned to Billy and said, 'Didn't Ah hear that you nearly got caught stealing a poster from Woolworths?' They were honest villains and Billy said, 'Yes, but that was more than a year ago.' Sam was laughing at him so I turned to him and said, 'And didn't Ah hear that you had been on the roof at the local shops pinching lead? You were both lucky you weren't caught. Get a record like tha' an' it will stay with you for life. There'd be no working with me if you had a record.' They seemed to take this in and were as good as gold.

On one occasion they arrived late. I wanted them to know it wasn't acceptable. 'But we missed the bus,' one of them tried to explain. 'Well, get up earlier an' get the bus before,' I told them. 'There's a group o' kids sitting in a school waiting for us tae come. Dae you think they'd say as they sat in the cold that it was okay as Billy and Sam had missed their bus? You're on time here every day, okay? Nae excuses.'

I found out later that they had to get a younger brother to school before they came to me and that was the reason for their lateness. There was a shopping centre across the road from the ground and I took them there on the day I heard about their sibling and bought them each a bike. Even then I was hard on them. 'Right, you have nae excuses now. Don't be late again. Late again and like Ah had to when Ah was a footballer an' late for training, you'll have some o' your wages docked. An' see these bikes? They're tae be used in getting you two aboot. None o' tha' dirt tracking nonsense on these. You understand?' I didn't give them an inch for the first year or so they were with me, but the tough-love approach seemed to work.

Sam still works as a community football officer, now in Bath. Billy has a job with Bristol Council. Would this have happened if they had not got involved in football and had the chance to see themselves as achievers, as people who could help others in their community? That's a hard thing to say for certain, but I do think the faith shown in them by James from the FA and the chance I gave them certainly did them no harm.

There were many more stories like these I could give, where the power of football helped to change the lives of the children we worked with. I loved my job and had no intention of retiring. However, after 11 years in Bristol, I felt I had to go. We had a new head of community at the club who thought our activities were being undersold. As well as providing coaching and other programmes for the community, we ought to be raising money for the professional side of the club. By this person's reckoning, we could be raising a million pounds a year. I said to John Relish from the PFA, 'If Ah could raise a million doing this, why would Ah be working for you?' This was very much tongue in cheek. The motivation was never money, it was always about helping to improve the lives of children.

The way this person viewed things was made clear when I tried to explain what it was we did. The comment was made, 'But you're only coaching kids.' They had no idea of what we tried to achieve through football and the programmes that we ran. The final straw came when I was told we were going to start charging schools. I told the powers that be in no uncertain terms that, as long as I worked there, I would never ask the schools for money. My job had become untenable and an agreement was reached that I should leave. The PFA fought my case and I left with six months' wages. It was a sour and sad end to my working life. I never even had the opportunity to say goodbye to the children or the teachers that I had worked with.

Chapter 42

Retirement

ON LEAVING Bristol, I discussed things with Irene and we came to the decision to call an end to my working days. Those paintbrushes and white dungarees that I had faithfully kept hold of would never see the light of day, at least not in a professional sense. Football had done me proud and had seen me through virtually the whole of my working life. We now had a decision to make. Where would we spend our retirement years?

When we had left Dundonald, we had said goodbye to both of our families. Because of the nature of a footballer's life, we had seen them for only brief periods over the intervening 40-odd years. During a brief visit back to Fife during my dispute, Irene and I made the decision that, subject to discussions with our children, we would like to come home. If we were to move back to Scotland, we would again be leaving our family behind – this time, our children. Our boys and our girl were grown and had flown the nest and were dispersed to South Wales, the Cotswolds and Lincolnshire. It was as easy to see us in Fife as it was in Chepstow, so once I left Bristol we returned to the kingdom!

I did receive a third and final award from the PFA for services as a development officer and for services to football. I was presented with it on the pitch at Ashton Gate before a City match, which was a nice touch. It was a lovely glass award that had hologram pictures of me playing for Coventry in a variety of kits and poses. On the plinth it detailed my career and the performances I had made for my various clubs. Unfortunately, they had spelled my name wrong, using an 'n', Hutchinson not Hutchison. It's an ill wind as they say. I was able to give the Hutchinson version to Lynn while I had a new model with the correct spelling!

We sold our house in Chepstow in double-quick time, two days to be precise. Irene's brother had a static home on a site in the seaside Fife village of Elie. We stayed there while we looked around for our new home. A new development was being built in a village not far from my old home in Dundonald. We liked what we saw and we bought a plot on which our new home would be built.

In the meantime, Irene's brother phoned me to say that he had heard that a static home just along from his own was up for sale. I contacted the guy selling it, we went to see it that day and we also bought it that day! It took nine weeks to build our new house and we spent a happy nine weeks in our new static home in Elie. On the day that we were to be given the keys to our new house, I said to Irene, 'Do we really need the house? Couldn't we just live here?' In reality, we wanted to have a garden, we needed more storage space and most importantly we needed somewhere for our children and their families to stay when they visited.

We still have the static home at Elie and most weekends we go there to enjoy the peace, the seaside and, for me, a game or two of golf. Our kids make good use of the static home too and stay there when they can. Having the new house gave me plenty to do. We wanted to have a nice garden so I spent many hours getting it into shape. We now have it as we like and make occasional additions from our frequent visits to garden centres.

On a slightly morbid note, growing older means you start to lose many of the friends you have made over a lifetime. Scottish team-mates such as Jim Holton and Gerry Gow have gone. My friend of more than 50 years, Derek Fontane, passed away in 2020. My abiding memory of Derek is his kindness. I wouldn't see him for three or four years and then he would suddenly pop into my life again, always with a thoughtful gift.

At the end of Scotland's 5-1 defeat to England, there was Derek, somehow in the officials' car park at Wembley, waiting to give me a lift back to Coventry in a dark-blue Rolls-Royce he was the chauffeur of – I didn't even know he was there. In Swansea, he turned up unannounced with trays of plants as he knew I liked my garden. At my son John's wedding, there he was again snapping away with his posh camera, trying not to get in the way of the official chap. By the time we sat down to dinner that evening, Derek had got his pictures developed and presented John and his bride with an album of their day. What a lovely chap he was!

Life now is very relaxed. I go for a walk with our neighbours across the way every day and we socialise with them quite a bit, popping into each other's houses for a chat and a cup of tea or visiting the local garden centre with them. My sport of choice these days is golf. I really enjoy the game and have been lucky enough to play at the home of golf, St Andrews, including a few rounds on the Old Course.

I suppose I enjoy golf so much as it is a game which, despite my advancing years, I can still play. I have always been a doer rather than a watcher. I rarely go to football matches now and, in truth, I never attended matches regularly. I do watch the occasional match on TV and I am soon drawn into the action, avoiding tackles by pulling my feet in and kicking and heading every ball. I have been known to give Irene a clip on the ankle through being engrossed in the action. However, even if I know that there is football on the telly, I don't always go out of my way to watch it, much to Irene's relief.

Of my clubs, I have only been back to Blackpool on a couple of occasions. Man City I have returned to a few times. Coventry is the place I revisit most frequently as they have an active former players' association. I really enjoy these occasions, meeting the fans and meeting up with old mates such as Willie Carr, Colin Stein and Chris Cattlin.

Family plays a big part in our lives. Moving back to Fife has allowed Irene to spend a lot more time with her brothers and sisters. I am able to meet up with my own sister Ann, who was still very young when I moved away to Blackpool. Unfortunately, my elder sister Lizabeth died a few years ago. We look forward to visits from our kids, Lynn, John and David, our son-in-law Peter, daughters-in-law Julie and Steph and our grandchildren Daniel, William, Olivia and Thomas. We also enjoy travelling to visit them.

I have no regrets about anything I have done in my life. I have had a wonderful time with a wonderful wife and children who fill me with pride. Everything we have done as a family, our travels and the lovely people we have met and who have befriended us, we owe to the fantastic game that is football. Considering that, as a boy, I was thought to be a useless footballer, I feel that I have been a positive force within the game and that I have done alright by football. However, that is all as nothing compared to what the game of football has done for me.

Acknowledgements by Kevin Shannon

THE FIRST acknowledgement, or thank you, is going to be a bit of a long-winded one!

I have been a Coventry fan since the age of nine, quite a late starter for a boy in the 60s. I had been badgering my dad for some time to take me 'up the City'. In February 1967 he finally gave in and he took me to Highfield Road, to see the Sky Blues beat Carlisle 2-1. I suppose my footballing debut could have gone one of two ways. I could have hated the whole experience and not wanted to go back, or I was going to love it and form a lifetime bond with my club. Fortunately, despite the occasional ups and the more frequent downs of being a City fan, I have never regretted falling in love with Coventry City.

By the time Tommy Hutchison arrived at my club, I was 15 and already six years into my obsession with the Sky Blues. Jimmy Hill was long gone and the reality of following a club like mine had started to dawn on me. For the two years prior to the arrival of Hutch, the football that I had watched had been dull and sterile. Attendances had fallen dramatically and the excitement and expectation that was a hallmark of the Jimmy Hill era had gone.

The new management team of Joe Mercer and Gordon Milne had promised exciting, attacking football. However, it wasn't until Tommy was signed that this was fulfilled. Hutch was sensational, as was the transformed team. We were blowing teams away with a brand of exhilarating football that I had never seen before. At the forefront of this was Hutch. He was a mesmeric figure with the control of a football that was unbelievable. He would take on and beat player after player. As soon as he got the ball, you just knew that something special was about to happen.

Tommy entertained and enthralled me and thousands of fellow Coventry and Warwickshire people for nearly nine years. The first acknowledgement or thank you then is to him for all of the wonderful footballing memories that he left with all who saw him play.

Fast forward to 2019. I was retiring as a teacher and drawing up a list of things that I wanted to do in my new-found freedom. I wanted to learn French, I wanted to master the intricacies of the Irish tin whistle and I wanted to write a book. As an avid reader, I reasoned that if I could read and mostly understand all the words in the books that I read, surely the writing process would be to simply reproduce some of those words on a page in some sort of cohesive order! I saw the writing and the publishing of a book as a challenge to be met.

If I was going to write a book, it would be about something that I both cared and knew a lot about. It couldn't just be about football in general because, as one of my sons probably correctly points out, I know very little about football but an awful lot about Coventry City. It would therefore have to be Sky Blue related. A book with Tommy as the subject was the obvious answer.

I had never forgotten my footballing hero of the 70s and I had never understood why Tommy had never had a book written about him. His 1,000 first-class appearances, made over a mammoth 28-year career, are a record for an outfield player in this country. This record, one that Tommy would dismiss with a shrug of his shoulders, is surely an indication that his was a career that needed documenting. Several Coventry players had been the subject of biographies or autobiographies, but never the person who is widely acknowledged as our greatest ever player, and who had such a long and varied career both before and after his time in the Midlands.

I checked with Jim Brown, the writer of several books about Coventry City, as to whether or not this was an undertaking he was likely to pursue. When he said it wasn't, I asked him if he would contact Hutch and see if he was interested in being the subject of a book. Jim put me in touch with Tommy who said he liked the idea and therefore the project could begin.

So it was that in September of 2021 that I found myself standing in the roadside in Burntisland, Fife, outside of the house we were renting for a week, waiting to be picked up by a man I knew well but who I had never met. My wife Susan had been pulling my leg, saying that I would be tongue-tied and starstruck when I finally met the man who had been my footballing hero for nearly 50 years. Had I met him when he played for my club, she would have been right. However, despite a few butterflies in the stomach that morning, I was fairly confident that this would be a meeting where two old blokes would discuss a subject dear to both of their hearts, namely football.

I had to admit to myself that it was going to be a bit strange. From my side, I would be meeting someone that I knew to see very well, had watched hundreds of times do his job of work, but who I had never spoken to (except on the phone to agree to write the book) and who I knew little or nothing about in a personal sense. From Tommy's point of view, he didn't know anything about me, not even what I looked like. I was some bloke from Coventry who had asked him to be the subject for one of my retirement projects.

Tommy rolled up in his Mercedes, I got in, shook hands, said hello and we were off. We had agreed to visit Tommy's hometown of Cardenden to have some background as to where his story began. As we rolled out of Burntisland, I immediately felt at ease as it was clear that Tommy was a relaxed and affable chap. Conversation flowed and there was no awkwardness between us.

Driving through Kirkcaldy, I saw the floodlight pylons of Stark's Park. This immediately prompted a conversation about the local team that played there, Raith Rovers. Further down the road Tommy pointed out the Port Brae, a pub formerly owned by the retired Scotland international, Willie Johnston. We then had a conversation on Willie himself but also about how he nearly lost all his footballing memorabilia, locked inside the pub when it closed due to financial difficulties.

It was as I felt it would be. Two old blokes talking about a mutual obsession. That morning we toured Cardenden. I saw the site of two of the collieries that Tommy's dad worked at and the ruins of what was once his secondary school. I visited the house where Tommy grew up and met up with some of his former neighbours who still live in the same street. I listened to the conversations and discovered two things. The first was that, although I knew Tommy and his friends were speaking English, it was a Fife version and I could barely understand what they were saying. The second was about Tommy himself. He obviously hadn't met these people in quite a while. Even so, there was an affinity between them that was immediately apparent. Each of the people we met obviously had a real fondness for Tommy.

We visited Denend School, Tommy's old primary, and then paid a visit to the Bluebell, his first club. As with his neighbours, the club steward greeted Tommy like a long-lost friend. As they chatted, I was pleased to see a picture of Hutch in a Coventry kit on the wall. Also there, in a frame, was Tommy's shirt from his Scotland debut, that he had donated to the Bluebell. We ended the morning talking about his childhood while eating bacon batches for lunch at a local garden centre.

On each of the next four days we met at Tommy's static home at Elie on the Fife coast. There, I started to record his story. By the time I came to leave Scotland, we were only halfway through despite nearly 20 hours of recordings. We would have to resume via Zoom when I returned to Coventry the following week. By the time we had finished we were approaching 50 hours of stories.

This is where my second thank you or acknowledgement comes in. Again, it is to Tommy, but also to his wife Irene for making both myself and Susan welcome during our week in Scotland. I loved it! Tommy is a funny man and we chuckled along as he told me his stories. The good time I had (and I think Tommy did too) has been very apparent when I listened back to the recordings from Elie and then watched and listened to our videos from Zoom. There was a fair bit of laughing going on. Tommy mentions in the book that he was thrilled to meet his hero Denis Law and to find out he was a thoroughly good bloke. I have to say I would feel the same about meeting and spending time with Tommy.

Besides Tommy and Irene there are a lot of other people that I need to acknowledge. My thanks go to Gordon Milne and Gordon Taylor for kindly taking the time to write the forewords for this book. Gordon Milne was particularly concerned that what he had written did Tommy justice.

I've mentioned Jim Brown above. He is the official Coventry City historian and is on the committee of the Coventry City former players' association. He gave up his time to talk to me and to give me sound advice on the writing process. He also made the contact with Hutch and gave me the details of his publisher, Pitch Publishing. My thanks to him.

Bernadette Cope has been a good friend for many years. When she heard I was writing a book she very kindly volunteered to proofread it. I'm really glad she did as the number of corrections needed for mistakes I had made and missed when reading back were huge. I thank her for her powers of concentration and for the many words of encouragement she gave about what she was reading.

My thanks to Jane Camillin at Pitch Publishing for giving me the chance to write this book. She asked me for samples of previous writing I had done. All I had was a single article I had written for a football magazine (inevitably on Coventry City) and some stuff that I had written to inspire creative writing among the children that I taught. I don't know whether she was genuinely impressed by stuff with titles such as 'My Dog Guinness' or whether she just felt sorry for me! Whatever the reason, I am grateful as without the publishing contract I would not have felt confident enough to broach the possibility of the project to Tommy.

Jane put me in touch with two of their published writers, Dave Thomas who writes books on Burnley and Jeff Holmes who writes about Rangers. My thanks to them as it was good to hear their advice and to be able to ask about the many things that I did not know or understand in the writing and publishing process.

The talk I had with Jeff in particular was really useful as he convinced me that using an autobiographical approach would be much more fruitful than the biographical one I had originally planned to use. He also asked me about Tommy's reasons for wanting to do the book. When I told him that he wanted something he could hand on to his grandchildren, Jeff said that I would have a good subject to write with. He mentioned that a former footballer had once approached him asking him to write his autobiography. Jeff turned him down when the chap indicated that he thought it would be a nice little earner and that he had been told that he could make up to £20,000 if the book was written. Jeff felt that he had the wrong attitude to having his story told and that this would be reflected in the quality of the book; that and the fact the guy was deluded enough to think he would make anything like that amount from an autobiography. Jeff felt Tommy's reasons for having a book written about him were spot on.

Lots of people have helped me with background information on Tommy's life and times. Drew Davidson, a friend of Tommy's since childhood, gave me a lot of useful stuff on Dundonald Bluebell FC. Jackie Watson helped fill me in on what it was like living and growing up in the Cardenden of the 40s, 50s and 60s. John Glencross, programme editor and historian at Alloa Athletic, has given up a lot of time finding out bits and pieces on Tommy's time at Recreation Park. For information on Tony Green's time at Albion Rovers I am grateful to Rob Crangle, historian at that club. For stories and pictures covering Tommy's time in Coventry, thanks to Greg Kenny. Tony Scholes has been a great help with information on Tommy's time at Burnley. Tom Fay of the Seattle Library Service supplied lots of links to information about Tommy's stay at the Sounders. Tony Tse, former general manager at Tommy's Hong Kong team, Bulova, has been very kind in supplying a lot of information, articles and photos. He also wrote a lovely tribute to Tommy that is at the end of the book. Tom Bates has also helped out with information and photos from Hong Kong.

My thanks to all of the people who were kind enough to write about their memories of Tommy at various clubs. Apologies that there wasn't room to put all of these in the book. Every one of these memories that I received I have passed on to Tommy.

My particular thanks to Malcolm Brown, Mandy Gardener, John Relish, Geoff Stevens and Sam Downes for the pieces they wrote about Tommy and his time as a football development officer. I think that what they have to say about him is very revealing, particularly with regard to the care and concern he had for the children in his charge. They all spoke about him with obvious affection.

My thanks to 'the committee', three people close to Tommy who helped to keep us both on the straight and narrow with their critique of each chapter as it rolled off the press. Tommy would refer each chapter I sent him to his children: Lynn, John and David. They would in turn offer advice and suggestions that were always gratefully received.

My thanks to my own committee, my own four sons: Tom, John, Michael and Patrick, who have all contributed technical (my IT skills aren't great) and creative advice. Particular thanks to Tom for proofreading and for organising the collection of the tributes to Tommy. Tom and John were only young boys at the time but managed to see Hutch play in Michael Gynn's testimonial match at Highfield Road in 2005. Both agreed with me that, even at 57, he was still the best player on the pitch.

Finally, a big thank you to my wife of nearly 40 years, Susan. For every one of those years she has had to share me with the other love of my life, a very unfashionable Midlands football club who play in sky blue. Even when I suggested a nice autumn break on the Fife coast, she later discovered that she would be sharing me with Tommy Hutchison! Thank you, Susan! X

Kevin Shannon

Tributes to Tommy

Blackpool

I was about nine years old when Tommy signed for the Pool. Great player, him and Tony Green used to terrorise defences. On the pitch I remember him running rings round full-backs. Probably his best game was against Blackburn Rovers when he gave the then England right-back, Keith Newton, a torrid time. Newton said of all the opponents he'd faced, including internationals, Tommy was by far the best.

One of the other things I recall was that he had a decent long throw, not as far as the other Hutchinson at Chelsea but very useful.

He was great mates with John Craven who also ended up at Coventry. I remember being with my dad in Blackpool town centre in the school holidays. Dad bought me the *Shoot!* summer special and got both Tommy and John to sign it.

Tom Heyes

I live in Coventry (the Sky Blues are my second team) and although Blackpool are my first, I spent many years with my dear dad at Highfield Road in the glory years through the mid/late 60s to 70s/80s (we had season tickets in the old Main Stand). We would go and watch Blackpool whenever we went up there to visit both grandmothers.

Sadly, my dad is no longer with us, but he too enjoyed watching Tommy Hutch at both clubs. Blackpool was his first club too – he used to watch them when he and my mum were courting – but he and I loved watching City too as they rose through the divisions. I stopped him going to the 1953 Cup Final (the so-called Matthews Final against Bolton Wanderers) as I was born the day before but he forgave me I think when I was able to go with him in 1987 to see City beat Tottenham at Wembley.

Tommy scored many a good goal, but the one that sticks in my memory was at Highbury when he beat most of the Arsenal side two or three times before scoring from close to the corner flag in 72/73. A great player, a great man and one of my Blackpool and Coventry heroes.

Rob Stuart

Tommy was definitely one of my Blackpool heroes growing up. I remember his great balance and obvious ability to beat players with skill and pace. One downside to this was the number of times he was fouled and one picture summed it up if you can find it.

Tommy is sat on the grass, knees up with his socks rolled down, smiling away displaying the state of his shins to the camera. Absolutely butchered! His smile though was a case of: you can cut me down as much as you like but you are not stopping me!

This picture appeared in one of the football annuals; apologies I don't have a copy but it left a great impression on me as it really was a case of 'a picture painting a thousand words'.

Colin McGown

When I first started watching the mighty Pool regularly, I used to sit on the 'Scratchers' wall, about the halfway line, and have very vivid memories of Hutchy with his scrawny legs, socks often rolled down, skittering down the wing, with equally bony elbows akimbo. I also remember the air of excitement when he got the ball, and the number of times he was clattered by some lunging full-back. A couple of years later, I remember a line in a *Guardian* footie report describing him being fouled and falling 'like a set of abandoned bagpipes'. Along with Micky Burns, my first Pool heroes. (Tony Green was injured at that time, and I was too young to appreciate Suddick's subtler skills.) He later played in a more midfield role for Coventry and won even more admirers. Ace player.

Discojohndeary

In all the years I've watched Pool, I can honestly say that 'Hutch' was the most individually skilful player we've ever had; when the ball was passed to him, there was an immediate roar of the crowd in anticipation, he would regularly dribble past five or six opponents with what seemed like ease. I can remember him a few times receiving the ball from our keeper, running the full length of the pitch dribbling past many players, he would very rarely go straight for goal, but would run out wide on the left to cross the ball and provide chances to team-mates.

The only way many teams could stop him was to hack him down, and in virtually every game they did just that, but he always seemed to just roll over and get back up and carry on as though nothing had happened. The press labelled him 'the India Rubber Man' as despite the rough treatment – and I mean this was late 60s/early 70s footy, when they chopped a player down it was with the intent that you wouldn't get up again or would be rendered ineffective for the rest of the game – he would bounce back up, and go at 'em again!

Many of us oldies would have fond memories of the top footy magazine of the era, namely *Shoot!*, and they used to have a feature where they would ask the top players of the time the same set of questions, one of which was: who is the most difficult opponent you have faced this season. Many would reply Tom Hutchison; we were at the time in the top division and they were the best players in the country. (I seem to vaguely remember one player – think it was a Leeds defender remarking that he'd suffered a nightmare after playing against Hutchison.)

We were all absolutely gutted when we sold him to Coventry, and one of our directors at the time told the Coventry board that Hutch was better than George Best at his best – this was how many of us felt about him. If he had been a more selfish player and scored more goals, he would have become one of the greats.

Our chant for him was ZAH ZAH ZIGGER ZAGGER HUTCHISON!!!

Bpool fan

If he'd known about having to wear the brown away kit later in his spell at Coventry he might never have signed.

Dirky

Coventry

Tommy Hutchison was a hero of my teenage years and 40-plus years after he left the Sky Blues remains my all-time favourite player, as he is for many of my generation.

Despite all the great memories of competitive games, the moment I remember the most was the very last thing he did on the pitch at Highfield Road, which was when he played in Michael Gynn's testimonial game in April 2005.

Despite bring 57 years old at the time, he gave as good a performance and was as fit as men 20 years younger. After an hour, the call came to make way for someone else. Tommy fell to his knees, kissed the turf, and departed to a standing ovation. From someone less classy it might have seemed a bit of a cheesy gesture, but from Tommy it summed up his greatness and the wonderful relationship he had with the fans.

Keith Bushnell

I was going on a regular basis to Highfield Road and stood behind the goal in the Kop. I was always on the right-hand side so used to get a good view of Tommy waltzing around and generally terrifying opposition defenders. I became a massive admirer and was in awe of his skill and football prowess.

I was 13 years old at that time and was watching some Sunday league football on this day at the council pitches at Sowe Common, just the other side of Potters Green next to the M6 motorway bridge. I was stood on the sidelines when a big car drove up and parked by the side of the road and the Hutch got out with his two small children and started kicking a ball with them dribbling past me. It was definitely him, you couldn't mistake the Hutchison swagger, the way he controlled this little ball; I just stood there open-mouthed at this sight and must have been a little starstruck as my hero was knocking a ball just inches away from me with all the skill and poise as he did on a Saturday afternoon. He did stop at one point and asked a gentleman the score. This chap did a double-take, then proceeded to shake his hand in disbelief that this was 'the' Tommy Hutchison stood before us, the all-time Coventry favourite, the Scottish international that would go on to grace the Wembley turf and the World Cup.

Obviously my friends at school didn't believe me when I related this story back to them at school on the Monday morning but I didn't care as he was my hero and the memory stuck with me forever.

Dave Mander

I count myself very fortunate to have been around during the Coventry City years of Tommy Hutchison. He was and is my favourite ever Coventry player. I saw his home debut against Manchester City where he was very much seen as the support act to the bigger signing, Colin Stein. I was aware of him coming from Blackpool and being part of a team that featured our new coach, Gordon Milne, future Sky Blue John Craven, the legendary Jimmy Armfield, Tony Green and Fred Pickering.

He was gangly, thin legs, thin arms and a lolloping gait when he ran. He was one of five Scots that started the Manchester City game. We went nine games unbeaten and he was a firm favourite by the time this run ended. It included his legendary run and goal at Highbury in a 2-0 win over Arsenal.

I saw most of his games including the Liverpool winner in 73, the day he tore the Spurs defence a new one in a 2-2 draw, the legendary Bristol City goals, a 4-4 draw with Boro at Ayresome Park up to his last goals v Brighton in the League Cup and Division One.

I can't help but feel he was let go too soon with such a vibrant young side that would have benefited from his experience as well as his skills which continued to be at a high level.

I went to the FA Cup tie in 1982 when we won 3-1 at Maine Road with him and Bobby Mac in the Man City side. It didn't look right. He was wearing the wrong kit.

Sometimes you can be accused of looking at things through rose-tinted spectacles when reminiscing where players never had a bad game, but Hutch was so consistently good and the standout performer of my 55 years supporters Coventry City. In my head I often chant 'Oh Tommy Tommy, Tommy Tommy Tommy Tommy Hutchison' to the tune of *Son of My Father* and 'Hutch on the Wing and Stein in the middle'. Always a boy within.

Dion Dublin comes closest in my affection and I look forward to one of the current crop retaining a place in my heart like Tommy Hutchison. To achieve this they would have to be truly excellent.

Stephen Quinn

It was a cold night in Mansfield. A midweek trip to friends coincided with Swansea's visit at Field Mill. This was Third Division football but as a Cov fan how could I pass up the chance to see Tommy Hutch play. Stuck with the Stags fans (Swansea bought about 30 but they wouldn't let me in the away end as I lacked Welshness). It was great to see even at 42 Tom could still show the young defender the ball, wait, jink and then dance past him even though the full-back at 20 was actually half his age. The crosses came in from deeper nowadays than at Highfield

Road but the balls were regularly hitting the danger area and there was a nervousness with the home fans every time Tom got the ball. Just a shame Swansea never took their chances that night. Despite the loss you could see how much Tom loved playing and it was a real thrill to see him play one more time.

Greg Kenny

The moments I remember Hutch best for were in Bill Glazier's testimonial match against the England 1966 World Cup-winning team. Alan Ball was constantly chasing around after him, trying to win the ball. In the end he was throwing his arms in the air in exasperation as he just couldn't get the ball off Hutch.

Roger Gurney

This man was my hero. The crowd gasped with excitement when he had the ball. Tommy Hutch is a true Sky Blue legend.

Ian Collins

We used to call him Mr Coventry. We would sit right by the touchline at Highfield Road. He had a wonderful skill of pushing the ball quite far in front of him and then just dink it past players who thought he'd lost it. This was his trademark. I have seen him leave international full-backs punching the turf many times.

Philip Gardner

Best player I ever saw play for us. There were some fairly grim days in the mid-70s, but there was always excitement when Hutch got the ball. Shouts from the crowd of 'Dazzle Tommy, dazzle' were frequent. With the protection players get from referees these days Tommy would have been unstoppable!

Mark Ryder

He used to help train a local team, Whitley Wanderers, based on the Old Church Road Courtaulds pitches. As a 15-year-old Sky Blues fan I was star-struck. Not only did he train us (360 stomach exercises were normal), he also joined in five-a-side games. I am very proud to say that he hit the ball into my nether regions on several occasions … and what a shot! He then turned up on Sundays, even if it was teeming with rain to shout encouragement from the touchline. I cannot see Premier League players doing that today. What a man! What a legend!

David Ward

After the last game at Highfield Road in 2005, which was against Derby, Tommy turned up at our house, which is situated at the top of King Richard Street, right beside the Main Stand. My dad had been sitting outside the house and as it was a hot day, he was drinking a cold beer. He saw Tommy coming out of the stand and called him over for a chat. When he saw my dad's beer, Tommy asked: where was his? We were all enjoying ourselves and he sat with us for a while, enjoying his beer and the chat. It was amazing having my favourite ever player sat with us. He stole the show as usual. Photos of this appeared in the *Evening Telegraph*. The pictures showed flags, etc. that we had decorated the front of the house with. We also had a banner that said thanks for the memories which Highfield Road and Tommy himself had both given us.

Bernard Bourke

I remember his first game back at Highfield Road as a player for Man City. The whole ground sung his name. The love and respect for Tommy will never leave Coventry City. What a player! As a kid I used to draw a lot and I'd done a drawing of Tommy that I'd copied from *Shoot!* magazine. I was about ten or 11 at the time and I walked from my home in Willenhall to Ryton with the picture. I watched the players train and when they finished, I nervously approached Tommy and asked him to sign my drawing. He looked at it and said in his strong Scottish accent, 'You draw this, son?' I replied yes. 'That's great that!' Tommy said, rubbing my head. I'll never forget that day. I wish I still had that drawing but it was over 45 years ago.

Mark Eardley

Manchester City

Just a little snippet into Tommy off the field. In the 90s I was chairman of the Prestwich & Whitefield Manchester City Supporters Club. We decided to try and get an evening together with Tommy, Gerry Gow (RIP) and Bobby McDonald who all played a prominent part in getting City to the 1981 cup final. Tommy was working with Swansea and for Welsh FA at the time.

The event was a Friday night and he drove after work from Swansea to Manchester to take part in the Q&A. I remember him answering one question by replying that his proudest moment in football was when he was selected to play for Scotland. He was brilliant with the fans, then after the event many of us went back to their hotel where we carried on drinking and he carried on telling us some great stories.

The next morning, I went with the three ex-players to Maine Road where they were guests of Manchester City. Before the game (I think it was against Bradford) all three were invited onto the pitch where they received a hero's welcome. After the game Tommy had to shoot off back to Swansea but not before many more fans had photos and autographs with him and he met many backroom staff and ex-players from his time at City.

He came across as a very humble person who was grateful that he lived the dream that we all had of being a professional footballer. Just to put it into context, after finishing a week's work, he drove hundreds of miles to meet up with a load of strangers to answer questions about football, then after the game because of commitments he drove back to Swansea. All of this without payment (I can't remember if he even took petrol money). We paid his drinks and hotel but to be honest he would have probably paid for them himself.

That was the only time I met him but he left me with everlasting memories.

Don Price

Tommy, along with Bobby Mac and Gerry Gow, completely turned our season round in 81, culminating in us reaching Wembley for the 100th FA Cup Final when I was 17. Tommy was *so* unlucky that day but we loved him even more for it as everyone at City was born unlucky.

One of my main memories (I think it was at home to Middlesbrough), the ball flew over to Tommy on the wing about two feet above head height from a Boro clearance and he feinted to head it, causing two Boro players to leap in the air as Tommy, nonchalantly, leant back, stayed on his feet and calmly picked the ball up to take the throw-in. The Kippax absolutely pissed themselves laughing as did half the Boro team.

One of the great characters of football. Rock on, Tommy!

Tim Crowther

Tommy Hutchison signed by John Bond, along with Gerry Gow and Bobby McDonald, transformed a very young Manchester City team after the departure of Malcolm Allison. Tommy was the creative winger who could drift past full-backs with ease. Even though he was in the twilight of his career he was still very influential and helped guide City to the 1981 FA Cup Final. He was my favourite player of that team, and I wished he had stayed longer. If only we had bought him earlier in his career! A great player who will always be remembered by the City fans of that era.

Percypawpaw

A wonderfully languid gangly skilful player who, when he played for us, always seemingly gave his all. As with all players who are blessed with technical ability, he seemed to find space easily and had time to do what he wanted to do. He used to beat people very easily and was very well balanced.

I watched him play against us many times and my dad always used to wish he was wearing our shirt. Needless to say, he and I were delighted when he signed for City and as others have said, the Scottish trio hugely lifted the team and gave us a much-needed harder edge.

I wished he had been with us for a much longer period.

Bongsblue

I seem to remember that we had quite a young team when he joined us along with Gerry Gow and Bobby McDonald. I remember reading that Tommy used to come off the field at the end of those early games totally knackered because as the senior player and someone who seemed to know what they were doing; the younger players were always looking to get the ball to him. Certainly, a very skilful wide player and was what we needed at the time to steady the ship.

Leveblue

Bulova

Tommy Hutchison's 17-month venture in Hong Kong soccer was a thrill ride, a fantasy of emotion, passion and adoration. He was only there for 17 months but he had firmly engraved an indelible footprint in the football circle in Hong Kong, a city known to the world as a Far East financial hub adjacent to Shenzhen, Southern China.

Hutchison remains till today one of the most, if not the most, beloved and talked about overseas imports. Hundreds of them had come and gone since the introduction of a professional football league in the early 1970s, but it was Hutchi who was ever to charm the Hong Kong scene. Forty years on, his photos and football videos still constantly appear in the local social media platforms posted by fans, remembering the good old days they all treasure.

Tommy's book, apart from giving me an insight into his wonderful past in the English game, provides me with a chance to look back into our time together in Hong Kong, the sweetness and joys and trove of memories that came in the thick of competitions all within a very short period of time. He was a joy to work with.

Hutchison arrived Hong Kong in February 1982 when the football season had already been six months old. At the age of 34, he stunned the crowd at the HK Stadium in his first appearance in the all-red Bulova FC shirt in dazzling style, passing defenders at will and delivering assists like an archer. Within four months, he almost single-handedly steered Bulova FC to two trophies, the popular Viceroy Cup and the FA Cup. We all fell in love with him.

The man of exuberant spirit received constant applause from every corner of the stadium ever since that first match. His passion for the game and his professional attitude was equally admired by his team-mates and by opposition footballers alike. Nobody begrudged him his popularity.

Hutchi, as we loved to call him, came at the strong recommendation of ex-Coventry coach, the late Ron Wylie, whom I signed as chief coach for the 1981/82 season before he joined West Bromwich. Hutchi, of course, worked under Wylie at Coventry City and they both spoke highly of each other.

The former Scottish international agreed to come to us despite playing regularly in the First Division with Manchester City. At the time John Bond was the manager and he duly agreed to let Hutchi come to us for free as a gesture for his loyalty. Hong Kong soccer at the time featured 12 teams in the First Division and most teams were boosted with signings from overseas, players who came from all over the world.

On his arrival, I urged Hutchi to shoulder the responsibility of becoming a role model for the local lads. He delivered on this with no fuss. As a heavy-weighted imported professional, he made a difference to the young footballers in Hong Kong by demonstrating his wonderful enthusiasm and affection for the game in training and in matches alike. He lifted his local team-mates from the depth of mediocrity to a new level, constantly spurred them to try harder. Towards the end of his time with us, the local lads were all eager to train, learn new things and give every effort.

Alongside the likes of Barry Daines (ex-Tottenham), Alan Dugdale (ex-Coventry City), Barry Powell (ex-Coventry and Wolverhampton), Derek Parlane (ex-Leeds United) and Clive Haywood (ex-Coventry), and later on Peter Foley (ex-Oxford United), he helped Bulova FC win two Viceroy Cups and two FA Cup trophies and to come second in the League Championship twice during his time with us.

Beneath his well-suited collar and tie, Hutchison spoke with a heavy Scottish accent and the local Bulova lads could hardly understand a word he uttered. But they adored him.

Hutchi often came down from his high level of achievement in order to push the local lads. He made fun with them, ate Cantonese Dim Sum with them and trained like a schoolboy. His patience was appreciated. He was doing the job of the manager and the coach on the pitch and got the team together, set the tone and gave the team energy. He was a rare breed.

Hutchi may well be hitting some golf balls through mud and wind in Fife these days, drinking a few beers at the 19th hole, but there would be time, I am sure, that he would spare a minute or two to recall from the memory slot within his brain the smiling faces of the Hong Kong lads he was once so happy to be associated with and the cheering and clapping from crowds he was used to. Those days were just so special.

I loved his talent and his desire for just playing football. I loved his sprints down the left flank and his flow of crosses into the penalty area. I loved the chill of terror he imposed to the opposition defenders. I loved his child-like love of the game on the football pitch.

But then, don't we all love him for what he is?

Tony Tse

I saw Tommy playing for Bulova on many occasions. I understand he played 22 games, but although he failed to score, he made such an impact in matches, and gave 100 per cent every game, that he is a HUGE favourite of Hong Kong football fans still. Gerd Muller also played in Hong Kong and was booed relentlessly as he made no effort. In addition to the football, Tommy played in the local darts league for a team called Pressstuds. I also played for them, but a few years later. My friend Peter Foley (ex-Oxford United) was a team-mate of Tommy's in both football and darts. Tommy was a phenomenal darts player and actually won the season-long award for the highest checkout – the maximum 60, 60, bull (170).

Tom Bates

Burnley

Good player who looked after himself well but who never got the credit he deserved from the Burnley faithful. We could do with someone who could cross the ball half as well as him at the moment.

Culmclaret

Hutch was excellent for Blackpool, Coventry and Man City and I thought he was a real class act at Burnley in those two years.

ClaretTony

I saw him play on the left wing for Blackpool against Arsenal in an early cup game when I was at Polytechnic in London. He was virtually unplayable and that against one of the best teams in England at the time. I think he was snapped up fairly soon after that. He was a handful in his day with his dribbling skills.

Warksclaret

One of the most underrated players of his generation. Without doubt Hutchison for me was the highlight of some very dark times for us at Burnley. Would I take Hutchison at his best tomorrow? In a heartbeat. I still remember how disappointed I was that Burnley didn't give him the player-manager job he wanted, yet he still scored one of the goals on the final weekend to do his bit to keep us up.

Absolutely love the guy. About time he got some recognition.

Elwaclaret

I was working in the sponsors' lounge after one game. Tommy came in and ordered two pints of lager and passed one to Roger Hansbury (goalkeeper) along with the comment 'Don't drop that'! I always found him pleasant with a very dry sense of humour. During the week he was always talking to the apprentices after training offering advice and encouragement.

XDS

A fantastic servant for us in the context of an undistinguished era. Gave his all and had real class in the way he conducted himself, and real quality as a player. A shining light in a relatively dark era.

Lewishamclaret

I remember the 1970/71 relegation season as an 11-year-old. It was the first season when I regularly attended Burnley games at the Turf. I only missed one game all season and that was because my brother and I had to go to stay at our grandma's in Poulton-le-Fylde which is a few miles from Blackpool, who were our opponents that weekend. I was disappointed that I missed what was one of the most vital games of the season and only consoled by the fact that we won 1-0 and saw Paul Fletcher score his first Burnley goal on *Match of the Day*. The next day (despite no doubt having a bit of a sulk), Grandma took us on the bus to Stanley Park in Blackpool where we settled to have a picnic in the sunshine. As we were sat there, we spotted a tall lanky feller with two considerably smaller older people walking along towards us. I nudged my brother and said 'I know who this is' and Grandma quickly found a pen and paper as we legged it over to Tommy Hutchison who was having a relaxing stroll with his parents. He signed our paper and before he handed it back to us, I couldn't resist asking him, 'Guess where we come from?' He looked at us with a serious face and said, 'Go on then, where?' When I told him 'Burnley', he grimaced and made as if to tear the paper up. His mum and dad were quite happy that we were chatting to them and were quite jovial. Tommy was great too, although he did have a quite serious disposition about him. We were over the moon as young boys to have met him and looked out for him in the papers and on TV thereafter. I thought that he was brilliant at Burnley and a class above most of those in the Third Division at that time.

Beesholeclaret

Swansea

I remember him playing for Swansea City U18 team (you were allowed two overage players) against my local team Pontlottyn sometime around

1989. Swansea won something like eight or nine-nil if my memory serves me right. After the game Hutch had the boys in a huddle for about 20 minutes to half an hour. Giving them a pick-me-up talk. That was a class gesture it must be said.

Andrew Lobodzinski

I played against Tommy in the 1989/90 season when he was assistant manager to Terry Yorath at Swansea City. After a 0-0 draw at The Vetch in a Welsh Cup match, my team, Caersws FC, played them on a wet February afternoon in a replay at our ground, the Recreation Ground, Caersws. Swansea fielded a very strong team including Alan Curtis, Alan Davies, Andy Melville, Paul Raynor, Andy Legg and a very young Chris Coleman. Anyway, as right-back I was tasked with trying to stop Tommy, I thought that I did a decent job but I do remember him trying to put me off all game by talking to me; he was saying things like, 'What time are you in to work tomorrow, son?' and 'We have got a day off tomorrow son.' His talking was constant. Anyway, we got beat 2-0, and for me it was wonderful to play against such a great player who had played for his country at a World Cup and also for Coventry and in a cup final. I think he was over 40 when I played against him.

After the game he sought me out in the clubhouse and insisted on buying my wife and myself a drink; he was a great player and a gentleman.

Gwyn Williams

Football Development officer

As deputy headteacher of a residential special school for pupils with severe learning difficulties, I received a telephone call from the school secretary to say that there was a Mr Tommy Hutchison, the Football in the Community officer for Taff Ely, wanting to speak to me about taking football lessons with our pupils. I invited Tom to call in to school for a chat with a view to organising lessons. I had never met Tom or indeed seen him play live despite working part-time for a Premier League club for over 15 years. Tom came to school to see me and was very enthusiastic, saying that he would take 24 students on his own every week for an hour at the local leisure centre.

I had to explain to him that our pupils had severe and other associated learning difficulties so the initial lesson was for a group of eight pupils accompanied by a teacher and nursery nurse, though I am sure by the end of his time with us he would certainly have been able to manage 24 students on his own.

Tom was always enthusiastic and structured his lessons in such a way that there was never any risk of behaviour problems because the students were enjoying themselves too much. Tom always ensured that his pupils achieved success in whatever activity they took part in, no matter how long it took them. These lessons certainly helped the students' hand–eye co-ordination, motor skills, spatial awareness and confidence. Tom, or 'Tommy' as he was known by his mates (the students), didn't just take his weekly lesson and then move on, he became a friend of the school, its pupils and staff, frequently staying for lunch and visiting the pupils in their classrooms when his time permitted.

I did come unstuck once when I insisted Tom be invited to the Christmas production and seated in the front row as a guest. The senior teacher organising the concert very professionally with stage lights readily agreed. Unfortunately when it came to the class of Tommy's mates to play their part, the lights went on which lit up not only the stage but also the first two rows of the audience brightly. Three of the students spotted their mate and ran to the front of the stage with their hands raised for a high five shouting 'Tommy!', for which I got a telling-off. Tom was always invited to school events but from then on he had to sit at the back of the audience where he couldn't be seen from the stage.

In 1994, BT Football opened a project for players with learning disabilities including both adults and young people. It began with a four-day coaching camp at Leicester University involving teams from all four home nations. I was invited to manage the Wales section and because of Tom's ability in working with our pupils I asked if he would like to join us as coach, which turned out to be a very successful decision. Tom gladly gave of his time freely and spent the week coaching players from all four nations in his usual enthusiastic way. The coaching camp was a great success in terms of football and also the social side in the evenings, where staff and players participated in a variety of activities together. This was followed up in 1995 with another four-day coaching camp for the same players at Surrey University followed by a coaching demonstration before the Charity Shield at Wembley between Blackburn Rovers and Everton.

Once again Tom joined us and freely gave of his time enjoying coaching and socialising with a group of adult players. He did question the organiser when he put Tom's group in the area of the field where Tom scored his own goal in the FA Cup Final.

While at the university and Wembley we were joined by Tom's great friend Derek who, as a keen photographer, took photographs of our players and helped organise the players during the day. He was of great assistance and did it all at his own expense, taking many photographs and giving them to the players.

Tom was certainly a great asset and friend to Ysgol Ty Coch, its pupils and staff. When I meet ex-pupils, their parents or staff they always ask me how Tom is getting on. He was also great friend and coach of adults with learning disabilities and is still strongly remembered. Tom was a very enthusiastic and popular member of our team and would have made a very good teacher had he not had such a long and successful career in professional football.

Tommy Hutchison is not just a professional footballer who had an exceptionally long and successful playing career, he's also an exceptional person. After he retired from playing, he became a Football in the Community development officer, coaching at all levels. He was equally at home coaching elite players, primary schoolchildren and children with special education needs and adults with learning disabilities. Tom has that special gift of being able to work successfully with players of all abilities and help them achieve success at their level. He obviously loved what he was doing and encouraged players to learn new skills and enjoy themselves. He has not only helped them learn those new skills but also improved their mobility, motor skills and confidence.

Malcolm Brown

This piece is really difficult to write as there are so many things that I could write about Tommy and the time that I was lucky enough to work with him at Bristol City Football in the Community that I could fill another book.

Tommy was an inspirational community coach and mentor. It wasn't about finding the next superstar player but about having fun and learning. He had a wonderful way with the young people that we worked with. He made sure that everyone had a role to play in all of the sessions, even the reluctant footballers were encouraged by making them the scorers or referees. He used the young people's love of playing football as a means of teaching them about life. The sessions were all about listening, working together as a team and taking these lessons back into the classroom.

Tommy loved working with the young people, and nothing was too much trouble, he would always turn up to our study centre celebration events, even though it meant having to wait around for a couple of hours before the event started. Both the Bristol City pro players and the parents were thrilled to see him, and he always answered their questions about his football career with good humour, even though he had been asked the same questions several times.

I had a flavour of his footballing celebrity status when Bristol City were playing away to Coventry. Tommy had been invited back for the evening and he invited Richard and I to join him. When we arrived at the new stadium we pulled into the car park and Tommy asked a senior policeman where he should park.

'Mr Hutchison, you can park wherever you like,' was his reply and that set the tone for the whole evening.

I have never been with a celebrity before, and we were treated as royalty that evening because we were with Tommy. Wherever we went within the stadium people were coming up to Tommy and greeting him. The obvious affection with which Tommy was held and the warmth of the hospitality that evening was overwhelming.

The Bristol City community team have all moved on to new roles over the years, but we have stayed in touch and some of us are now working back together again at Bath City FC Foundation. Even after all these years we still find ourselves working to the same values and methods that we learnt from Tommy. His legacy lives on in our team and through the young people that we work with now.

Mandy Gardener

Context: In the late 80s I was working for the PFA as a regional manager (South West and West Midlands) tasked with expanding the Football in the Community schemes to every club in England and Wales. Another remit was to encourage and support ex-players who wanted to work in this community sector.

Of course, I knew Tommy from watching his amazing career but I was fortunate enough to work closely with him for many years.

It was in the late 80s that I watched Tom coaching a group of youth players at Swansea City. I noticed immediately the effect that Tom had on the group. He was demanding the best from them but I could tell that they all bought into the session. I knew then that Tommy would make an excellent Football in the Community officer.

In the early 90s Tommy moved to Merthyr Tydfil where he ended his playing career in 1994. He started his community work at the club but quickly moved on to Rhondda Cynon Taff as a local authority community officer. This is where I got involved as I was able to access funding from the PFA to support his work.

It was here that Tommy started to build his reputation as a first-rate football community officer. In 2001 I recommended Tommy for the vacant community position at Bristol City. He was duly appointed to the role.

One of the national schemes, which is still in place today, is where a community officer would visit an inner-city estate where anti-social activity was prevalent with a bag of balls, bibs and cones and set up impromptu coaching sessions, drills and games. The idea was to divert young people from hanging around street corners and get them involved in sport, particularly football. This initiative has been a great success over the years.

Tommy worked on some of Bristol's toughest estates to great effect. He insisted on high standards of appearance, behaviour and respect from everyone he worked with. Somehow, he had the ability to get youngsters to buy into his work ethic. Over the years Tommy turned around the lives of many young people who were in danger of making poor choices with their lives. It was tough love with Tommy, no shortcuts, but he seemed to inspire people, possibly because deep down, they knew Tommy cared.

He also ran boot camps in the summer in South Wales for teenagers. They would stay the week near Ogmore by Sea and be responsible for cleaning their room, washing their kit and keeping their football boots spotlessly clean. At the end of the week when their parents arrived to pick them up, there would be a prize-giving ceremony for the winners of various categories. It was priceless to watch the parents' faces when they realised that their offspring who had never cleaned their own room or washed their kit was given an award for exactly that. They were genuinely amazed at the change of behaviour.

Over the years I saw scenes like that play out over and over again. Sometimes, he turned down opportunities to get involved in areas of work that he deemed fluffy or not important. He loved the nitty-gritty of working with hard-to-reach youngsters and he was successful so many times.

It was an honour and a privilege to work with Tommy for so many years, a top player and a great man.

John Relish

It's difficult to sum up in a few words the impact and effect Tommy had on me and how that would shape my career in later life. As a young person of 21, having left university and just starting out on my coaching journey, I was fortunate to be given an opportunity to work in the community department at Bristol City. After a few months I found myself applying for a position to work alongside Tommy with Football in the Community and work in some of the more challenging parts of Bristol. To see first-hand, not only how I could develop young people as footballers, but also as individuals and change lifestyles and life skills, this would give me a passion and drive to strive and embed the skills I learnt from Tommy, not just for myself but for those that I worked with.

I couldn't have asked for a better mentor in Tommy, not just in terms of his leadership skills, but how to ensure everyone worked together as a team. There wasn't a day went by that I didn't look forward to going into work. He gave me the chance to develop my coaching skills by ensuring I worked with a variety of community groups, young and old. To see that by using football as the 'carrot' you could do so much good for so many. I always felt that coaches would use community coaching as a stepping stone to work in an academy. Tommy's words stuck with me when he said, 'I'm setting up 99 per cent of players to fail when I work at an academy. When I work in the community, I can have a positive effect on 99 per cent of those we work with.' That gave me the reason to do what I do.

When Tommy previously worked in South Wales, he brought part of that with him. Every summer we used to go to Ogmore in South Wales and run residential camps. They were long days filled with football from nine in the morning until seven at night. Making sure those attending had fun but were also well behaved with being away from home. Later in the evenings all the coaches would get together to review some of the day's activities and plan for the next day. It was here that we would hear many of the amazing football stories Tommy had from his time in the game and from his work in the community. It was always great to listen to but the thing that captured my imagination was the passion and enthusiasm he had for his community work as much as he did his playing career. It was infectious and drew you in and made you want to be part of it. To make that difference.

Having now spent over 20 years working in community coaching with Bristol City, Weston-super-Mare and now Bath City, I still draw on that ethos that Tommy instilled from the first day. It doesn't matter if I'm working with a five-year-old in a primary school or a 75-year-old playing walking football, the goal remains the same. To see them achieve, however that looks for them, making them believe in themselves and feel better about themselves. Being positive and being part of a team, a community. That's how Tommy made me feel and all those around him.

Geoff Stevens

I first met Tommy when I was nine years old. Tommy was one of the few people who supported me growing up and then went on to give me my first job at Bristol City. Tommy always set very high standards from those who worked for him but was always approachable and made it enjoyable and a good place to learn and get experience. There are still things I do now 13 years later in my day-to-day work that I learnt from Tommy.

Sam Downes